MARYLEBONE LIVES
Rogues, romantics and rebels

Character studies of locals since the 18th century

Edited by Mark Riddaway & Carl Upsall
*Published in association with the Marylebone Journal
and The Howard de Walden Estate*

Published June 2015 by

Spiramus Press Ltd
102 Blandford Street
London W1U 8AG
United Kingdom

www.spiramus.com

© Spiramus Press Ltd

Paperback   ISBN 978 1 910 151 03 7
Ebook   ISBN 978 1 910 151 04 4

Printed and bound in Great Britain by
Grosvenor Group (Print Services) Ltd

Cover design by Mike Turner of Em-Project Ltd
Cover image: Portrait of Mary Anne Clarke, by Adam Buck (1803)

Contents

CONTENTS

MARYLEBONE LIVES

Foreword

As the main landlord for a large part of Marylebone, The Howard de Walden Estate is always looking to the future. Over the past few decades, the Estate has gained plaudits for its highly strategic, long term approach to development; one which seeks to both anticipate and influence the changes inherent to this most dynamic of cities.

But as well as looking ahead, the Estate understands the importance of heritage. We know that Marylebone has to evolve to meet the changing needs of our diverse mix of tenants, but we also have to understand and respect the rich history that helps make this such a special place. The Estate's roots to the area can be traced back for centuries, and with that longevity comes a sense of guardianship. This feeds into the approach we take towards Marylebone's extraordinary period buildings, and it also drives our willingness to provide access and support for projects that help unlock the door to the area's past: historical surveys, academic research, journalistic features. And, of course, the *Marylebone Journal*.

In 2005, when the Estate handed the production of its popular *Marylebone Journal* magazine into the safe-keeping of a new editorial team, our instructions were clear: publicise all that is new and exciting about the area, but celebrate its past as well. For 10 years now, Mark and his colleagues have been following this remit to the letter, with features on the latest shops and restaurants sitting comfortably alongside intelligent and engaging essays on the people and places that have over the centuries given such colour to this most fascinating of areas. We are delighted that, thanks to the input of a local book publisher, these essays can now find a new audience.

Jenny Hancock
Creative director
The Howard de Walden Estate

Acknowledgements

Thanks must go to Cecilia Hallpike who suggested that there should be a book about the interesting people who have lived in Marylebone.

We would also like to thank the Marylebone Journal's staff and contributors:

Donna Earrey, Viel Richardson, Clare Finney, Ellie Costigan, Stephen Harrison, Steve Kidd, Mike Turner, Jean-Paul Aubin-Parvu, Tom Hughes, Glyn Brown, Louisa McKenzie, Rupert Butler, Oliver Bradbury, Todd Swift, Andrew Lycett, Dr David Miller and Richard Bowden.

Their hard work over the past 10 years has formed the basis of this book.

INTRODUCTION

This is a collection of Marylebone lives, but not necessarily the ones you might expect. This is not a check-list of the grandees of Marylebone, although plenty do appear in these pages. Some of have been commemorated with blue plaques or statues, but many have not. This book makes no claim to completeness. In fact, some of the area's most famous names are almost entirely absent: Charles Dickens, Michael Faraday, William Gladstone, John Lennon.

Alongside the great and the good sits a litany of rogues, villains and eccentrics. While some of them led vaguely notable lives, many of our subjects left behind nothing but an entertaining story. But entertaining stories are what this book is all about.

As befits an area of such genteel charm, some of the lives recounted here provide a shiny veneer of high society glamour. But others offer a glimpse into the hardship and squalor that often scarred the parish—as was graphically illustrated in Charles Booth's poverty maps of London in 1889.

The essays have been grouped into themes: politicians and warriors, culture and sport, love and marriage, crimes and misdemeanours, science and medicine, buildings and places. There is also a chapter featuring a fairly random collection of colourful characters and ne'er-do-wells— those whose stories don't fit a convenient box but are too good not to tell.

In all, we hope that these individual lives will between them tell a bigger story: the life of an area, in all its messy glory.

Mark Riddaway & Carl Upsall

A brief history of Marylebone

By Mark Riddaway

The Marylebone of today is a busy, vibrant place, deeply embedded within the centre of London—but it wasn't always so.

When London was first settled by the Romans, this space by the banks of the River Tyburn sat several miles beyond the city. In the Middle Ages, it was occupied by two manors belonging to religious orders. To the west, Lilestone Manor belonged to the Knights Templar, until it was confiscated and given to the priory of St John of Jerusalem (hence, St John's Wood lies to the north of Marylebone). To the east was Tyburn Manor. When William the Conqueror was compiling the Domesday Book in 1086, the manor of Tyburn, which had been granted by the crown to the abbess and convent of Barking, had a value of 52 shillings and a population of no more than 50 people—fewer than the current number of traffic wardens on the high street at any given time.

In 1400, the old Tyburn church, located in a lonely and dangerous spot just off Oxford Street, was pulled down and rebuilt at a more salubrious location at the top of what is now Marylebone High Street.

The new church was named St Mary's. The area soon became known as St Mary's on the Bourne, then—with a rather pretentious French flourish—St Mary-la-Bourne, then finally St Marylebone, although the fluid standards of historical spelling saw it rendered as Marybone, Mary-le-burn, Mary-la-bonne, Mariburn and even, in Pepys's diary, Marrowbone. Still today, its correct pronunciation is the subject of impassioned—and ultimately fruitless—debate.

Having earlier relieved the priory of St John of Lilestone Manor, the Crown leased the property to Lord Chief Justice Portman in 1532. He bought the land outright in 1554, and it remained as agricultural land for the next 200 years.

Tyburn manor passed through a bewildering succession of aristocratic hands until 1544, when the large, tempestuous and no doubt extremely persuasive Henry VIII encouraged its owners to swap the area for some freshly plundered church lands elsewhere. Henry had his eyes on the fields and woodland to the north of the area, and Marylebone struck him as the perfect place for a hunting lodge. That land became a royal park and—now known as Regent's Park—has remained so ever since.

Henry's heirs soon leased the manor back to a fresh succession of royal favourites until, in 1611, King James sold it for £829 3s 4d to Edward Forset, one of the prosecutors of Guy Fawkes and author of *A Defence of the Right of Kings*—a good piece of work to have on your CV if you're looking for a cheap royal land grant. Almost a century later John Holles, Duke of Newcastle, was made to pay rather more for the estate—£17,500—and in 1711 the manor passed to the duke's daughter, Henrietta Cavendish Holles, who later married Edward Harley, 2nd Earl of Oxford.

Marylebone was then still a quiet country village. Henry Platt's survey of 1708 shows a small number of houses dotted along the high street, beyond which lie open fields. In 1719, the wealthy and socially ambitious Lord and Lady Oxford commissioned the architect John Prince to draw up a plan to convert this rural backwater into a fashionable estate, based upon an elegant grid of streets, with Cavendish Square at its focal point.

At the time, Marylebone was viewed by the gentry as a place to visit rather than a place to live. To the east of the high street stood the Rose of Normandy pub, which had been famous since Stuart times for its bowling greens and garden. In 1738, the landlord of the tavern, Daniel Gough, saw a chance to make some money by setting up the grounds as a pleasure garden and charging admission. Marylebone Gardens became a popular place for London's wealthy to promenade and listen to specially commissioned works by Handel and Arne. The gardens were also famous for their fireworks. Fireworks of the metaphorical variety were also available—despite lacking the bacchanalian spirit of the famous Vauxhall Gardens, Marylebone was a place where the rich came to find love or, failing that, buy it.

As the development of the estate spread slowly but inexorably north towards Marylebone Road, the pleasure gardens were forced to close and in 1791 the old manor house, which had been used as a boys' school since 1703, was pulled down. The Rose tavern became a music hall, which enjoyed a modicum of success before being converted to a cinema. It was bombed out in 1941.

Progress on John Prince's 1719 plan for the estate in was initially very slow, not helped by the financial shambles of the South Sea Bubble of 1720 which battered London's economy. The development scheme accelerated under Lord and Lady Oxford's daughter, Margaret Cavendish Harley, who married the second Duke of Portland. Building continued on what was then known as the Portland Estate, and today's tall Georgian houses began to emerge along the wide roads of Harley Street, Portland Place and Wimpole Street.

John Rocque's map of London of 1746 shows that building had only reached as far north as Wigmore Street and Mortimer Street, while the Portman Estate remained as farmland, with just a few houses on Oxford Street. That started to change in the 1750s, when Henry William Portman started to build on the Portman Estate, beginning with Portman Square and the Portman family house and gardens, which were erected at the north-west corner of the square.

By the 1740s, the traffic on Oxford Street was so bad that proposals were put forward for a relief road be built to the north. The problem then wasn't buses, taxis and delivery vans, it was cattle being driven from Hyde Park to Smithfield Market—blocking the coach route to Oxford. The New Road (now the Marylebone Road and Euston Road) opened in 1757, and this made the land in between much more attractive for development.

By 1799 virtually the whole area from Oxford Street to Marylebone Road was covered with houses. Numerous architects placed their stamp upon this burgeoning quarter, the most celebrated being the Adam brothers, who designed Chandos House and much of Portland Place, and John Nash, the architect of Park Crescent.

Marylebone became home to the city's wealthy elite, but it was also scarred by pockets of extreme poverty. In Marylebone's large and notorious workhouse, opened in 1775 on land donated by the Portland Estate on the north side of Paddington Street, society's poorest and most vulnerable exchanged unpaid labour for food and shelter. A Ragged School, founded in 1846 on Grotto Passage, was set up to provide education for destitute children. The Ossington Buildings estate, off Moxon Street, was built between 1888 and 1892 to house some of the area's working class poor, who had previously lived at the same site in miserable slum dwellings. It was also in Marylebone that the social reformer and general force of nature Octavia Hill began her campaign to improve accommodation for the poor. Supported by John Ruskin, she took over several slum buildings and turned them into model housing.

The Portland Estate flourished for five generations until 1879 when the death of the childless fifth Duke saw the land pass to his sister, Lucy Joan Bentinck, widow of the 6th Baron Howard de Walden. The Portland Estate became the Howard de Walden Estate, and the development of the area continued apace. Most of the buildings on the high street today date from around 1900 when the area was given a major facelift.

Medical men began arriving in Marylebone in the mid-19th century. By the 1860s there were a dozen or so doctors on Harley Street. By 1873 there were 36. After that, the numbers increased rapidly. There were around 200 doctors in 1914 and 1,500 by 1948.

The last hundred years have seen the area continue to evolve. Marylebone escaped relatively unscathed from the Second World War, but it did begin to stagnate somewhat in the second half of the century, losing some of the lustre of its heyday. This all began to change in the 1990s, thanks in part to some inspired management from the Howard de Walden Estate, which surmised that a distinctive retail environment, with an emphasis on independent retailers and a careful balance of tenants, would have a positive impact on every aspect of Marylebone life. As more and more high streets became clones of each other, Marylebone opted instead for character, quality and distinctiveness. As a result, Marylebone has slowly evolved into the highly prosperous, culturally vibrant and hugely popular urban village that we see today. And it will continue to evolve—carefully and thoughtfully—in the years to come.

POLITICIANS & WARRIORS

At times there have been almost as many politicians in Marylebone as voters. Local residents have included several prime ministers (Gladstone, Asquith, Pitt the Younger) and countless members of both houses of parliament, some of them fine, civic-minded servants of the nation, others shameless charlatans. The establishment has been well represented around these parts, but so too have more radical voices, from Charles Stanhope—the Tony Benn of his day—to the Victorian housing campaigners Octavia Hill and Emma Cons.

The area has also been home to many a great military man, endowed more often than not with vigorous facial hair and a hard earned reputation for suppressing uppity colonials. Their multi-barrelled names adorn blue plaques and statues throughout these estates. But Marylebone's warriors haven't always been so visible. During the Second World War, the Special Operations Executive (SOE) conducted many of Europe's underground resistance movements from a dull-looking building on Baker Street.

Edwin James, the dishonourable member

By Tom Hughes
MJ8.3, Jun-Jul 2012

In 1832, the Great Reform Bill gave Marylebone its first two seats in the new House of Commons. Those who feared that the barbarians were at the gate were reassured that Marylebone's voters could be trusted as they fit the "better description of persons resident in that opulent and extensive quarter of the town". And, in fact, the first two gentlemen sent to parliament by the voters of Marylebone were good and worthy men, the banker Sir Samuel Horne and the Hon Edward Berkeley Portman. Neither gentleman found life in the Commons all that compelling and their stays were short; Portman soon found himself in the ermined comfort of the House of Lords.

It must be said that the men who held the seats for Marylebone in those early years achieved no great distinction in the House. There was Lord Dudley Coutts Stewart whose views on Polish independence were thought to be quixotic. There was Edmund Burke Roche (Lord Fermoy) who sat in the House for more than a decade but passes down to history only as Princess Diana's great-great-grandfather. The long forgotten but deliciously named Sir Samuel St Swithin Burden Whalley was actually run off by the locals amid claims that he had purchased his knighthood. In truth, no one really trusted the chap anyway, as he resided in St Johns Wood. Say no more.

One of the more interesting early members for Marylebone was Sir Charles Napier, a crusty Regency naval hero who was known as either Dirty Charlie, Black Charlie or Mad Charlie depending upon his toilette, his mood or his battiness at any given time.

But by far and away the most controversial figure ever to represent Marylebone in the halls of Westminster was Edwin James QC. He came before the people of Marylebone in 1859, a man in his mid-40s. His father had been a solicitor and he too had been called to the bar and made himself a very wealthy, if not overly well-respected, barrister. James was known for taking all the "flash" briefs. The Spectator said he was the man to see in "all cases involving the reputation of an actress or a horse". He was quite popular with the radical set after he successfully defended a French refugee who'd been implicated in a plot to assassinate Napoleon III. For his legal labours, James was earning—in today's money—about £500,000 a year. He was fat, rather coarse looking, unmarried (but never lacking for feminine companionship) and he lived in Belgrave Square.

The man who stood between James and the House of Commons was Colonel Frederick Romilly, a relation to the prime minister, Lord John Russell. It looked like nepotism. James took to the hustings with the always reliable claim to be the "man of the people" battling against the aristocrats. He asked the voters: "Is the great constituency of Marylebone to be treated like a pocket borough?" Beyond rhetoric, however, James knew how to spend his money wisely.

By this time, Marylebone had become known as the most expensive constituency in all of Britain. "There is something so filthy in the humiliation that a Marylebone candidate has to undergo that none but mere adventurers will stand... the publicans and their customers have fairly driven out the inhabitants of the stately streets and squares." That more or less summed up the James campaign strategy. He openly courted the "licensed victuallers"—the publicans. He rented their rooms for "committee meetings", he hired their relatives as canvassers and "thank you men". He bought drinks for all. He bought votes and he won the poll handily. The *Westminster Review* was aghast: "The people of Marylebone did themselves no honour by electing Mr Edwin James."

James had stood for the House as a supporter of the Liberal Party, not that he held any serious political views. One of his early speeches was to oppose a bill permitting wine to be sold at eating places; his publican friends resented the competition. Still, James sat amongst the supporters of the new prime minister, Lord Palmerston, and the talk of Westminster was that this brash chap was on his way to the Woolsack, to become Lord Chancellor.

There was one little, but rather expensive, problem. Five months after James has been voted in, Palmerston dissolved parliament and new elections were required. There was no serious opposition in Marylebone, but that mattered not. The voters still expected to be "refreshed" at all their political meetings. They even demanded the cab fare to go to the polls. James wrote the required cheques and the happy voters of Marylebone swept him back into parliament by a wide margin.

Edwin James's sudden rise was outdone in rapidity by the sublime and terrible suddenness of his fall. The reasons behind the great crash that cut short this flowering career are tangled and murky but, suffice to say, they involved money. Despite his great income, James's expenses far outpaced his earnings and his parliamentary duties were limiting his time in court. Among his clients was a Colonel Dickson who was being sued for libel by the 2nd Earl Wilton. Dickson had claimed that the earl had brought his mistress along to a military review. Well, of course, the randy earl had done just that (although to his great credit, he later married the woman). Still, this was a great scandal at the Horse Guards and mighty efforts were made to hush it all up. It seems clear that James took money from Lord Wilton to go easy on him. Alas, Colonel Dickson could smell a set-up and he published a pamphlet that made it appear that he had been betrayed by his lawyer, the honourable member for Marylebone.

But the biggest problem for James was his relationship with Lord Worsley, son of the 2nd Earl of Yarborough. James had known this young peer for some time and had sufficiently gulled Worsley into serving more or less as his personal cash point. The foolish toff, still in his 20s, had co-signed insurance policies and other notes to the extent that he was now in debt for £30,000—well over a million today. The earl was not pleased and bearded James with a demand that he pay everything back.

On 9 April 1861, the voters of Marylebone—who knew nought of these transactions, of course—were stunned to read in their Times that Edwin James was resigning his seat, citing the demands of his profession. "My memory will treasure to the last hour of my existence the recollection of the honour you have conferred on me." The shock this generated was not contained within the boundaries of his constituency as James had freely borrowed money from many individuals; even his home in Belgrave Square was on loan. Many of these supporters had lent their money in anticipation of the time when their great friend would receive the high legal position that was due him. Now that he had fallen, "every one of them rushed in to save what he could out of the ruins".

Edwin James took a boat to America. In New York, he quickly applied to be a member of the Bar and told the papers that he was the victim of a conspiracy mounted by vengeful men driven by professional jealousy. The *Saturday Review* declared: "There never was such a triumph of pure unadulterated impudence." James was promptly and publicly disbarred in London. He remained in New York for several years, practising law and even trying his hand on the stage. But he eventually returned to London and applied for reinstatement to the Bar. They rejected him, and he died in rooms near Bedford Square in 1881.

After James had resigned in 1861, a bye-election was held and Marylebone chose a gentleman named John Harvey Lewis, a wealthy Irishman who ran a shipping company. He held no views anyone cared to know about; he treated the thirsty voters in the style they demanded and he went to Westminster where he caused no trouble for 14 years.

Leo Marks and the code wars

By Mark Riddaway

MJ2.2, Apr-May 2006

Baker Street, 1943. Leo Marks, head of coding and ciphers at the Special Operations Executive (SOE, was in the middle of a dressing down from the secret warfare organisation's finance director for yet another case of unauthorised spending when he was hit by a stunning revelation. Marks had spent several months trying to work out why a nagging doubt about the wellbeing of SOE's Dutch agents had been bubbling away in his gut.

Suddenly it all became clear to him. Every secret agent everywhere else in Europe had at some point sent a message coded so badly it was impossible to read—an 'indecipherable'—and some rarely sent anything else. But not the Dutch. The hundreds of messages received from operatives in the Netherlands had all been completely perfect. Far too perfect. As far as Marks was concerned this could mean only one thing: the Dutch resistance network had been compromised. Its communications weren't being sent by agents in the field, struggling with complex coding under terrible pressure, but by the Nazis.

SOE's senior commanders considered Marks to be a bit of a maverick. He was incapable of suffering fools, no matter what their rank, and was in constant trouble for his inability to follow orders he didn't agree with. Marks bombarded his superiors with criticisms and recommendations, but even a voice as demanding as his struggled to be heard above the political manoeuvring and in-fighting that dominated the secret services. His suspicions about the Dutch traffic were ignored or covered up.

The cryptographer, whose father ran the famous Marks & Co bookshop at 84 Charing Cross Road, was blessed with a restless intelligence and a life-long obsession with secret codes. When the war began, his ill-discipline at school meant he had to rely on the influence of his godfather, a Special Branch major and a prominent Freemason, to win him a place on a special government course for cryptographers. The course was designed to groom potential recruits for Bletchley Park, the government's secret communications headquarters and a Xanadu for coding boffins. But Marks proved incapable of keeping his feet out of his very smart mouth. At the end of the course, 14 of the 15 students were applauded off to Bletchley.

Marks, the sole failure, was farmed out on a month's trial to the Inter Services Research Bureau—a place described to him as "some potty outfit on Baker Street, an open house for misfits". But the Inter Services Research Bureau was no ordinary stable of misfits. It was, in fact, a cover name for SOE—the secret organisation responsible for training, arming and coordinating a network of resistance fighters, saboteurs and assassins in occupied territories across Europe and North Africa.

SOE had been formed in 1940 in the aftermath of the Dunkirk retreat, when Winston Churchill famously instructed the organisation to "set Europe alight". By the time Marks arrived at Baker Street in 1942, aged just 22, the organisation had expanded to take over large swathes of Marylebone.

Its operations—blowing up bridges, railways and power stations, murdering German soldiers and coordinating local resistance groups— were characterised by incredible courage and wholehearted sacrifice, coupled with bureaucratic ineptitude and political wrangling. SOE was, said Marks, "pitted and pockmarked with improbable people doing implausible things for imponderable purposes and succeeding by coincidence".

Marks quickly started stirring up what he saw as a moribund and dangerously slack coding operation. All agents were equipped with radio transmitters through which they were able to keep in touch with Baker Street by sending and receiving morse code messages. These communications were vitally important, but the codes being used to protect them were, he thought, an absolute disgrace.

Messages were hidden using a code based upon poetry. Each agent chose a poem or a passage from a book and committed it to memory. When sending a message, the agent would choose five words from the poem, which would then be written out with each letter numbered. The resulting code would then be used to encrypt the message.

There were two serious flaws with the poem system. The first was that the ongoing security of each agent's messages could easily be undermined by any German cryptographer with a reasonable grasp of English literature. If, for example, a message was intercepted by the Nazis and its coding painstakingly traced back to the words 'wandered', 'lonely', 'cloud', 'vales' and 'daffodils', it would not take long for the Germans to work out that William Wordsworth was supplying the source of the cipher. Decoding that agent's past and future communications would thereafter be child's play.

The second fatal weakness in the use of poems was the scope for errors. Any mistake in transposition, spelling or numbering could lead to the message being completely indecipherable, and such mistakes occur all too easily when the Gestapo are on your trail.

When Marks arrived at SOE around 20 per cent of messages received from the field were indecipherables. Each indecipherable meant that the agent had to be contacted and told to resubmit the message. As agents were putting their lives at risk every time they went on air—the Nazis were constantly tracking wireless transmissions—Marks considered this to be an unforgivable risk. Believing that there should be no such thing as an indecipherable message, Marks set about recruiting and training teams of young women from the First Aid Nursing Yeomanry (FANY) to use thousands of potential solutions to attack and solve any garbled messages that came through, thus avoiding the need for retransmission. Within months, almost all indecipherables were being cracked.

He also insisted that agents' poems should be original compositions instead of hoary old familiars that were likely to figure on the curriculum of any decent Berlin Gymnasium. He began churning out reams of his own poems, and encouraged his FANY recruits to do likewise. He reasoned that no German agent, however familiar with the canons of English verse, would be likely to have come across the L Marks composition "Tickle my wallypad / Tongue my zonker / And make an oak tree / Out of a conker."

One of Marks's poems has since become widely known. It begins: "The life that I have / Is all that I have / And the life that I have / Is yours." He wrote it in memory of a girl he had loved who had died in a plane crash in Canada. In 1944 he presented it as a code poem to a beautiful young agent in the French resistance—Violette Szabo. In 1958, the story of

Szabo's heroism and violent death was turned into a successful film called *Carve Her Name With Pride*. Marks's poem featured in the film and built a huge following among tear-stained romantics.

Marks's initiatives did a great deal to patch up the unreliability of the poem codes, but he was convinced that a completely new form of coding was required. He came up with two new methods: Worked Out Keys (WOKs) and Letter Onetime Pads (LOPs). Both systems used a series of random letters printed on pieces of silk that would provide the coding for each transmission. After using each code only once, the agent would destroy it. Silk could be easily concealed, and the simplicity and random nature of the codes meant they were safe from being cracked by Nazis or garbled by agents.

Marks endured months of fighting with a reactionary hierarchy before his new systems began to be accepted. Even after the benefits of WOKs and LOPs became apparent, Marks faced a constant struggle to secure the silk and man-power required to produce them.

Marks managed through persistence, persuasion and occasional gross insubordination to revolutionise coding practice in SOE, and his ideas were gradually incorporated into other areas of the secret services. By the time D-day came around, Marks's silks were being used for almost all operational coding. His methods saved hundreds of lives, but his failure to convince his superiors that the Dutch operation was rotten to the core drove the young cryptographer to distraction.

As his frustration mounted, he deliberately disobeyed orders by sending an indecipherable message to a Dutch agent, mangled in such a way that only an experienced cryptographer would be able to decipher it. Normally if an agent received an indecipherable from SOE, a message would wing its way back asking Baker Street to retransmit. In this instance, just as Marks feared, nothing was returned. Whoever had received the message—clearly not the code-shy agent it had been sent to—had unravelled it without a second thought. Shortly afterwards, a signalmaster named Ken Howell, who shared Marks's suspicions, signed off from a message to Holland with the letters HH—the standard Nazi sign off. The response come straight back from Holland without a pause—HH. There was a German at the other end of the line.

Marks and Howell had stumbled upon the Englandspiel, a devastating Nazi counter-intelligence operation that almost destroyed SOE. It had begun in April 1942 when a Dutch SOE agent codenamed Abor had been captured by the Germans following a tip-off. He was forced by his captor—Lieutenant Colonel H J Giskes—to continue transmitting misleading messages to London. Abor correctly, and bravely, attempted to alert Baker Street to his capture by omitting a series of security checks from his coding. But instead of being alarmed by the tip-off, it was the considered opinion of the SOE Dutch section that Abor was just being slack. Shortly afterwards, SOE instructed him to prepare to receive another agent. Giskes and his men created a giant fiction that fooled the Baker Street hierarchy completely. By April 1943, the Nazis were controlling 18 radio channels to London, sending reams of misinformation. Of 56 agents sent into the field, most landed straight into the waiting arms of the Nazis. Only eight survived.

Despite Marks's shrill warnings, the SOE hierarchy's incompetence, fear, cynicism or treachery—it has never been entirely clear which—stopped them from acting. Even the escape of two captured agents—Sprout and Chive—from Haaren concentration camp and their subsequent confirmation of the extent of the Dutch disaster, didn't entirely convince the SOE leadership. The escaped agents were assumed to have been 'turned' by the Nazis and were locked up in Brixton prison. Further Dutch operations were nonetheless cancelled.

On April Fools' Day 1944 a message arrived at Baker Street sent simultaneously from 10 different SOE transmitters in Holland: "In the last time you are trying to make business in the Netherlands without our assistance. We think this rather unfair in view of our long and successful co-operation as your sole agents. But never mind, when you come to pay a visit to the Continent you may be assured that you will be received with the same care and result as all those you sent before. So long!" The Englandspiel was over, and despite the best efforts of Leo Marks, SOE's reputation had suffered a terrible blow. Marks, disillusioned by the politics and infighting of the secret services, walked away from coding as soon as the war came to an end.

The lonely demise of Benedict Arnold

By Louisa McKenzie
MJ5.2, Apr-May 2009

If you know anything at all about Benedict Arnold, it's probably that, in America, his name has become a byword for treachery. But even those who are acquainted with his story are possibly unaware that he lived out his final days here in Marylebone. He died, largely unmourned, at 62 Gloucester Place on 14 June 1801.

As is so often true, Arnold was a more complex figure than the demonic caricature of popular imagination. In recent years, there seems to have been some rehabilitation of his image, with greater consideration given to his motives. But to many, he will remain the archetypal traitor at the gates—a turncoat willing to sell out his country for a few pieces of silver.

Arnold was born in Connecticut in 1741 into a prosperous, well-connected family. His grandfather, whose name he shared, had been a governor of Rhode Island. On his mother's side, Arnold was descended from John Lothropp, a dissenting clergyman from Yorkshire who emigrated to New England and was an ancestor of four future presidents: Ulysses S Grant, Franklin D Roosevelt, George FW Bush and George W Bush. The family's prosperity was not to last, as Arnold's father made a series of ill-judged business decisions and, buffeted by debts, drifted into alcoholism. This reversal of fortune forced Arnold to leave school at 14 when he was sent off to work as an apprentice at an apothecary.

Not long afterwards, Arnold gained his first military experience. During the French and Indian War, at the age of 15, he enrolled in the Connecticut militia. Although Arnold saw no direct action, this was a formative period in his life. When the British Fort William Henry fell to the French and their Native American allies, the French promised the British they could evacuate under truce conditions. Instead, Native American troops massacred the fort's men, women and children as the French looked on. Arnold is said to have gained his life-long hatred of France from this brutal episode. Some argue that Arnold's later treachery only occurred when he learnt that there would be a Franco-American alliance against the British.

After this early interlude in the militia, Arnold set up a business in New Haven, Connecticut and was soon very successful. Arnold also went into partnership with another local merchant and they began trading with the West Indies. But like his father, Arnold was not to have long-lasting commercial success. The pressures wrought by the 1765 Stamp Act pushed Arnold to the brink of bankruptcy.

Arnold was not alone in feeling the pinch from the British exchequer. The American colonies were growing increasingly dissatisfied with the taxes and instruments of oppression being forced upon them from across the Atlantic. Flashpoints such as the 1770 Boston Massacre (during which five civilians died at the hands of British soldiers) and the 1773 Boston Tea Party (in which crates of tea belonging to the British East India Company were destroyed in Boston harbour) soon led to sustained rebellious sentiment, then revolution.

All spectra of society chafed at the constraints placed upon colonial citizens by the British. Arnold was no exception. Of the Boston Massacre, he wrote: "Are the Americans all asleep and tamely giving up their glorious liberties?" He soon became deeply involved in the revolutionary cause, becoming captain of the Governor's Second Company of Connecticut Guards in 1775. The same year, the company marched to Massachusetts to join the revolution.

A capable man, Arnold moved up through the military hierarchy, becoming a colonel in the militia. During much of the War of Independence, Arnold distinguished himself as a daring soldier and a good leader. But his military career was characterised from first to last with what he probably considered to be personal slights. In 1775, Fort Ticonderoga, with its large cache of munitions, was captured by a force under the joint command of Arnold and another man, Allen. Allen then withdrew with his troops, leaving Arnold in sole command, but another company soon arrived from Connecticut, with its colonel taking command of the fort. Arnold was left in a subordinate position. Arnold resigned his commission and returned home.

But Arnold could not stay out of the revolutionary cause for long. He was soon part of an expedition to invade Canada overland. George Washington, then a general, gave Arnold a colonel's commission and put him in charge of an attack on Quebec. The campaign ended in defeat, with the British proving far too strong for the American forces. But despite this set back, Arnold was promoted to brigadier general and given the key task of blocking a British invasion over water from the north. Although Arnold's forces would have been outnumbered, they were saved by the onset of winter, which repelled any thought of invasion.

But Arnold was soon to face more disappointment. In 1777, he was passed over for promotion in favour of a less experienced man. Again he impetuously resigned his commission, but was soon recalled by Washington, who admired Arnold's bravery. This courage was further demonstrated in the Saratoga campaign when the British were forced to surrender after Arnold had cut them off from retreat despite being badly wounded. He again received very little public credit.

Arnold had become a bitter and conflicted man. "Having become a cripple in the service of my country, I little expected to meet ungrateful returns," he wrote. He began to live extravagantly, which led him into debt. Several lawsuits were launched against him and he was court martialled for corruption in 1779. Arnold's bitterness and financial woes led him down the path to treachery. In 1780 he sought out command of the strategically important Fort West Point. For a while previously he had been secretly corresponding with a major in the British forces. Arnold offered to betray the fort to the enemy for a cash payment of £20,300 and a brigadier's commission.

Years later, in a letter entitled *To the Inhabitants of America*, Arnold attempted to justify his treachery as coming from a true patriotic love of his country. Whether he really believed this, or just succeeded in convincing himself of this after his treachery had not provided the power and money he sought, remains a matter for interpretation. Although his courage as a soldier cannot be denied, it was a bravery characterised by impetuosity. Perhaps his treachery was another impetuous act, but it was the demand for money that sealed the fate of his reputation. An idealistic turncoat is one thing, a mercenary one is quite another.

The British major with whom Arnold was corresponding was captured and the plans for Fort West Point discovered. He was then hanged.

Arnold, amazingly, managed to flee to a British ship which was waiting for him.

After his treachery, it was Arnold's turn to be betrayed. Although made brigadier general by the British, he never received the £20,300 he had been promised. But he still fought on the British side, proving himself to be a true turncoat. As the British tried to extricate themselves from the war, Arnold was recalled to the UK. Living in London, he was treated with contempt by the British hierarchy, who, ironically, disliked his treachery as much as anyone. One MP is reported to have demanded Arnold not be given a position of power in the British Army in case he affect "the sentiments of true honour, which every British officer holds dearer than life". Instead, Arnold moved into a moderately successful shipping business in Canada, but left after a mob burned an effigy of him on his front lawn. Arnold once more returned to London, where he died in Marylebone after a short illness.

The very model of a modern major general

By Tom Hughes
MJ9.3, Jun-Jul 2013

We have, with some very good reasons, lost the taste for venerating our military leaders, present and past. The great commanders of yore, the generals and admirals of the fleet, may still strike a determined pose from atop their various plinths around the city but the civilian population often scuttles by without a thought or look, let alone a silent salute. But it was so different in the simpler days of Nelson and Wellington and Wolseley.

Wait a second, I hear the cry, Wolseley? I have never heard of the man. Tell me more.

General Sir Garnet Wolseley was ever at the ready for his imperial Queen. "With portmanteaus packed and warpaint always fresh," he was prepared to serve. Whether it was on the wild western plains of Canada or the steaming tropics of Africa, Sir Garnet sallied forth to crush any resistance to the spread of British pink across the map. Wolseley believed that the best way to advance his military career was to try to get himself killed. He put in the effort. When a teenage subaltern out in Burma, in his first military action, a formidable gingall ball passed through his leg and he nearly bled to death. In the Crimea, at Sebastopol, an exploding Russian shell destroyed his right eye. His greatest campaign came in 1874; though struck down by fever, he led his forces against the rebellious Ashantees in West Africa. From Kumasi (Coomassie), he returned to London to a reception worthy of a national hero. Disraeli called him "our only soldier". Victoria knighted him and the expression "all Sir Garnet" was coined to mean that everything was ready and correct, bang on. He was, as Gilbert wrote to Sullivan's score, "the very model of a modern major-general".

Soon after the conquering hero's return to London, Wolseley and his wife purchased 23 Portman Square, at the northwest corner of the square. It was one of the most aristocratic purlieus in the capital. The Hyatt Churchill Hotel occupies the entire block today. The Wolseleys were a remarkable couple. He was strikingly slight—in his youth, he was even thought to be "girlish". But, of course, he had the requisite bearing. He spoke in a strong voice, "its tones quite suave and courteous, but tinged with the decisive authoritative utterance of the soldier accustomed to command and to be unhesitatingly obeyed". Lady Wolseley, the former Miss Louisa Erskine, from a military family herself, was a renowned beauty. She once boasted that she had the exact figure of the Venus de Milo.

Some of the neighbours thought the Wolseleys arrogant and snobbish. But Henry James, the novelist (and snob), who became a regular visitor to "exquisite" Portman Square, found them delightful company. "Sir Garnet is a very handsome, well-mannered and fascinating little man with rosy dimples and an eye of steel; an excellent specimen of the cultivated British soldier." Lady Wolseley, James wrote to his brother, "is pretty, and has the air, the manners, the toilets and the taste of an American". Toilets, by the way, meant something rather different back then.

In March, 1878, the general and Lady Wolseley opened their home to Edmond Hodgson Yates, editor of the society weekly, *The World*. Yates created that ever fashionable genre of the glossy magazine, the 'Celebrity at Home'. The reporter described 23 Portman Square as a comfortable mansion of the old-fashioned type. He praised the elegant style of the home that her ladyship had made for the general. "It is an artistically-planned abode, furnished and decorated with the charming taste that speaks of a refined lady's governing hand."

But rather than the tapestries and Chippendale chairs, the high point for Yates was the general's gracious invitation to enter his private sanctum, a room festooned with the trophies of war. Alas, most of Wolseley's collection of loot had gone up in flames when the Pantechnicon, a massive Victorian self-storage pile in Belgravia, burned to the ground in 1874. Nevertheless, the visitor to Portman Square was begged to admire "the quaintly-carved wooden stools of African kings, trophies of arms, Kaffir assegais, and cowhide shields. Many other memories of the stirring scenes through which Sir Garnet has passed are to be found scattered here and there up and down the house."

Though the general was happy amid his uxorious comforts at home, smoking and pouring over his maps, he freely admitted, that "without a moment's hesitation", he would leave for service if called. Yates thought the empire was in good hands: "It would be difficult to find a man more absolutely free from what is commonly called 'nerves'. This faculty of high courage, combined with a perfectly cool head at moments of great emergency, augurs most strongly Sir Garnet's probable success as a commanding general in the days to come."

His rivals thought the article was typical toady puffery and slated Wolseley as a self-promoter. While at home, although ostensibly employed at the India Office, the general used Portman Square as the base camp for 'the Wolseley ring', his cadre of like-minded young officers. The 'ring' railed and plotted against "the false gods of worm-eaten tradition and reactionary routine" they saw crippling the army. The symbol of all they loathed was that "disgusting anachronism", the aging commander-in-chief, the Duke of Cambridge. The old duke, however, had the un-assailable good fortune to be the Queen's cousin. Hence, HRH did not care for the Wolseleys. He was "full of new fancies", she grumbled.

She was delighted when he was sent out to run Cyprus, a place he loathed. But Wolseley was soon recalled from the Mediterranean. Hicks-Beach, the colonial secretary and neighbour at 40 Portman Square, needed the general to hasten out to crush the Zulus who had recently thrashed the British army at Isandlwhana. Wolseley returned in triumph escorting the captured king, Cetawayo, who—if anything—was the greater celebrity of the season.

The Wolseleys sold 23 Portman Square in 1879, making something like a 25 per cent profit. They moved to Mayfair and we shan't follow them there. In truth, the general was rarely at home. Lady Wolseley tired of socialising without him: "I really felt as if every Jill had her Jack, and I belonged to nobody." While he was away, they corresponded daily, his letters to "beloved Loo" reaching London from cantonments afar.

Wolseley went on to command a victory at the great battle of Tel-el-Kebir in Egypt, for which the Queen, however reluctantly, made him a viscount. But his greatest disappointment came when he was too tardily given command of the expedition to march up the Nile to save General Gordon, besieged by the Mahdi's army in the Sudan. They arrived too late, of course. Wolseley had quite fancied the idea of being someday the Duke of Khartoum. He died a field marshal but "just" a viscount in 1913. In one of his journals, he had written, "All other pleasures pale before the intense, the maddening delight of leading men into the midst of an enemy."

The Great War, which began soon after his death, and ensuing wars, has given such talk a decidedly outmoded ring. Today, Wolseley, no longer bronzed by the imperial sun but by the sculptor, the greatest of the now forgotten colonial commanders, sits placidly astride his steed outside the Horse Guards. But he had once pitched his tent in Portman Square

Profile: Earl Charles Stanhope (1753-1816)

Politician and inventor, lived at 20 Mansfield Street

Charles Stanhope was born in London in 1753, the second son of Earl Philip Stanhope. After a couple of years at Eton, Charles was taken to live in Geneva where his older brother Philip was being treated for tuberculosis. Philip died, but the family stayed in Switzerland for the next 10 years, partly out of concern for Charles's own delicate health.

The Stanhopes returned to England in 1774. Later that year Charles married Lady Hester Pitt, sister of William Pitt the Younger, and took his first steps into politics by unsuccessfully standing for parliament as a candidate for the City of Westminster. It wasn't until 1780 that he finally entered the Commons after his ally the Earl of Shelburne engineered for him an uncontested seat at Chipping Wycombe. Stanhope proved himself to be a hardworking, independent-minded and highly passionate MP. A vocal opponent of prime minister Lord North, he developed a reputation as a somewhat eccentric radical and a ferocious campaigner for electoral reforms and jury trials. Although initially a supporter of Pitt the Younger, Stanhope was never slow to criticise his brother-in-law for his moving away from liberal ideals.

In 1786, Stanhope's father died and Charles succeeded to the earldom. Within weeks Stanhope had taken his seat in the Lords, where he carried on agitating for reform. It was the outbreak of war between Britain and revolutionary France in 1793 that came to define his political career. The earl had been an active supporter of the French Revolution and was chairman of the Revolution Society, set up to celebrate the centenary of the Glorious Revolution of 1688. In 1790 he had written an impassioned refutation of Edmund Burke's attack on the new French regime.

When war finally broke out, Stanhope consistently opposed the conflict, introducing bills into the Lords urging recognition of the French republic and an end to interference in France's internal affairs. Completely isolated in parliament, the earl was given the soubriquet 'minority of one'. It was well earned—Stanhope wrote a series of protests in the House of Lords to which his was the sole signature. His reputation shifted from harmless eccentric to dangerous political fanatic.

In 1795 the earl seceded from the Lords in frustration. He didn't return until 1800. While maintaining his opposition to the war, he became involved in the campaign for a united Ireland and was also a prominent supporter of abolition of the slave trade, although here at least he found himself closer to the political mainstream.

In the political satire Rolliad, Stanhope, who is dubbed "the Quixote of the Nation", is accused of having "all his sense at his fingers' ends". This was a cutting reference to the earl's parallel career—as well as being a hugely committed politician, Stanhope was an engineer, scientist and inventor of considerable renown.

He registered patents for steamships in 1790 and 1807, devised a new printing press (which was adopted by the *Times*) and worked on a system of fire-proofing. He also dabbled in optics, electricity and the development of an adding machine. The earl was more than just an enthusiastic dabbler—he invested a large amount of money in his work, and his scientific achievements were, if anything, more lasting than his political legacy.

The earl's political isolation was sadly mirrored in his personal life. His first wife, Lady Hestor, died of dropsy in 1780. He remarried but it was not a happy union, ending in separation in 1806 following his affair with a music teacher. He fell out with all of his children from both marriages and eventually disinherited the lot of them. The only member of his family mentioned in his will was his mother, and she died before him. By the time he died of dropsy in December 1816, he was a lonely figure.

Profile: Talleyrand (1754-1838)

Politician and diplomat, lived on Harley Street

Charles Maurice de Talleyrand-Périgord, Prince de Benevente, was born into an aristocratic family on 2 February 1754. By his death 84 years later he was universally regarded as one of the greatest of all European diplomats. The Talleyrand family took its aristocratic duties seriously and each duke was expected to adopt a military career. As the first child, Charles was in line to inherit the dukedom but a leg injury during childhood led to him being stripped of his title, as he could not continue this military tradition, and he was directed towards the clergy. The Talleyrands were not particularly wealthy and an ecclesiastical career offered access to the vast fortunes controlled by the church.

After his Ordination in 1779, Talleyrand's diplomatic talents were quickly recognised and he was made the Agent-General of the Clergy—the Catholic Church's representative to the French crown—in 1780. He helped make an inventory of church properties throughout France, and was instrumental in drafting a defence of the "inalienable rights of the church". In 1785 Talleyrand was made Bishop of Autun through family influence, even though his lack of belief was well known.

When the revolution struck France, Talleyrand found himself at the centre of events representing the church—the First Estate—at the revolutionary councils. He supported the revolutionary cause, helping to write The Rights of Man and proposing policies that effectively nationalised the church, a position that led to his excommunication by Pope Pius VI.

In 1792, while Talleyrand was in England trying to prevent another Anglo-French war, the revolutionary council issued a warrant for his arrest, leaving the diplomat unable to return home. His stay in Marylebone was short-lived—he was expelled by Prime Minister William Pitt in 1794 and found himself moving to America. While there Talleyrand became embroiled in what was known as the XYZ Affair, where accusations of diplomatic corruption flew back and forth when he was asked to represent France in negotiations about shipping rights with America. The affair marked his return to favour in France and he returned home in 1796. A year later we was foreign minister, in which capacity he met Napoleon and the two became close allies.

Three years later Talleyrand was involved in the coup that brought Napoleon to power and was later confirmed as foreign minister in the new Napoleon Consulate. He was also released from excommunication, which while being of no spiritual relief, made his diplomatic duties somewhat easier. In March 1804, he may have been involved in the kidnapping and execution of the Duke of Enghien, a cause célèbre in European politics. If so it would have been out of character as Talleyrand was a lifelong opponent of violence both personally and on a national basis, which brought him into frequent conflict with Napoleon. In May 1804, Napoleon made him grand chamberlain and vice-elector of the Empire. It was the highpoint of his time under Napoleon as the Little General's increasingly expansionist policies began to drive a wedge between the two.

Talleyrand began taking bribes from enemy agents and betrayed Napoleon's secrets firstly to Russia, and eventually to Austria and England. These actions ensured him a good name amongst the European aristocratic elite, and would set the scene for his last great diplomatic mission. Talleyrand became one of the key figures at the restoration when the Bourbons were returned to power in 1814.

Napoleon's brief return in 1815, marked the end of Talleyrand's career as a major European figure. He was by now considered an elder statesman and his opinions confined to the sidelines.

Talleyrand was a great conversationalist, gourmand, and wine connoisseur, all of which added to his effectiveness as a diplomat, but in the end diplomacy was his first love. He was a political animal who enjoyed the game as much as the results, and whose skills allowed him to navigate the shifting sands of European politics.

Profile: William Pitt the Younger (1759-1806)

Prime minister, lived at 120 Baker Street

William Pitt the Younger was born in Hayes, Kent on 28 May 1759, the second son of the Earl of Chatham, the inspirational prime minister who led Britain against France during the Seven Years' War. As a child he held the conviction that he was born to do great things. Aged 14, he entered Cambridge to study Latin and Greek, receiving his MA in 1776.

Pitt was fascinated with politics and often attended parliamentary debates. On 7 April 1778, he was present when his father collapsed whilst making a speech to the House of Lords. He helped to carry his dying father from the chamber.

In 1781, Pitt began his political career as Tory MP for Appleby. Lord North, then prime minister, described his maiden address to the House of

Commons as the "best speech" that he had ever heard. Both eloquent and forceful, Pitt's immense powers of debating allowed him to dominate parliament. His political ascent was spectacular. In July 1782, he became Chancellor of the Exchequer. In December 1783, King George III dissolved parliament and invited Pitt to form a government. He was only 24, Britain's youngest ever prime minister. Initially hamstrung without a parliamentary majority, he used his position as the dispenser of royal patronage to build support. After calling an election in March 1784, he returned with a clear majority.

Pitt set about restoring public finances, ravaged by the cost of the American Revolution. He imposed new taxes, took measures to reduce smuggling and fraud, and simplified customs duties. His premiership ran uninterrupted until 1801 and involved him leading Britain in the long wars against France. Initially, the French Revolution of 1789 had little impact on Britain. However, relations between the two nations deteriorated sharply because of the French promise of military assistance to any European radicals wishing to depose their rulers.

The execution of Louis XVI in 1793 outraged the British. Pitt stated: "On every principle by which men of justice and honour are actuated, it is the foulest and most atrocious deed which the history of the world has yet had occasion to attest." The French, confident of victory, declared war on 1 February 1793. Pitt's government sought to crush any radical activity. It issued a proclamation against seditious publications and suspended habeas corpus, the protection against detention without trial. Anyone advocating parliamentary reform risked arrest.

To pay for the war, Pitt introduced a new income tax, placed duties on horses and tobacco, and levied taxes on tea, sugar and spirits. A series of bad harvests only worsened the economic climate. Pitt often needed protection against angry mobs.

In Ireland, the French war worsened old religious feuds, igniting a rebellion in 1798. Though easily crushed, Pitt believed this showed the need for Ireland to be united with Britain under a single parliament, with the Catholic majority being granted legal equality with the protestants. The Act of Union was passed in 1801, but George III fiercely opposed Catholic Emancipation, resulting in Pitt's resignation.

He was brought back to power in May 1804 at a time of threatened invasion by Napoleon. Pitt's greatest triumph came when the French and Spanish navies were destroyed at Trafalgar on 21 October 1805. He was hailed as the saviour of Europe. His glory was short lived. Napoleon hit back, destroying Britain's allies at Ulm and Austerlitz. These victories broke Pitt, who became seriously ill. He died on 16 January 1806 and was buried in Westminster Abbey.

William Pitt devoted his life exclusively to politics, showing no interest in literature, science or the arts. He neither married nor displayed any interest in women. His only apparent vice was a devotion to the consumption of port. Though always prudent with the nation's finances, he had allowed irresponsible servants to squander his own income. When he Pitt died in 1806, parliament had to raise £40,000 to pay off his creditors.

Profile: Lord George Bentinck (1802-1848)
Politician and horse breeder, buried in Marylebone

In the middle of Cavendish Square stands an imposing statue of a tall Victorian gentleman with a regal stance and vigorous whiskers. His name was Lord George Bentinck, although those with a sense of decorum and plenty of time on their hands knew him as Lord George William Frederick Cavendish-Scott-Bentinck.

This impressively multi-barrelled aristocrat, the second son of the Duke of Portland, was famed in his day for two things: politics and horse racing. In the 1820s, before the advent of racecourse bulimia, it was possible to be both a champion jockey and a strappingly masculine six footer. Lord George won his first public race at the age of 22, and continued racing for the next 20 years. But it was as a horse owner, breeder and prodigious gambler that he really made his name. Disraeli said of his turf activities that they were "on a scale that perhaps has never been equalled". Horses owned by Bentinck won every major honour bar the Derby.

Lord George thought betting to be an honourable pursuit and he hated being swindled. One disputed bet with Squire Osbaldeston resulted in

Bentinck challenging his opponent to a duel. Lord George shot first, missed by a mile, smiled at his rival and shouted: "Now, Squire, I suppose this makes you two to one on." Osbaldeston, recognising brass balls when he saw them, let him off.

Being of good family, Lord George was a shoo-in for parliament, even though he rarely bothered attending if there was any racing business to concentrate on instead. When he did show up, it was often in his gaudy racing pinks.

In the mid-1840s, Bentinck suddenly discovered some convictions that had nothing whatever to do with horses. The prime minister, Robert Peel, whom Lord George despised, started toying with the new-fangled free trade ideas that had become fashionable in some circles. Bentinck became a central figure in the campaign to retain trade tariffs and keep imports from uppity foreign countries well and truly out. His tooth and nail fight against the repeal of the Corn Laws and other Peelite innovations meant he had no time left for his beloved horses, so he sold his entire stud operation. One of his former horses straight away won the Derby, much to Lord George's chagrin.

Political life placed a heavy strain upon Bentinck's health. His unusual distain for food didn't help—he often failed to eat anything at all until past midnight. In 1848, aged just 46, he dropped dead from a heart attack while walking near his Nottinghamshire manor. He was buried in Marylebone in the family burial patch. The statue in Cavendish Square was erected in 1851, allowing Lord George Bentinck's straight back and manly sideburns to be admired for countless generations to come.

Profile: Earl Frederick Sleigh Roberts (1832-1914)
Field marshal, lived at 47 Portland Place

Frederick, the son of General Sir Abraham Roberts, was born at Cawnpore, India on 30 September 1832. Educated at Eton, Sandhurst and Addiscombe, aged 19 he obtained a commission from the British Indian Army as a Second Lieutenant in the Bengal Artillery. He would become one of the most distinguished, successful and highly decorated military commanders of the Victorian era.

Frederick Roberts rose to prominence during the bloody suppression of the Indian Mutiny of 1857-58. After fighting rebel Indian sepoys in the Punjab, he arrived at Delhi and was delighted to find it still occupied by the enemy. "I could hardly believe my good luck," he wrote. "I was actually at Delhi and the city was still in possession of the mutineers." British forces vanquished the rebels and took the city.

On 2 January 1858, during hostilities at Khudaganj, Roberts captured a standard from two sepoys in singlehanded combat. He also risked his life to save one of his own men. His bravery earned him the Victoria Cross. Home on sick leave, he married Nora Bews in Waterford, Ireland on 17 May 1859. With an empire to protect, Roberts soon chose the roar of cannon over tranquil domesticity, fighting lengthy campaigns in Umbeyla, Abyssinia and Lushai.

By 1880, he was a major-general commanding troops in the Second Afghan War. On taking Kabul, news arrived that Lieutenant-General Primrose lay besieged in Kandahar. Leading 10,000 troops, Roberts started a forced march through Afghanistan. His relief mission became the stuff of legend. Covering 313 miles in 22 days, his forces reached Kandahar on 31 August. On the following day Roberts scored the decisive victory in the campaign, crushing Ayub Khan's Afghan army. Roberts received the thanks of parliament and a whole load of initials after his name. In July 1885, he became commander-in-chief in India, instituting major developments in frontier communications and defence. Now a general, in January 1892 he was elevated to the peerage as Baron Roberts of Kandahar and Waterford, and was promoted to field marshall three years later. At Queen Victoria's diamond jubilee in 1897, he became Lord Roberts.

This national hero was not about to retire. After the disastrous actions in the Second Boer War at Magersfontein, Stormberg and Colenso, where his son Frederick was killed, Roberts was dispatched to South Africa as commander-in-chief. With strategic brilliance, he reversed British military fortunes, relieving Kimberley, Ladysmith and Mafeking, capturing the Boer strongholds of Bloemfontein and Pretoria and routing enemy commandos at Bergendal.

Arriving in the Solent on 2 January 1901, Roberts was handed the

Insignia of the Order of the Garter. The next day he was met at Paddington by the Prince and Princess of Wales and driven to Buckingham Palace to be entertained as a guest of Queen Victoria. On 14 January, on his elevation to an earldom, he was received at Osborne, the final audience given by her majesty before her death.

Roberts became the honorary Colonel of the Irish Guards, which gained the regiment the nickname 'Bob's Own'. He died of pneumonia at St Omer, France on 14 November 1914, whilst visiting troops fighting in the First World War. He lay in state in Westminster Hall—the only other non-royal to do so in the 20th century was Sir Winston Churchill in 1965—and was buried in St Paul's Cathedral.

Earl Frederick Sleigh Roberts epitomised the Victorian ideal of muscular Christianity: he had courage, faith and honour in abundance and stood willing to make the supreme sacrifice for queen and empire. He cared deeply for the soldiers under his command, who affectionately knew him as 'Bobs'. To Rudyard Kipling, Robert's personified the very best of the army in India. He dedicated two poems to him: *Bobs* and *Lord Roberts*. Roberts became known as 'Kipling's General'.

Profile: Emily Faithfull (1835–1895)
Writer and campaigner, lived at 52 Bryanston Square

The position of legal equality and emancipation in which women living in the UK today find themselves is due in no little part to the actions of their foremothers. Among the canon of women's rights campaigners, some names are better known than others—the Pankhursts, for example—but one particularly influential group of women's rights activists used to meet in Marylebone. This group was called the Langham Place Circle, named after the location of the offices of the *English Woman's Journal* at 19 Langham Place, where the group would gather.

The Langham Place Circle was composed of likeminded middle-class women determined to improve the standards of women's education and their employment prospects. These issues were the major themes dealt with by the English Women's Journal, for which the majority of the circle wrote and worked.

One member of the circle was Emily Faithfull. Born into conventional Victorian gentility—the daughter of a vicar, presented at court, educated—she devoted her life to attempting to better the prospects of women in the workplace. Faithfull began to work at the *English Women's Journal* in 1858, soon after its creation (and only a year after she had been presented at court). She was described by Elizabeth Rayner Parkes, one of the founders of the circle, as being 'a most hearty young worker who has brought us a host of subscriptions'. In conjunction with the other members of the circle, Faithfull began to seek roles in which women could be gainfully employed.

One possibility was the role of compositor. Fundamental to the printing industry, the compositor was in charge of composing the individual letters and punctuation marks in the frame to provide the plate for printing. This was a fiercely guarded, male-dominated industry, so the ladies of the circle certainly ruffled some feathers in exploring this avenue. Unperturbed, in 1860 Faithfull, backed by another interested individual, invested her own capital into the creation of the Victoria Press.

The Victoria Press was a commercial success and gained the recognition and support of no less influential a backer than its namesake, Queen Victoria. Although the Victoria Press, with its mixed workforce, marked a definite step forward, its women still did not fulfil all the functions of the compositor's role. Instead they acted much as a sub-editor would today—writing, tidying and proof-reading copy. It would be another body, the Women's Printing Society (1876), which would allow women to take on the full role of a compositor. Faithfull was also associated with this body, although it was the brainchild of other members of the circle.

The Victoria Press produced some exemplary work, including a *Te Deum Laudamus* with exquisite illustrations, printed in 1868. It was both a printer and a publisher, turning out books and periodicals including, from 1863, Faithfull's own *Victoria Magazine* to which she was a tireless contributor.

In 1869, Faithfull was bought out of the press by a male associate, WW Head. From then on she dedicated herself to writing and lecturing in order to further the cause of women. Her works included a novel (whose theme was the need for a change in the status and treatment of women), articles in journals, periodicals, gazettes and propaganda documents.

She made three lecture tours of the USA where she became a renowned speaker and contributed to developments in education and employment. In the UK she was one of the few of the circle who was unafraid to speak out about the need for women's suffrage. Some were afraid that this controversial topic would deter politicians and the public from supporting smaller improvements. Not Emily Faithfull—she managed to speak out and still retain her place as a favourite of the Queen, by whom she was awarded several honours.

Profile: Emma Cons (1838-1912)

Housing campaigner, lived and worked at 136 Seymour Place

Looking around the blue plaques of Marylebone, there is one significant characteristic that almost all of the area's celebrated luminaries had in common: they urinated standing up. And had beards too, for the most part. But among this parade of Victorian men, a handful of women did force their way into the plaque-makers' plans—including the formidable Emma Cons.

Born in 1838, Cons grew up near Goodge Street in a working class family with artistic aspirations—her father Frederick was a skilled cabinet and piano case maker. At the age of 14, Cons joined the Ladies Art Guild, a Fitzroy Square cooperative run by Caroline Hill, which helped turn the creative talents of women into gainful employment. It was here that she made friends with the principal's daughter, Octavia Hill—a relationship that would shape her life.

After graduating, Cons found work as a watch engraver, then a stained glass painter. Meanwhile, her friend Octavia, angered by the ugly slums that scarred London, had started a campaign to provide proper housing for the city's working poor. With investment from John Ruskin, she purchased some previously squalid tenements in Marylebone, known as Paradise Place and Freshwater Place. Her intention was to help the poor, but without sentiment: the business was run for profit, and its strict rules encouraged thrift, hygiene and personal responsibility. Emma Cons was brought in to manage the estates and collect the rent. She threw herself into the job with genuine zeal, proving utterly fearless in dealing with the rough and ready tenants.

She was unafraid of hard work, rolling up her sleeves to help out with the renovations. Henrietta Rowland would recall her "mounting ladders, mixing colours, ordering and laughing at the men who, when too inexperienced, backward or perhaps indolent, would show resentment at or disinclination for the job."

In 1869, Julia and Hester Sterling, inspired by Hill and Cons, purchased a block of 38 houses in Marylebone: Walmer Street and Walmer Place. Cons became manager and moved into the building. With a £10 donation, she immediately established a library for tenants, with 300 books. It was a huge success. Less successful was the pub next door which lacked one essential component: plentiful booze.

Having witnessed first-hand the destruction wreaked on poor families by drunken husbands and fathers, Cons became deeply involved in the temperance movement. She was honorary secretary of the Coffee Taverns Company, which sought to compete with the city's dens of iniquity by providing wholesome coffee shops. In 1873, the Walmer Castle coffee tavern was opened right next door to her home, with Cons as its manager. It became a base for her campaigning work, and thrived for a while, but the coffee tavern idea never quite caught on. After moving out of Marylebone, Cons made even more of a mark on London's Southbank. It was here that she helped found Morley College, an adult education centre for the working classes, and turned the Old Vic theatre into an alcohol-free venue which put on great plays at prices affordable to London's poor.

CULTURE & SPORT

Marylebone is currently home to three major cultural institutions—Wigmore Hall, the Royal Academy of Music and the Wallace Collection— as well as a whole host of galleries and exhibition spaces. Other famous venues have been and gone: the famous Marylebone Pleasure Gardens, where Arne and Handel both unveiled new works; Queen's Hall on Langham Place, home of the Proms before it was destroyed by a bomb in 1941; and Trinity College of Music, which resided on Mandeville Place until 2001.

Some of the true giants of British culture made their homes here: Charles Dickens, JMW Turner, Gabriel Dante Rossetti, Lord Byron. Marylebone looms large in Beatles lore, with the ill-fated Apple Boutique opening on Baker Street, Paul McCartney writing Yesterday while living at 57 Wimpole Street, and Ringo Starr leasing a basement flat on Montagu Square where John and Yoko were busted on trumped up drugs charges.

While hardly a hotbed of sporting endeavour, Marylebone has one major claim to fame in this sphere: as the birthplace of the MCC and, therefore, the game of cricket as we know it. Less trumpeted is its pedigree in the bare-knuckle boxing game.

John Ruskin's tea shop

By Tom Hughes

MJ3.4, Aug-Sep 2007

The great critic and commentator John Ruskin has been poorly treated by us moderns. I imagine a few architecture critics still get a bit heated over the old boy's Stones of Venice but for the rest of us—or the select few who give any thought at all to the bloke—Ruskin has been written off as the man who came over all unnecessary on his honeymoon at his first sight of female body hair, survived a scandalous annulment, wrote scads of meddlesome letters, and was sued for calling James McNeill Whistler a coxcomb. After such a full life, Ruskin ended up a barking-mad recluse living in splendid seclusion in the Lake District.

Well, if you're enjoying this marvellous publication while sipping a 'cuppa' or a cappuccino in one of the—at last count—794 coffee shops in W1, I'd like to give some props to JR. He had the idea 130 years ago. Mr Ruskin's Tea Shop was at 29 Paddington Street, on the northwest corner of the present day intersection of Paddington and Chiltern Streets.

Ruskin was not a Marylebonian. In fact, he spent most of his time in London living south of the river in Herne Hill, save for a few excruciating years of unsatisfying (literally) married life in Mayfair. Upon the death of his father, however, he inherited a goodly bit of property in Marylebone, which was then rather down-at-heel and not the chic purlieu of Michelin-starred restaurants and glossy magazines it is today. It was a working class area and Ruskin saw his new landlord status as an opportunity to put some social theories into action.

On 1 January 1871, Ruskin had started writing a weekly open letter to the "working men and labourers of England". The series of letters had the title of *Fors Clavigera* (presuming that said workmen and labourers were familiar with Latin and classical mythology). Ruskin thought the poor—who lived from payday to payday—were getting jobbed when it came to buying staples for the home. Be it bread, eggs or even tea, most people were unable to get the price advantages enjoyed by wealthier shoppers who bought in bulk. So Ruskin decided to open his own teashop, declaring his intention to supply the poor of Marylebone with pure tea, in packets as small as they chose to buy, without making a profit on the subdivision.

Alas, Ruskin's own eccentricities probably doomed the tea shop to failure. While standing firm against "catchpenny tricks of the trade" is a praiseworthy business practice, then as now, Ruskin also decreed that there would be no advertising at all. Even the sign above the door became an issue as Ruskin explained with either disarming naivety or just damned silliness: "Owing to that total want of imagination and invention which makes me so impartial and so accurate a writer on subjects of political economy, I could not for months determine whether the said sign should be of a Chinese character, black upon gold; or of a Japanese, blue upon white; or of pleasant English, rose-colour on green; and still less how far legible scale of letters could be compatible, on a board only a foot broad, with lengthy enough elucidation of the peculiar offices of Mr Ruskin's Tea Shop."

While Ruskin stood outside in deep contemplation of the perfect sign, the tea scales and cash registers inside were to be managed by the Tovey sisters, Harriet and Lucy, who were long-time servants of the Ruskin family. Through no fault of the tireless Toveys, the Ruskin revolution failed.

As a professional critic, Ruskin had no shortage of theories as to why the whole venture was a dismal failure. First, there were too many local topers whose idea of a refreshing beverage wasn't to be found in a teashop. Ruskin noted with sadness "a steady increase in the consumption of spirits throughout the neighbourhood faster and faster slackens the demand for tea". There were two public houses in Paddington Street at the time—the Apollo across the street, and the Pitt's Head further down the road.

But it took more than simply a couple of competing local boozers to put paid to Ruskin's tea trade. In a subsequent issue of *Fors Clavigera* (letter XLVIII for those of you inspired to seek out the original text), Ruskin put the heaviest blame on an "uncalculating public". He dourly concluded that "the poor only like to buy their tea where it is brilliantly lighted and eloquently ticketed". The tea-historian Osbert Lancaster imagined the few stragglers who did find their way to Ruskin's corner shop entering a world of "a correct but a possibly slightly forbidding Gothic gloom". But no glowing chandeliers and sconces would illuminate Ruskin's tea shop for he proclaimed that he would not compete with other tradesmen "either in gas or rhetoric". The Ruskin business model, however artfully conceived and passionately held, was a failure. Poor Ruskin finally faced reality: "The business languishes, and the rent and taxes absorb the profits, and something more, after the salary of my good servants has been paid."

After one of the faithful Tovey sisters passed on, Ruskin turned the business over to the famous Marylebone-based housing reformer Octavia Hill who tried to make a go of the shop for a while.

In one of the last decisions Ruskin made in the tea shop, he gave in to the not unreasonable request from the Toveys that they perhaps could also sell coffee. Ruskin's friend and biographer GW Collingwood said: "This was not at all in Ruskin's programme, and there were great debates at home about it. At last he gave way." One can almost hear Ruskin's blustering fulminations, "What, tea and coffee? Next, they'll want to be selling fresh cut sandwiches, carrot cake and marzipan ducks." It is for the best that he never saw a Starbucks.

But we should not mock Ruskin. He understood, he cared and he tried to help the poor in his comical street corner tea shop in Marylebone. But he always knew where he stood with the "uncalculating public": "I am far more provoked at being thought foolish by foolish people, than pleased at being thought sensible by sensible people; and the average proportion of the numbers of each is not to my advantage."

The tragi-comedy of Edward Lear

By Glyn Brown
MJ7.2, Apr-May 2011

Head down Seymour Street, away from the thunder of Edgware Road, toward the relative peace of Portman Square and an attractive row of Georgian terraces. Number 30 catches the eye for a couple of reasons: it's bedecked with window boxes of tumbling blossoms, and it boasts a blue plaque which states that nonsense poet and painter Edward Lear once lived here.

Today the hotel named after him will let you sleep in one of the rooms where he—well, for the most part worried, but also joked, drew, and kept company with the person he loved most in all the world; apart from Foss, the cat he had in his declining years. Though plagued by "the morbids" (Lear-speak for depression), he was a kind and charming man whose teenage fame began on this very street.

Lear was born in north London on 12th May 1812, the 20th of 21 children to be born to parents Ann and Jeremiah Lear. Life wasn't difficult: Jeremiah was a city stockbroker and kept his family in a large and comfortable house in the village of Holloway.

It was here in the painting room that young Edward took his first steps in drawing, under the tutelage of his sister Sarah. But it was Ann, 21 years his senior, to whom Edward was closest and who would eventually be given the task of taking her favourite brother under her own wing—their mother being somewhat preoccupied.

Ann took on the job with delight, educating Lear herself (he never went to school) and trying to reason away his dislike of his appearance. Judging by the eulogies his nose would come to receive, her success in this was limited: *The Dong with the Luminous Nose* is still one the most recognisable of Lear's comic rhymes. Yet it was upon experiencing his first epileptic fit at a fair near Highgate that his big sister's support really came into its own.

At first the five-year-old Lear was frightened. Then he was deeply embarrassed. In the early 19th century, epilepsy was thought to be linked to demonic possession. Coping with up to 18 attacks per month, Lear played on his own, kept himself hidden away, and was sensitive about the feelings of others. Much of the adult Lear's self-imposed isolation was driven by his need to hide his 'Demon' condition. Growing up, Ann's unfailing support was often the only thing standing between him and a depression that would become increasingly severe with adulthood, caused by the shame of epilepsy and his father's iron discipline.

When Edward was 13 Jeremiah Lear made a disastrous speculation, ruining the family finances and landing himself in King's Bench Prison. Mrs Lear had no choice but to sell Bowman's Lodge and move her 15 children to lodgings within easy reach of her husband's jail. Later, Edward would write a poem about his distress at leaving the home he was born in: "In dreary silence down the bustling road / The Lears, with all their goods and chattels, rode". Yet as Mrs Lear was busy taking full six-course dinners to Mr Lear, Edward's suddenly-suffering brothers and sisters were forced out to work.

 Four of Lear's sisters died over the next four months. Two of his brothers emigrated to America, one to Africa. But Ann, the eldest daughter, had been left £300 a year by her grandmother. She found pleasant lodgings at 30 Seymour Street, and moved there with Edward. It was a happy time and later, when he lived away from England, Edward would write Ann—who he saw as his mother—letters full of tenderness and affectionate teasing.

A little money didn't let Lear off earning a living however. By 15 he was doing "uncommon queer shop-sketches, selling them for prices varying from ninepence to four shillings; colouring prints, screen, fans; awhile making morbid drawings for hospitals". By 18 he was teaching drawing in London houses, and was also named unofficial draughtsman of the new zoological gardens.

His first task was to record the parrots, a job which had previously been done by the renowned John James Audubon using stuffed models. An American, Audubon, would shoot hundreds of the same species of bird, then select one or two to mount on wires in various positions. Lear couldn't countenance such a thing, and worked only from live sitters. Biographer Peter Levi describes what this entailed: "A young zoo keeper would hold the bird while Lear measured it in various directions. Then Lear would sit in the parrot house for days, drawing. Some of the sketches contained caricatures of the public who came to goggle at him." The resulting likenesses meant his reputation as a naturalist was established by the time he was 20.

High profile assignment followed high profile assignment, and it wasn't long before the Earl of Derby was asking Lear to draw the animals at his vast private menagerie at Knowsley Hall near Liverpool. The undertaking would change his life.

Though he and Ann kept their rooms in London, Lear spent the next four years at Knowsley, being introduced to society and entertaining the old Earl's children and grandchildren with limericks adorned with whimsical drawings.

At first Lear ate his meals in the servants' quarters—a formality that was quickly rectified when Lord Derby found his dinner guests vanishing downstairs to hear Lear's witty conversations. From then on the young Lear was invited to take his meals upstairs, meeting family and guests who would prove invaluable to him as future friends and patrons.

It was this that led to Lear giving the young Queen Victoria 12 drawing lessons. Nevertheless Lear was still barely out of his teens, and sometimes found the large house oppressive. "The uniform apathetic tone assumed by lofty society irks me dreadfully," he wrote to a friend. "Nothing I long for half so much as to giggle heartily and hop on one leg down the great gallery—but I dare not."

By 1836 the earl's books were finished—and so, at the age of 24, was Lear's precarious eyesight. Years spent straining to capture the finer points of feathers and beaks had taken its toll. With funds and instructions from the kind Earl on how to set himself up as a painter of topographical landscapes, Lear took himself off to Italy where the light and the warm climate helped considerably with the depressions he was fighting.

"Always have 10 years' work mapped out before you if you wish to be happy," Lear claimed—and thus he spent 10 years in Rome, travelling through Europe, all the while working prolifically to help ward off depression. So things were—and so things would have continued had he not decided on a whim to publish a *Book of Nonsense* under the name Derry Down Derry.

The book was hugely popular. In Lear's lifetime alone it went through 30 editions—though having sold the copyright for £125 he didn't make a great deal from it. What the book did make, however, was his name.

There were to be more books, more travelling (about which he loved to write—even an owl and a pussycat head off to sea) and there was of course more painting. But it was a solitary life. Even poems obliquely about himself show Lear as a sad clown and an outsider. He proposed twice, both times to the same, much younger woman, and twice was turned down. When Ann died, aged 70, Lear sank into depression and couldn't work for months.

He picked up to an extent. At 59, he built a house at San Remo, Italy and lived a settled existence with his adored cat Foss—by all accounts an ugly beast with half a tail. He wrote regularly and wittily to the 440 or so friends he had made over the years. He even had a parrot named after him, the blue Lear's macaw (for himself, his round spectacles and snowy beard made him look much like a barn owl.)

Nevertheless, when Foss passed away in 1887 his devoted owner was quick to follow. His depression worsened, and his prevailing ill health culminated in him dying alone at his villa on 28 January 1888.

While it has been pointed that not one of Lear's friends attended his funeral, this has not stopped Lear from being remembered as someone with an acute sense of beauty and delight—nor stopped his particularly good friend Chichester Fortescue from describing him as: "a delightful companion, full of nonsense, puns, everything in the shape of fun—and brimming with intense appreciation of nature and history."

In the modest words of the good poet himself: "How pleasant to know Mr Lear / Who has written such volumes of stuff. / Some think him ill-tempered and queer / But a few find him pleasant enough."

The bitter end of Anthony Trollope

By Tom Hughes

MJ5.6, Dec-Jan 2009-10

One of the first critics to visit the newly developed Marylebone residential purlieus of Montagu Square and its western neighbour Bryanston Square called them "twin deformities". They are rectangles not squares, he scoffed as he wallowed in his geometrical purity. Whingeing on, he declared that the central gardens were made so narrow as to be un-tillable and were likely to be given over to "perambulating nursemaids and exiguous cats".

Despite the sneers, the new Georgian area prospered. In the late Victorian years, Montagu Square, because it was "north of the Park", was quite affordable. In 1873, the prolific and frugal novelist Anthony Trollope—using the earnings from his latest in the Palliser series, The Eustace Diamonds—purchased 39 Montagu Square, on the west side of all those nursemaids and cats.

The author was not overly impressed at first with his new digs. He wrote to a friend: "It is not a gorgeous neighbourhood but one which will suit my declining years and modest resources." Trollope settled in, taking most of his time to organise a library of some 5,000 books, a collection more important to him than the "wine in the cellar". The bibliophilic chore having been done, Trollope recalled, "I began a novel, to the writing of which I was instigated by the commercial profligacy of the age". In 1875, he published *The Way We Live Now*.

"Commercial profligacy", you must have read somewhere, still exists in the world. But 1870s London saw a series of financial scandals and resulting panics. Even Trollope's beloved Post Office—where he'd been employed for decades—was tainted by misappropriated revenues that ruined the careers of some of his long-time colleagues. Thousands of Britons had lost their investments in the failed Emma Mine fiasco—silver diggings in Utah that had been touted across society dinner tables by the American minister to London (hastily recalled to Washington in disgrace). But the poster child of profligacy was the Baron Albert Grant, an Irish-born financial schemer and self-promoter whose dodgy title was bestowed upon him by the Italian King Victor Emmanuel. So shady was his reputation that a London clubland wit wrote: "Honours a king can grant; Honour he can't / And Grant without honour is a Baron Grant." Well played, sir. And in passing, do clubland wits still exist?

Grant, in his flushest days, purchased himself a seat in parliament. He bought up the unkempt, litter-strewn land off Piccadilly and re-claimed it for Leicester Square and gave it to the people of London. He built a monstrous home off Kensington High Street. But he never moved in, because, by 1874, it was all over. His empire of companies such as The Cadiz Waterworks and the Lisbon Steam Tramways Company collapsed in litigation and scandal. Grant was hounded from parliament. The home in Kensington was pulled down. His magnificent art collection was sold at auction. He slunk away to die unmourned in Bognor.

Grant's most lasting memorial is in the character of Augustus Melmotte, the corrupt and doomed financier of Trollope's imagination. In his book-lined study in Montagu Square, Trollope fleshed out his villain: "It was said that he made a railway across Russia, that he provisioned the Southern army in the American civil war, that he had supplied Austria with arms and had at one time bought up all the iron in England. He could make or mar any company by buying or selling stock, and could make money dear or cheap as he pleased. All this was said of him in his praise—but it was also said that he was regarded in Paris as the most gigantic swindler that had ever lived.; that he had made that city too hot to hold him; that he had endeavoured to establish himself in Vienna, but had been warned away by the police; and he had at length found that British freedom would alone allow him to enjoy, without persecution the fruits of his industry."

The Way We Live Now was a one off, of sorts, for Trollope. He was known (then and now) for his comfy tales of genial country parsons in Barchester and his world-weary politicians in Westminster, like good old honest Planty Pal. In *The Way We Live Now*, however, he loosed what one critic called "an indiscriminate assault" on London society.

None of the characters emerges in a very pleasant light. The usual booby aristocratic dupes appear, slurping at Melmotte's trough in Grosvenor Square, lending their names to his letterhead and trying to inveigle their wastrel sons to marry his daughter. All London, even the women, are frenziedly chasing money. The only "hero"—and he bears the significant name of Paul Montague—dares to quarrel with the great Melmotte's hazy business model.

Yet, Montague meekly went along with his fellow directors in endorsing the gaudy plans to launch the South Central Mexican and Pacific Railroad, following a circuitous route across trackless deserts from the Great Salt Lake to Mexico City and then out to the Gulf at Vera Cruz. Montague's anguished worries about engineering issues or costs are derided as "off the mark". And he backed down, because "the money was very pleasant to him". After all, the share prices were soaring, helped along by glossy illustrated prospectuses with "gorgeous maps, and beautiful little pictures of trains running into tunnels beneath snowy mountains, and coming out of them at the margin of sunlit lakes".

Inevitably, Melmotte's ponzi scheme collapsed, fortunes were lost, and the great man took his own life with prussic acid. There was no alternative. "Fraud and dishonesty had been the very principle of his life... Not to cheat, not to be a scoundrel, not to live more luxuriously than others by cheating more brilliantly, was a condition of things to which his mind had never turned itself." Montague could only tell everyone that he had always known that the great Melmotte was a scoundrel and a swindler.

Trollope was shaken by the generally negative reviews that his first major Montagu Square effort had received. It was un-Trollopian, they shouted. It didn't help that one character in the book writes a novel—a storyline used by Trollope to gleefully bash the whole review-shopping gambit. Not the recommended way to ingratiate an author with his critics.

Back at 39 Montagu Square, Trollope soon returned to more familiar subjects and continued to produce at a remarkable rate, if not up to the same mark as before. He was older and tired. Maybe it was the German bands and Italian organ-grinders that infested the square and menaced his peace and quiet with their incessant oom-pahs and hurdy-gurdys until they were paid to sod off. They were a constant bane to him and he suffered a mild stroke after exchanging heated words with one especially importunate bandleader.

According to his autobiography, Trollope had planned to live out his years in Marylebone: "I took a house in Montagu Square, in which I hope to live and I hope to die." That was not to be; for reasons of health he finally moved to Harting, near Petersfield. He actually died in Marylebone, however, at a nursing home in Welbeck Street in October, 1882.

In 1914, Westminster City Council honoured Trollope with a (quite rare) black plaque beneath the ground floor bay window at 39 Montagu Square. During one of Trollope's last trips abroad, to see a son in Australia, he came home via South Africa. The trip was exhausting. Although he had seen much, he wrote to a friend in London, "the grandest scenery to me would be in Montagu Square".

Wilkie Collins: Marylebone man

By Andrew Lycett

MJ9.6, Dec-Jan 2013-14

A smart blue plaque is displayed outside his revamped house, 65 Gloucester Place, leading northwards from Oxford Street to Marylebone Road. A cheery mosaic showing his features can be seen behind the tills in the unlikely setting of the Marylebone High Street branch of Waitrose.

But otherwise the popular Victorian novelist Wilkie Collins's associations with Marylebone, the area of London where he was born, died and lived most of his life, are little trumpeted. This is a shame since his most famous book, *The Woman in White*, has enduring connections with the neighbourhood.

At the time of Wilkie's birth on 8 January 1824, Marylebone was enjoying a late Georgian boom. John Nash's Regent Street had recently joined up with the Adam brothers' grand Portland Place and opened the way to the rural delights of Marylebone Park, where a number of elegant stucco terraces with Hanoverian names were being built. This would soon be known as the Regent's Park, bordering the New Road, which would become the Marylebone Road.

To the west of Portland Place stood the burgeoning property holdings of the Duke of Portland (now the Howard de Walden Estate), in the centre of which stood New Cavendish Street, an east-west thoroughfare which incorporated part of the Portland family name. Wilkie was born here, at number 11.

His family had lived locally for a couple of generations. An immigrant from Ireland, Wilkie's grandfather, William, had flourished as a picture dealer in nearby Great Titchfield Street. His father, also called William, was a prominent painter and Royal Academician, who settled in New Cavendish Street. The artists and writers of the area would feature throughout Wilkie's life.

William Collins met his wife Harriet Geddes—Wilkie's mother—in Marylebone. She came from the village of Alderbury, near Salisbury. In 1814 she was visiting her sister, Margaret, who had moved to London, and, unusually for a woman, was making an excellent living as an artist, initially from a base in Mortimer Street. She introduced Harriet to her fellow painter William.

William Collins and Harriet Geddes did not marry until 1822. Less than two years later Wilkie was born in New Cavendish Street and was christened nearby in the parish church of St Mary the Virgin on the New Road (now Marylebone Road). Although there had been a place of worship there for centuries, this latest building dated only from 1817, when it had been refashioned and greatly expanded by the architect Thomas Hardwick to cater for new parishioners from the Portland Estate and its environs. It had notable artistic connections, represented in the transparency, or picture window, by Benjamin West, president of the Royal Academy, an institution revered by William Collins. It would later become the local, if seldom frequented, church of Wilkie Collins's friend Charles Dickens, when he lived in Devonshire Terrace.

Baby Wilkie appears in his father's drawings as a fat-cheeked infant with dark hair, though with no indication of the prominent bump on his forehead which he retained through his life. He had grey eyes and was generally small for his age, though he would grow to five foot six inches, an average height for a man of his time. He was called after his father's friend, the Scottish painter, David Wilkie, later Sir David, who was his godfather.

As a child Wilkie Collins flitted between various addresses in north London. After the death of his father in 1848, he, his mother and brother Charley settled in Hanover Terrace, one of the attractive Georgian terraces surrounding Regent's Park. Four years later he wrote *Basil*, his first adult novel, which tells of a young man who, after falling instantly in love with a young girl in an omnibus, follows her back to her home in the fictional Hollyoake Square, which is identified as part of a new housing development north of Regent's Park—probably St John's Wood.

Four years later, as his career as an author began to develop, Wilkie left the family home. However he unexpectedly moved to Howland Street, one of the seedier thoroughfares in neighbouring Fitzrovia, where he settled in with Caroline Graves, a married woman with a chequered past. Caroline, who was five years younger than Wilkie, liked to portray herself as the respectable daughter of an army captain. In fact she was the illegitimate offspring of a jobbing carpenter from Gloucestershire. In an effort to escape her surroundings, she had married young and had a daughter, Harriet. Two years later, her husband died and she was left alone to bring up her child.

At the time her mother in law Mary Ann Graves ran a tobacconists' shop in Hertford Street, Fitzrovia, where many of Wilkie's artist friends had homes. Caroline was forced to open a marine or junk store in the less salubrious Charlton Street nearby. This was a lowly form of mercantile life, even by Victorian standards. As Mayhew's great sociological study London Labour and the London Poor shows, she was surrounded by labourers, carpenters, charwomen, seamstresses and prostitutes.

Wilkie portrayed these surroundings in an article for Charles Dickens's magazine *Household Words* in June 1856. Laid up in Two Lodgings contrasted his experiences in two hostelries—one in Paris, where he had delighted in the view from his window, and the other in London, where he "looked out upon drab-coloured walls and serious faces through a smoke-laden atmosphere". In 'Smeary Street', his name for Howland Street, his room was flea-ridden, generally dirty and uncomfortable; the other tenants passed through rapidly—as did the maids.

Three years later, in 1859, Wilkie wrote his novel *The Woman in White*, which starts with an unforgettable scene in the Finchley Road, where Walter Hartright, a 'drawing master', is accosted and asked directions by a hysterical woman in white. Shortly afterwards, in Abbey Road, St John's Wood, he meets two sinister men who ask him if he has seen such a woman who has escaped from their asylum. So Collins launches into his masterly 'sensation novel'—part page-turning mystery, part psychological thriller—about the attempts of the villainous Count Fosco and his associates to benefit financially from incarcerating the wrong woman in an asylum.

Because Wilkie was secretive about his relationship with Caroline Graves, several myths developed. One was that she was a prostitute. Another was that she was the model for *The Woman in White*. Neither is likely, though Wilkie did use her as a rather generalised inspiration for the kind of fallen woman he wrote about in his later novels.

Wilkie subsequently moved with Caroline and Harriet Graves to addresses in Albany Street, New Cavendish Street, Harley Street and Melcombe Place, before settling with her in 65 Gloucester Place in the summer of 1867. By the autumn the carpenters and painters had finished their work, and Wilkie was enjoying the spaciousness of his new dwelling. To ensure his creature comforts, he hired three servants, two of them women, whom he provided with new 'gowns'. His centre of operations was a double drawing room, dominated by a large writing table with a smaller inlaid desk, similar to the one used by Dickens.

He had a separate study and a large, airy bedroom. At the back of the house was a stable which was surplus to requirements, so Wilkie was able to let it out at £40 a year. However Wilkie's happiness was short-lived because, the following year, he established another girlfriend, Martha Rudd, in lodgings less than a mile away at 33 Bolsover Street, just east of Portland Place. He had met her while researching his novel *Armadale* in Norfolk. She was working in a pub in Great Yarmouth and was barely educated.

Shortly afterwards Caroline decided that she was not prepared to share Wilkie with another woman. In 1868 she left Gloucester Place and married a much younger man, Joseph Clow, whom she had met through his cousin Leonard, a prominent licensed victualler in Fitzrovia. Bizarrely the couple married in Marylebone parish church with Wilkie in attendance, and then went to live in Clow's family home in Avenue Road.

To ease his pain, which was primarily caused by excruciating gout, Wilkie increased his habital intake of laudanum, or tincture of opium, while he finished The Moonstone, his gripping detective novel which drew on the techniques of sensation fiction. As a result Wilkie spent more time with Martha, who bore him three children. Extraordinarily, three years later Caroline tired of her marriage and returned to live with Wilkie in Gloucester Place, while Martha tended his progeny in Marylebone Road and Taunton Place.

Wilkie left further descriptions of Marylebone in novels such as The Law and the Lady, where a central character, the libidinous Major Fitz-David, lives off Portman Square, close to Wilkie in Gloucester Place. Portman

Square featured in Wilkie's life because Harry Bartley, a young solicitor who married Caroline's daughter, Harriet Graves, had an office there.

By then Wilkie was used to living with two families—one in Gloucester Place and the other in Taunton Place, less than a mile away. When Wilkie's son William was born in 1874, Wilkie appeared on the birth certificate as William Dawson, his pseudonym when dealing with Martha. He liked to spend summers in Ramsgate, Kent, where Caroline and Harriet stayed in a house one side of the harbour, and Martha, as Mrs Dawson, with her children on the other.

After a dispute with his landlord in Gloucester Place, Wilkie moved in 1888 to Wimpole Street, where he rented a house from a doctor. By then his health was failing. Laudanum was only one of a cocktail of drugs, and Wilkie died from heart failure on 23 September the following year.

He was buried in Kensal Green cemetery where Caroline followed him seven years later. Martha lived on in reduced circumstances. Her share of Wilkie's estate, originally a tidy sum, dwindled after Harry Bartley absconded with most of the money.

Today Wilkie's star is again in the ascendant. His intricately plotted novels provide inspiration to authors such as Sarah Waters and Booker Prize winner Eleanor Catton. His off-beat novels, which looked at the problems of women, the disabled and the otherwise disadvantaged are much admired in academia. It is time for him to be fully and appropriately celebrated in his home borough of Marylebone.

The ghost of Sarah Siddons

By Louisa McKenzie
MJ10.4, Aug-Sep 2014

A rustle of satin skirts, a glimpse of lily white flesh, the lingering smell of some long forgotten scent. Venture to the first floor of 228 Baker Street, now an electrical substation, and you may even see her: Sarah Siddons, the former first lady of the London stage, who is reputed to haunt the building.

Until it was demolished in 1904 and the street naming system altered due to an extension of the London Underground, 228 Baker Street was known as 27 Upper Baker Street, the site of Siddons's final London residence. The area still bears a trace of its former inhabitant in the nearby Siddons Lane. When Siddons retired to 27 Upper Baker Street in 1817, the area was still something of a rural idyll. It is said that Siddons built a special bow window at the property so that she could sit and look out over this unspoiled landscape.

The Marylebone into which the actress settled was undergoing a process of rapid development. According to a 1904 article about Sarah Siddons in the *Otago Witness*, the lady herself was so enraged about the possibility of the putative Cornwall Terrace obstructing the view from her house that she went straight to the Prince Regent himself to complain.

Although her complaint ultimately went unheeded—Cornwall Terrace was built as planned between 1821 and 1823—this gives a sense of the circles in which Siddons, as famous in her own lifetime as Angelina Jolie is today, was able to move.

Born Sarah Kemble in Wales in 1755, into a famous theatrical family, Siddons acted in family productions from a young age. As a teenager she became infatuated with another member of the theatre company, William Siddons. Despite her family's initial disapproval, the couple married in 1773. At the same time she started her acting career in earnest. The early years were hard.

She initially tried her luck in London, but was not successful. This led to several years spent touring the country in a variety of theatrical companies: wilderness years, but ones which laid the foundations for her stardom. Returning to London a few years later, Siddons was luckier, proving to be a huge success in David Garrick's Drury Lane theatre.

Although Siddons played the whole pantheon of Shakespearean female (and some male) characters, it was the role of Lady Macbeth with which she became indelibly associated, repeating the role multiple times on stage. Perhaps fittingly, her farewell performance before retiring was in Macbeth. The audience weren't there for the Scottish play. They were there for Mrs Siddons. Accordingly, it was impossible for the play to continue after Lady Macbeth's final lines, so great was the audience reaction.

Throughout her career, Siddons found herself rubbing shoulders with the elite of the day. This didn't stop after her retirement, when she established a sort of informal salon at 27 Upper Baker Street, attracting writers, painters, politicians and society friends for tea, toast, discussion or to listen to her famous readings. Sir Thomas Lawrence, the painter, with whom she had a long relationship, painted a portrait of her at one such reading.

Throughout her career, Siddons was a regular subject for portraitists, including luminaries such as Gainsborough and Reynolds. These portraits, the publicity shots of their day, give us some clues about the power of her presence. In the Reynolds portrait of the actress as a tragic muse, her personality jumps from the canvas. These paintings offer a clue as to how Sarah Siddons held her audiences in such thrall. Contemporary or near contemporary reports cite the realism and believability of her acting. Onlookers felt her pain, her love, her terror, her cruelty, her evil. Samuel Taylor Coleridge, a fan of Siddons from a young age, published the poem *To Mrs Siddons* in 1794 as part of his *Sonnets on Eminent Characters* in a London newspaper (although scholarly opinion now attributes at least some of the credit for this poem to Charles Lamb). The final couplet captures the effect Siddons had on her audience: "Ev'n such the shiv'ring joys thy tone imparts/ Ev'n so thou, SIDDONS! Meltest my sad heart!"

This naturalism was a break with the prevailing acting style of the time, whereby each part had its own convention and was played in exactly the same way, regardless of the actor. It was the part, and not the player, which was memorable. By becoming more spontaneous and individual, Siddons enchanted audiences, paving the way for a more modern style of acting in which both the actor and the part were memorable.

Although her marriage to William ultimately failed, it endured long enough for Siddons to have seven children (only two of whom survived her) all the while continuing on the stage. The nature of her relationship with Sir Thomas Lawrence has long been debated. Most agree that it was nothing more than a friendship, which began when he saw Siddons in a production in Bristol during her wilderness years. Lawrence painted and sketched Siddons many times. He also, somewhat confusingly, fell in love with two of her daughters, Sally and Maria. He courted one, broke it off, courted the other, then went back to the first. He broke both their hearts—and both died young. This did not, however, stop Sarah Siddons from continuing to welcome the painter as part of her salon at 27 Upper Baker Street.

The final curtain fell in June 1831. Sarah Siddons died in her home and was buried in St Mary's Cemetery, Paddington. Even in death, she could still attract an audience. Reportedly, more than 5,000 people attended her funeral. And so the story ends. Or, if you happen to visit that electrical substation, maybe it doesn't.

The Hollywood tale of Edgar Wallace

By Rupert Butler
MJ10.1, Feb-Mar 2014

It was a familiar image worldwide: a dynamic, supremely successful business tycoon facing the world with total confidence from behind an aggressive cigarette holder. This was William Horatio Edgar Wallace, master creator of crime literature and drama, who opted to move from Clarence Gate Gardens near Baker Street to the more opulent splendour of Portland Place with a brace of secretaries and servants, later shifting to the equally luxurious Carlton Hotel as his base for churning out his 170-odd novels and plays—netting, incredibly for the late twenties and early thirties, around £50,000 a year.

Edgar never knew his true antecedents. Born on 1 April 1875, he was adopted by the family of Dick Freeman, a fish porter. With money tight, Edgar was put to work barely out of childhood, landing a job in a Newington Causeway printers at five shillings a week, producing nothing more literary than paper bags inscribed with the names and addresses of grocers and bakers. In disgust and boredom he walked out. Scarcely more congenial was being a milk roundsman and selling newspapers at Ludgate Circus, on the edge of Fleet Street. The stimulation he craved was instead sought during afternoons spent at race courses or poker tables.

Edgar's first steps towards writing were taken when he began devising competitions for Tallis Press, a newly formed publishing company. It was here that he masterminded a "guess the murder method competition" in the *Daily Mail*, with a suggested top prize of £1,000, which he expected would be provided by the newspaper's proprietor Lord Harmsworth. As it happened, Harmsworth turned Edgar down flat.

Undaunted, he pressed ahead with a costly promotional campaign, on "1,250 sites all over London, placed on buses, hoardings, flyers", reaching a daunting bill of £2,000. Advertising space was bought in the *Evening News* and the *Daily Mirror* and a detachable competition form was placed on the Mail's back page, informing the reader: "In the foregoing pages, Mr Edgar Wallace has told in a style which, we submit, at once places him in the forefront of living impressionist writers, a story of enthralling interest."

Then came the blow. In the course of running the competition in the Mail, Edgar's draft of the rules had failed to include any limitation clause which would restrict payment of the prize money to a single winner. The number of successful entrants rose alarmingly, and with them the inevitable clamour for payments. An enraged Harmsworth was obliged to pay out more than £5,000 to protect his newspaper's reputation. Edgar's promising career in journalism came to an abrupt end.

Edgar was saved from total insolvency by hasty enlistment in the Royal West Kent Regiment. Upon his posting to Africa, he was quick to gather material for a novel, *Sanders of the River*, about a colonial administrator battling against a devious tribal king. Published in 1911 at the height of Edwardian imperial power, the book caught the mood of an empire intent on civilising its colonies through tough, paternalistic rule. Its runaway success quickly spawned an entire series of West African stories with Sanders as the hero.

At Clarence Gate Gardens, Edgar's secretary and future wife Violet – succeeding Ivy, his first, after a mountain of his debt ruined their marriage – was faced daily with a formidable array of cylinders containing the writer's rapid-fire dictation.

She later recalled: "The words flowed from his lips uninterruptedly – almost as if he were reading from an invisible page." His dictation speed became a standard joke. If someone telephoned him and was told he was writing a novel, the caller would reply: "I'll wait."

The daunting speed was witnessed by his friend, the celebrated barrister Sir Patrick Hastings, who during a week's stay had gone one evening to Edgar's study, where he found him sitting at his desk in a dressing gown, still dictating, drinking cups of sweet tea brought to him every half hour by a servant. By the next day Edgar had completed his novel, and went to bed for two days, satisfied in knowing that he'd earned £4,000 in serial rights in just 60 hours.

Edgar made his mark with a succession of plays, above all *The Ringer*, staged at Wyndham's Theatre in London during May 1926, featuring

Henry Arthur Miller, a legendary assassin who kills for vengeance. The play was a huge success with audiences. In swift recognition of an obvious talent, leading publisher Sir Ernest Hodder-Williams snapped up Edgar. Another highly successful drama *On The Spot*, set in gangland Chicago, was penned in four days in 1931, and a 75,000 word novel, The Coat of Arms, was completed in just over a weekend in the same year.

The move to 31 Portland Place was accompanied by the recruitment of an additional secretary and numerous servants, as well as the installation of a sound-proof glass cabinet for unencumbered dictation. This was followed by relocation to the opulent Carlton Hotel where Edgar thought nothing of taking over the entire restaurant for as many as 200 guests. Although much had changed, his supreme passion remained racing, with his telephone bets seldom less than £100.

Never one to have just a single iron in the fire, he was briefly attracted to politics in 1931, becoming active in the Liberal Party and contesting Blackpool with singular lack of success due to his spectacular lack of political experience and mutterings about his excessive gambling. There were few signs that he was overly bothered. Infinitely more enticing were the substantial offers arriving from Hollywood's burgeoning talking picture industry.

On 21 July 1931 he sailed for New York on the Empress of Britain, fully intending, he declared, to rest on the way. Few believed him. Within two days he was hard at work in his state-room, producing a scenario, 16 articles and one broadcast as well as assisting with the script for the 1932 film adaptation of *The Hound of the Baskervilles* and creating a 110-page draft of a story about a giant ape and a beautiful movie actress. Successively titled *The Beast*, then *Kong* and finally *King Kong*, this rough draft, with its climactic scene at the top of the Empire State Building, was eagerly pored over by the studio on his arrival in Hollywood.

Edgar would never get to see the completed film. There had been increasing signs that his seemingly dauntless constitution was under serious threat after years of chain smoking, endless cups of sweet tea and a reckless intake of aspirin. Beset by diabetes, cerebral haemorrhages and severe headaches, Edgar found his illnesses impossible to conceal. Newspaper hoardings outside Wyndham's Theatre, proclaimed "Edgar

Wallace gravely ill". He died on 7 February 1932, making his final journey home by sea with the ship's flags at half-mast when it reached Southampton Water and the bells of Fleet Street and London's theatres gravely tolling.

King Kong was published as a novel in December 1932, credited to Wallace but actually largely written after his death by Merian C Cooper and Delos W Lovelace. The film adaptation was first screened in California during January 1933. Audiences reacted by screaming, leaving the theatre and fainting in droves. Nonetheless, the movie was a huge critical and commercial success, although most of the honours rested with the technocrats for the special effects and stop motion sequences. The studio sound effects department came up with some 40 sound-making instruments to produce menacing hisses, grunts and groans.

The book has been adapted for the cinema many times since, as have many of Wallace's stories. *The Green Archer*, dating from 1923, has been filmed three times, telling the story of a man found murdered after a quarrel with the owner of a haunted castle. A decidedly pale series version of *The Four Just Men* came onto British television screens in 1959 with Dan Dailey, Richard Conte, Jack Hawkins and Vittorio De Sica as the wealthy vigilantes, killing in the name of justice. There was something of a cult following in the late 1960s for *The Mind of JG Reeder*, which sets a shabbily dressed 1920s detective with a criminal mind in conflict with his corpulent, monocled boss, starring Hugh Burden.

Margaret Laing's biography of Edgar Wallace, published in 1964, was a relentless saga of "spending, losing, owing, squandering and again compulsively making money". At the time of his death, creditors' claims amounted to £140,000 and his assets virtually nil, but robust earnings from his work over the years meant that all were eventually satisfied.

"But Edgar Wallace who?" a generation may well be asking. The answer can surely be seen on the plaque at Ludgate Circus on the edge of a Fleet Street which no longer holds the nation's newspapers. It says: "He knew wealth and poverty, yet had walked with kings & kept his bearing. Of his talents he gave lavishly to authorship—but to Fleet Street he gave his heart."

The urban idyll of Patrick Lichfield

By Glyn Brown
MJ9.4, Aug-Sep 2013

Built by Decimus Burton, Clarence Terrace is the smallest and prettiest terrace at the edge of Regent's Park. It was here, at number 22, that one of Britain's best-known photographers, a man whose work came to define the excesses of 'swinging London', lived with his family.

The flamboyant Patrick Lichfield was never a settled married man, but he gave it his best shot, and in Marylebone, for a few years at least, he seemed to have everything. Years later, when the hurly-burly was over, it was to Clarence Terrace that he would return to at last live a domestic and contented life.

Thomas Patrick John Anson was born on 25 April, 1939, the son of Viscount Anson and Princess Anne of Denmark, the Queen Mother's niece. He grew up at the family seat, the 200-room country estate of Shugborough Hall in Staffordshire, set in 6,000 acres of woodland. Lichfield was given his first camera at the age of six to take his mind off being shunted away to boarding school.

It was at Harrow, as he played cricket against Eton, that he snatched his first pictures of the Queen—it was immediately confiscated, and Lichfield was punished.

Unacademic, a bit of a scamp, he was bullied at school—but the camera gave him something to be good at. He spent any spare money on equipment, covered Harrow's sporting and theatrical events, and quite shockingly, even undercut the town's portrait photographer, who charged the school half a crown a shot for leaving photographs—the entrepreneurial Lichfield got the gig, charging a rock-bottom ninepence.

After Harrow, Lichfield headed to Sandhurst and from there, in 1959, to the Grenadier Guards. After semi-imprisonment at public school, Lichfield revelled in the travel and adventure. He found himself a home—a big, tatty flat in Belgravia—and there installed a darkroom. Obsessed by photography, he used girlfriends as models and printed late into the night, hanging the results on his walls in the morning.

Lichfield's father had died in 1958, aged just 44, so when his grandfather died in 1960, Lichfield inherited the title. He resigned from the Guards, preparing to become a landowner—only to find that his grandfather had made arrangements to sell Shugborough to the National Trust in lieu of death duties. This left Lichfield still proprietor, but with no money worries. At 23, he turned his attention to becoming a photographer.

In its early days, photography had been dominated by those who had the money and leisure time to pursue it. Julia Margaret Cameron, Fox Talbot, Henri Cartier-Bresson, Diane Arbus, Cecil Beaton—all were from privileged backgrounds. But in the sixties, Britain's social fabric was a blur of change. Working class snappers bristling with raw talent stormed the barricades, with Terence Donovan, David Bailey and Don McCullin leading the charge. Though the 5th Earl of Lichfield was proud of his title, he could sense something in the air. He dropped the 'Lord', and told his relatives he'd be buckling down to a job in trade. Said one of them: "Photography. It's far worse than being an interior designer, and only marginally better than hairdressing."

Lichfield found a job as assistant to two photographers, Dmitri Kasterine and Michael Wallis, who he'd met while they worked on an advertising shoot outside his Wilton Place flat. During his last months in the army, he'd begged them virtually every day to give him a job, any job. Lichfield described the resulting four-year apprenticeship, on £3 a week, as the most formative time of his life.

Lichfield used his connections shamelessly, offering to shoot portraits of London's smart set at a flat five guineas a pop. He began to put together a little black book of potential models, including a 19-year-old Joanna Lumley and Jacqueline Bisset, who his flatmate met on a bus. He also had easy access to debutante dances where he took the society pictures that, despite the changing face of Britain, papers like the *Sunday Mirror* and the *Daily Express* still cried out for. He worked hard, soon earning enough to buy a yellow Mini Cooper. He also started earning respect. Photographer Terry O'Neill said: "We were from the poor side of town, he was from the posh side, and he took a lot of stick at the beginning. But he proved himself. He stuck to the task. He just wanted to be 'one of the chaps'."

Lichfield set up on his own, with a studio in Holland Park's Aubrey

Walk. He found regular work with Jocelyn Stevens's *Queen* magazine. Around 1966, Stevens asked him to catalogue the movers and shakers of what *Time* magazine had dubbed 'swinging London'. It was the start of a hallucinogenic decade. Lichfield took pictures of Roman Polanski, David Hockney and Michael Caine, and shot singer and actress (and Mick Jagger's girlfriend) Marsha Hunt naked apart from her huge afro, earning massive publicity for the musical Hair.

As his reputation grew, he was signed to a contract with American *Vogue* by the legendary Diana Vreeland, taking his place alongside Bailey, Cecil Beaton, Norman Parkinson and Lord Snowdon—becoming the youngest photographer on her books. She'd tested him out by sending him to photograph the Duke and Duchess of Windsor at their home outside Paris. The resulting shots were legendary in their intimacy. It later transpired that Lichfield had got his hatchet-faced subjects to relax by deliberately falling through his chair.

He covered the wedding of his friend, Bianca Rosa Perez Macias, to Mick Jagger in St Tropez in 1971, producing casually beautiful results—and, society boy despite himself, also managing his role of giving the bride away.

By now, Lichfield was a staple of the gossip columns, thanks in part to his relationship with actress Britt Ekland. He was irresistible fodder—Borzoi-thin, and with a wild mop of hair that had him compared to Roger Daltrey (and occasionally Lionel Blair). He dressed in cowboy boots, Levi's and big-buckled belts: the boho gypsy. An urbane and witty bon viveur, he was a dandy who made every shoot fun, but had manners and charm. And he had a fatal eye for the ladies.

It seemed that particular characteristic had been brought under control when, in 1975, he married Lady Leonora Grosvenor, daughter of the fabulously wealthy Duke of Westminster, and bought Clarence Terrace as their home. In an American interview in 1976, Lichfield said he'd got bored with being a playboy. "I'd done all the adventuresome things a playboy does. Actually, I was beginning to repeat myself." He'd met Leonora when, at 18, she'd modelled for *Vogue*. He bumped into her again eight years later, fell in love and quickly proposed. "It was over dinner. Leonora thought I asked if she wanted more coffee and uttered a prim, 'No thank you.' But of course, I explained more explicitly."

Once married, Lichfield explained, there had been a metamorphosis. He'd given up his king-size bachelor bed ("with music coming from the mattress") and his 19 motorbikes. The man who had his family crest tattooed on his arm continued: "Leonora knows all about me—for years she's read about me in the columns. I wasn't 26 and unreliable. I'm 36, and experienced." Heartbreakingly, in retrospect, he finished: "Even more dazzling than the romance I've found with my wife is the friendship between us. This marriage flows with strength I never thought possible."

You can just see it coming. For several years, Lichfield found fulfilment and happiness in Marylebone—creatively successful, with a loving wife and young family, all installed beside one of London's most bucolic parks. Then in 1979, he was invited to shoot a calendar for Unipart, Britain's poor relation to Pirelli's much hotter operation. Apparently, he thought he'd be taking glossy photographs of cars—only when he got the brief did he realise the company wanted glossy nudes.

Every year, Lichfield would head to some far-flung location—Kenya, Bali, Death Valley—with some astonishingly pneumatic nymphets. The pictures were mind-blowing: a woman walking up an escalator at Moscow's underground, her buttocks mesmerising; a naked model lying on white fur in snow; a sinuous girl suspended from a crane hoist. Lichfield was nothing if not inventive, and the style is Helmut Newton crossed with *Penthouse*. Jilly Cooper, who accompanied him on one of these trips, said: "He was just a gorgeous man, lovely and intensely glamorous. He was charming and very kind to the models." Journalist Richard D North, who accompanied another shoot, had a slightly different story. "I told Lichfield he should work harder at seeing the merit of women of his own age. He told me I could only think that if I had not properly explored the pleasure a man could have with a bottle of baby oil and a young enthusiast."

Lichfield's taste for women had begun to strain his marriage. At last, stories of an affair brought it to an end. But he deeply regretted the pain he caused his wife. In 2004, the year before he died, he ruefully observed: "To marry a photographer who charges around the world with the most beautiful girls is not a reliable prospect. I might have broken a few hearts, but my own was pretty much intact. That shows how spoiled I was."

Separated, Lichfield was so miserable he "forgot to eat", but he worked with dogged tenacity—no commitment problems here. In 1981 he was the official photographer for the wedding of Prince Charles and Diana, capturing the occasion in a radical way. Said *Tatler* editor Geordie Greig: "He got the intimacy of the royal family. There was almost Hollywood magic dust spread throughout that shoot." Lichfield later admitted he'd controlled the massive group of royals with a whistle. "Blow it sharply and you get a surprised look, quickly followed by laughter." His relaxed, intimate results, obtained under pressure, became some of the most syndicated photos in history.

Lichfield continued to hone his skill, becoming an early master of digital technology. ("Ah," he shrugged, "but it's just so much easier to lie your arse off with digital.")

In 1994, when he was 55 and she was in her early 40s, he began his relationship with biographer Lady Annunziata Asquith. "I've become content in the last few years," he told an interviewer at his home (one of many) on the island of Mustique. He relaxed more and more at Clarence Terrace, and eased into a quieter social life. As the millennium arrived, he admitted, "My greatest thrill is that I'm now shooting pictures for the British Tourist Board; at last something I'm proud to identify with." He added wistfully, "I'd like to be taken seriously before it's too late."

He already was, of course; and as for too late, well, that was just about the case, too. On 10 November 2005, Lichfield suffered a major stroke, and died the next day, aged 66. He was buried at St Michael and All Angels Church, less than a mile from Shugborough.

Former royal press officer Dickie Arbiter said: "Patrick was passionate about his work. It was more important to him than any hereditary title."

And that does seem to have been the case. In his last-ever interview, Lichfield said: "I sometimes wake up in the morning and think, this is just another amazing day. I'm not doing anything that I don't want to do. It's fantastic. What a life!"

George Stubbs and the equine obsession

By Rupert Butler

MJ 10.3, Jun-Jul 2014

If, using an aged map of Marylebone, you hope to find yourself on Somerset Street off Portman Square, forget it. You are going to end up standing confused and lost outside Selfridges. This was the site of the home and studio of the ultra-obsessive painter and engraver George Stubbs, who in 1763 acquired the lease of No 24 Somerset Street. Here he lived and worked until his death in 1806. The street itself survived until it was pulled down after the Second World War.

Stubbs, born into a family of skilled Liverpool artisans on 25 August 1724, was a painter whose fanatic interest in animal anatomy drove him to just about any lengths to acquire previously unseen models, including those that stood upright, carried their young in pouches and moved in giant leaps. A kangaroo, subject of a Stubbs painting in 1772, was inspired by a skin he acquired from Australia. This kangaroo painting, together with one of a dingo, has recently been saved for Britain in the face of a bid from Australia after the National Maritime Museum managed to raise the required £5.5 million. Among his exotic subjects were a nylghau, a moose, a baboon, an Indian rhinoceros, a macaque monkey and a yak, some stuffed and some living.

In the 1750s Stubbs had visited Italy, many years later revealing to a fellow artist that his motive had been "to convince himself that nature was and is always superior to art". In 1756 he rented a farmhouse in Lincolnshire and spent 18 months dissecting horses, then moving to London after the death of his father with the encouragement of his common law wife Mary Spencer, together with their son, George Townley Stubbs, later also a painter and engraver.

In just five years, Stubbs senior was securing commissions from some of the most prominent of the country's citizens. All the while, he continued with his own personal obsession: a minute study of the anatomy of the horse, dead specimens of which had been dragged with his immense strength into his Somerset Street studio. The corpses were dissected, layer by layer, with drawings portraying muscles, sinews and entire skeletons.

In 1766, Stubbs published *The Anatomy of the Horse*, illustrated with engraved plates. These were made available for likely clients to study in what became an expanding market, particularly among wealthy aristocrats, including the Marquess of Rockingham, the Duke of Grafton and the Earls of Spencer and Grosvenor. Prominent was the 3rd Duke of Richmond with his Chichester country seat at Goodwood House. Stubbs produced three notable pictures of the Richmond family, fellow statesmen and servants, including Racehorses Exercising on the Downs at Goodwood. In his 2002 study of George Stubbs, Martin Myrone, a curator at Tate Britain, writes that the pictures "present a vision of the land taken, quite literally from an aristocratic perspective, confirming the right of the landowning class to view and hold authority over the nation".

Making himself available for sittings had its perils though. Rockingham's fiery Arabian stallion Whistlejacket, a rich coppery chestnut, later immortalised on a canvas nearly 10 feet high, had turned on Stubbs viciously, causing him to defend himself solely with a thin metre-length pole. Tireless when it came to seeking out menageries like the one at Windsor Great Park, Stubbs created for the Duke of Cumberland paintings of lions, tigers and zebras which had been brought from the Cape of Good Hope as a present for the Royal Family. A truly outstanding prospect for a commission turned out to be Viscount Bolingbroke. In 1765 Stubbs painted a work for Bolingbroke entitled *Gimcrack on Newmarket Heath, with a trainer, a stable-lad, and a jockey*. It sold at Christie's in July 2011 for a sensational bid of over £22 million.

The 1790s saw a major coup with a highly-prized commission from the Prince of Wales. But the decade was not without scandalous associations for Stubbs, with his spirited equestrian portrait of hard-swearing Laetitia, Lady Lade, notorious wife of racehorse breeder, owner and inveterate gambler Sir John Lade, who dressed at all times in riding clothes, perpetually carried a whip and matched his wife when it came to foul language. Among her numerous alleged liaisons, one of the most notorious was with John Rann, a debt-bogged former coachman turned highwayman, apprehended after robbing the chaplain of Princess Amelia, King George III's youngest daughter. Rann was held in custody at Newgate Jail where he was said to have entertained seven women to a farewell dinner shortly before his execution which was accompanied by farewell banter with the hangman in the company of an ecstatic crowd.

In his later years Stubbs persisted with his vigorous lifestyle, conserving his energy with a strict diet. Unlike so many of his hard-drinking contemporaries, he was reputed to have touched nothing but water for 40 years. In his late 70s he still trudged the 16 miles between Portman Square and Lord Clarendon's house in Hertfordshire, producing pictures of countryside workers' activities, subject of two oils, *Haymakers* and *Reapers*. In 1799, the 28-year-old rakish and wealthy Sir Henry Vane-Tempest, with his passion for racing and gambling, commissioned Stubbs to paint his stately bay colt Hambletonian. Hambletonian won a famous race at Newmarket against Diamond, a previous victor there, for a massive 3,000 guineas. The race was vicious beyond imagining, both horses being slashed and whipped until they bled. The event, according to *Sporting Magazine* "drew together the greatest concourse of people that ever was seen at Newmarket. The company not only occupied every bed to be procured in that place, but Cambridge and every town and village within 12 or 15 miles was also thronged with visitors." Hambletonian won by a mere half a neck. The painting, *Hambletonian, Rubbing Down* is dominated by the horse, in the care of groom and stable boy.

By then, though, Stubbs had returned to the obsession which likely had never left him—producing a long dreamed-of sequel to the Anatomy of the Horse: the extraordinarily ambitious *A Comparative Anatomical Exposition of the Human Body with that of a Tiger and a Common Fowl*. But by the winter of 1804 his previously keen eyesight was notably lessening, possibly blurred by cataracts. A fairly regular visitor, George Dance, reported at their final meeting, that Stubbs had appeared "so aged, so in-jawed and shrunk in his person".

Death, on 10 July 1806, came suddenly. Mary Spencer revealed that, an hour or so before his final breath, he had declared: "I had indeed hoped to finish my Comparative Anatomy e'er I went, for other things I have no anxiety."

James Figg, king of Marylebone Plains

By Mark Riddaway

MJ3.3, Jun-Jul 2007

Nobody really knows exactly when James Figg was born. Being from a poor, illiterate agricultural family in the small Oxfordshire town of Thame, his birth wasn't notable enough to be properly recorded. It was probably 1695, maybe earlier. By the time of his death in 1734, and his burial in the grounds of the St Marylebone parish church, Figg had managed to batter his way firmly into the national consciousness as the most brutal and successful prize fighter in Britain.

Details of his early life are scarce, but it seems that he initially made a living fighting for money at local fairs, before his growing reputation and the diminishing ranks of local lads stupid enough to share a ring with him forced the young bruiser to head for London.

The first mention of Figg fighting in the capital comes from an advert in the *Daily Courant* from June 1714, which suggests that he was a pupil of one Timothy Buck of Clare Market, off The Strand. Around the same time the young fighter was sketched, muscles rippling, by the portrait artist Jonathan Richardson. Figg soon caught the eye of the Earl of Peterborough, under whose patronage he was able to open an arena in Marylebone Fields, just north of Oxford Street. The arena, known as either Figg's Amphitheatre or the Boarded House, became home to an academy at which Figg taught other young fighters. In the centre was a ring—demarcated with wooden boards rather than ropes—in which Figg fought regular bouts in front of large, noisy, blood-thirsty, drunken crowds.

During the 1720s Figg became a celebrity of huge public standing. This was the result partly of the savage beatings he handed out to most of his opponents, and partly of his publicity material being produced by the great painter, engraver and satirist William Hogarth. Hogarth not only designed Figg's flyers ("James Figg—Master of the Noble Science of Defence") but also managed to sneak Figg's likeness into some of his most famous works of art. There he is in the second plate of *A Rake's Progress*, holding a pair of quarterstaffs and looking distinctly menacing.

And there he is again in *Southwark Fair*—a depiction of the annual festival in Borough at which Figg would earn easy money by offering to fight any member of the public stupid enough and drunk enough to want to take him on. In Hogarth's painting Figg can be seen wielding a sword while sitting on a horse, waiting patiently for a challenge.

Figg was a big man with a shaven head and an imposingly muscular physique. Pierce Egan, one of the first historians of pugilism, described the fighter in his 1812 *Boxiana* as being "more indebted to strength and courage for his success in the battlefield than to the effects of genius". At a time when prize fights often consisted of a round of sword fighting, a round of cudgels and a round of boxing, Figg was actually far more technically accomplished with weaponry than he was with his fists. Captain John Godfrey, who was taught to fight by Figg and was himself a talented swordsman, wrote of his mentor: "Figg was the Atlas of the sword, and may he remain the gladiating statue! In him, strength, resolution and unparalleled judgement conspired to form a matchless master." He heaped praise upon Figg's use of "time and measure" and described his way with a sword as "charming".

According to Egan, Figg's way with his fists was far less elegant: "If his methods of fighting were subject to the criticism of the present day, he would be denominated more of a slaughterer than a neat and finished pugilist." But early 18th century boxing wasn't the subtle chess match of gloved fists and tight defences that characterise the modern sport. Instead it was a brutal bare-knuckle brawl in which fighters were expected to use their elbows and fingers, throw their opponents to the floor and land punches and kicks even after their opponents were down and out.

This was a form of boxing in which blood and broken bones were accepted, even demanded. Godfrey, in his book *A Treatise Upon the Useful Science of Defence*, recommended that boxers aim their punches between the eyebrows as this causes the eyelids to swell, obstructing the sight. "The man thus indecently treated and artfully hoodwinked," he wrote, "is then beat about at his adversary's discretion." He also advised that blows to the stomach "may be attended with a vomiting of blood". Queensbury Rules this wasn't.

Back-sword fighting was a brutal pursuit which made bare knuckle brawling look like a bit of a picnic. The back-sword was a small one-sided blade designed for slashing and cutting, far removed from the elegant movements associated with fencing. Fighters wore no protective clothing, with the result that Figg's body was a web of scar tissue. Godfrey recounts a back-sword bout between William Gill—one of Figg's pupils—and an Irishman named Butler. Gill was renowned for aiming at his opponents' legs, and on this occasion he wounded the Irishman with a cut "more severe and deep" than Godfrey had ever seen before. "His leg was laid quite open, his calf falling down to his ankle." Butler was stitched up but surgeons who operated on lowly brawlers weren't up to much. The wound became infected and after a botched amputation the Irishman "soon expired". In such circumstances, the fact that Figg retired with all his limbs in place was proof of his considerable skill.

The most famous of Figg's hundreds of fights were with Ned Sutton, a pipe maker from Gravesend—"a resolute, pushing, awkward swordsman," according to Godfrey. Figg vs Sutton was the Ali vs Frazier of its day. The first time they fought, Sutton won—the only recorded instance of Figg ever losing a fight. A rematch was arranged in which Figg exacted his revenge, setting up a third bout in 1725, to be held at the Boarded House.

The fight was attended by John Byrom, a well-known poet whose works were often published in the *Spectator*. According to Byrom, in a poem published soon afterwards and reprinted in the London Journal in 1727 to mark yet another epic rematch, the bout started with a round of the back-sword, during which Figg—after breaking his own sword with a stroke so brutal it would have "discarded" Sutton's head had it not been deflected—soon found himself wounded in the side, an injury he treated with "sullen disdain" and some smart-mouthed banter with the crowd. After breaking for a quick dram of strong booze, the fighters resumed, with Sutton taking a cut on the arm. Following a further break, they returned with cudgels. Finally, after a punishing exchange of blows, Figg made the breakthrough: "So Jove told the gods he had made a decree, / That Figg should hit Sutton a stroke on the knee. / Tho' Sutton, disabled as soon as he hit him, / Would still have fought on, but Jove would not permit him; / 'Twas his fate, not his fault, that constrain'd him to yield, / And thus the great Figg became lord of the field."

Figg retired from fighting in 1730, after which he devoted his time to passing on some of his skills to the students who flooded to his academy. Godfrey rated him as the best teacher around: "I chose to go mostly to Figg partly as I knew him to be the ablest master and partly as he was of a rugged temper and would spare no man, high or low, who took up stick against him." It was a painful experience: "I purchased my knowledge with many a broken head and bruise in every part of me."

As well as being a fighter, teacher and national celebrity, Figg was also a bit of a promoter—an early Don King, but with far less hair. One of the most famous fights of the era was arranged by Figg in 1725—an epic scrap between a boxer from Venice known imaginatively as Gondolier and a grazier named Bob Whitaker. The fight came about through a wager made at Slaughter's coffee house between a foreigner, who was talking up the Venetian, and an English gentleman who thought this a slight on Blighty.

The Englishman "sent for Figg to procure a proper man for him". On arriving at the coffee shop, Figg was warned that the Venetian was a "man of extraordinary strength and famous for breaking the jaw-bone in boxing". His response was almost King-like in its sass: "I do not know, Master, but he may break one of his own countrymen's jawbones with his fist; but I will bring him a man and he shall not break his jaw-bone with a sledge-hammer in his hand."

Figg chose Whitaker—"a hardy fellow and would bear a deal of beating". According to the *London Journal*, Whitaker was "entertained at Mr Figg's house for instruction and proper diet till the day of battle". The fight caught the public imagination, and thousands of pounds were wagered: "In a word, the public daily enter into this affair with so much passion for the event, and gentlemen are so warm on both sides, that it looks like a national concern."

On the night of the fight, Figg's Amphitheatre was filled to the brim with what Godfrey called "a splendid company, the politest house of that kind I ever saw". The high class of the crowd at first worked painfully to Whitaker's disadvantage. Early in the fight the muscular Italian struck the Englishman so hard that he was knocked off the stage. "Whitaker's misfortune," wrote Godfrey, "was then the grandeur of the company, on which account they suffered no common people in, that usually sit on the ground and line the stage round. It was then all clear and Whitaker had nothing to stop him but the bottom."

After scrambling back into the ring the Englishman soon twigged that Gondolier's superior reach was causing him trouble, so he moved inside to fight up close. "He, with a little stoop, ran boldly in beyond the heavy mallet, and with one English peg in the stomach (quite a new thing to foreigners) brought him on his breech." The Italian decided that "the blow carried too much of the English rudeness for him to bear", and the yellow-bellied foreigner threw in the towel.

Figg was delighted by the turnout at his arena, so quickly "stepped up and told the gentlemen that they might think he had picked out the best man in London on this occasion, but that if they would return he would bring a man who should beat this Whitaker in 10 minutes". A week later Figg rolled out another of his protégés, Nathaniel Peartree, to give Whitaker a solid hiding.

Figg's fighters weren't always men. Fights between women were a huge draw, with the most famous female brawler being Mrs Stokes, the self-proclaimed "Invincible City Championess". In 1725, Figg hosted a battle between Mrs Stokes and an Irish boxer. An advertisement in Mist's Journal ramped up the excitement: "The gentlemen of Ireland have been long picking out an Hibernian heroine to match Mrs Stokes; there is now one arrived here, who, by her make and stature, seems mighty enough to eat her up." It was expected to be a well-attended fight: "This being like to prove a notable and diverting engagement, it's not doubted but abundance of gentlemen will crowd to Mr Figg's Amphitheatre."

But boxing wasn't the only show on the bill at Figg's place. Paying customers were also entertained by extraordinary displays of barbarity against animals. An advertisement in a 1721 edition of the Weekly News—a journal specialising in foreign affairs coverage—promises a mind boggling spectacle: "At the Boarded House in Marybone-Fields on Monday 24 of this infant July will be a match fought between the wild and savage panther and 12 English dogs." The ad goes on to explain that this bout resulted from the boasts of an unnamed foreigner who had been putting it about around London that a panther could easily take on any number of British dogs. Stung by this insult to his country's canine stock, an English gentleman strongly objected. Today, this kind of pub debate would result in a few spilled pints and an agreement to disagree. In 18th century London it led instead to the procuring of a panther (God knows where from), the hiring of an arena and the collection of a £300 purse.

The advertisement then spirals off into an almost comical list of the other entertainments on offer in the arena on the same evening. "NB, also a bear to be baited and a mad green bull to be turn'd loose in the gaming place with fireworks all over him and bull dogs after him, a dog to be drawn up with fireworks in the middle of the yard and an ass to be baited on the same stage." Let me run that by you again: after watching a panther fight 12 dogs, the crowd would be entertained by a bear being attacked, a bull being killed by dogs, and then a dog being blown apart with fireworks. And finally, for a nice gentle coda, a donkey would be slaughtered. Happy days.

All this violence did have its critics and there were frequent bouts of moral panic played out in London's burgeoning new journals and newspapers. In 1724 the *Daily Journal* attacked the boxing arenas "for calling raw tradesmen out of their shops, students from their books, apprentices and hired servants, and even his Majesty's soldiers from their duty, to attend at the rude and savage diversions, where prophaneness reigns triumphantly, vollies of the most dreadful oaths being pour'd out incessantly, and picking of pockets practic'd openly with impunity". The Journal's solution to this growing social problem was a novel one, and one that was never likely to succeed: "Mr Jones, the famous High-Constable of Holborn, in whose division this nuisance chiefly lies, will speedily be commission'd to take one single bout at staff with this terrible Mr Figg, he being as well vers'd in the true exercise of that weapon as Mr Figg, or any of his fraternity." But Mr Jones and his moral crusaders had about as much chance of success in Mr Figg's notorious arena as that poor donkey.

Thomas Lord and the MCC

By Jean-Paul Aubin-Parvu
MJ1.2, Summer 2005

First played in the countryside by the masses, cricket was adopted by public schools during the 17th century. The game was seen both as a manly pursuit and a welcome opportunity for serious gambling. Around £20,000 was bet on a series of games between Old Etonians and England in 1751.

One of the earliest London cricket clubs, the Je-ne-saisquoi, spawned another that played its matches on White Conduit Fields. The exclusive White Conduit Cricket Club boasted several members of the aristocracy among its numbers, who were unhappy at the manner in which the watching hoi polloi chose to voice their opinions. They wished to have a private ground and so turned to Thomas Lord, a practice bowler and attendant at the club.

Lord, a Yorkshireman, was also a shrewd entrepreneur, trading in wines and spirits and dabbling in property. He only agreed to develop a ground provided the club indemnify him against any financial loss. He leased land from the Portman Estate and built his pitch on Dorset Fields, the area now covered by Dorset Square, Marylebone. He named the ground Lord's and erected a high perimeter fence. Grazing sheep kept the grass short.

The first match was played at Lord's between Middlesex and Essex on 31 May. With crowds often several thousand strong, Lord made a handsome profit charging each spectator sixpence for admission. In 1787, the Marylebone Cricket Club (MCC) was founded.

One year later, the MCC played its inaugural game against its parent, the White Conduit Club. The MCC laid down a Code of Laws, requiring the wickets to be pitched 22 yards apart and detailing how players could be given out. These laws were quickly adopted throughout the game.

In 1805, the first Eton versus Harrow schools cricket game was played there. Lord Byron was in the Harrow team. The following year saw the first Gentlemen versus Players match, a tradition that lasted until 1962.

With cricket purely a summer pursuit, Lord needed to diversify in order to raise income during other months. He allowed other sports to be played on his ground and even sanctioned a balloon ascent.

With land values rising the ground was sold in 1809. Lord dug up the pitch and relocated to North Bank, Regent's Park. He was on the move again five years later as the Regent's Park Canal was about to be cut through the middle of the wicket. The ground was moved to its present site in St John's Wood, with the first game played between the MCC and Hertfordshire on 22 June 1814.

In 1825, at the age of 70, Thomas Lord sold the ground to the famous cricketer and Bank of England director William Ward. Lord retired to Hampshire and died there in 1832. Lord's transformed over the years with taverns, grandstands, a new pavilion and telegraph scoreboards. The grazing sheep were finally evicted and replaced with a mowing machine, and in 1864, the first groundsman was appointed to push it.

In 1877, the MCC invited Middlesex County Cricket Club to adopt Lord's as its county ground. Seven years later, in the first Test match played there, England beat Australia by an innings.

The future of Lord's lay in jeopardy during 1888 until a bill to take over the ground for extensive railway development was rejected in Parliament.

In recent times Lord's has hosted prestigious one day and world cup finals, and in 1987, the MCC celebrated its bicentenary with an MCC versus the Rest of World match. In 1998, the club broke convention by voting to welcome women as members. At the 100th test at Lord's in 2000, England beat the West Indies in three thrilling days.

The MCC continues to enjoy a prominent role in the game, especially in promoting the laws of cricket and safeguarding its spirit. Lord's remains the world's foremost ground. Every international team desperately wants to win there. Australian legend Sir Donald Bradman perfectly summed up the special appeal of the place. "It does not have the best of pitches, it does not have the best of playing fields but it has got an atmosphere you can feel."

Profile: Arthur Wing Pinero (1855-1934)

Playwright, lived at 115A Harley Street

Ask you to name the greatest playwright of the late Victorian period, and your answer would probably be fairly predictable: Henrik Ibsen, Oscar Wilde, George Bernard Shaw. But the same question addressed to the London theatre-goers of the time would doubtless have thrown another name into the mix: Arthur Wing Pinero.

Born in London in 1855, Pinero at first seemed set to follow his father and grandfather into the legal profession, but at the age of 19 he left his law school and travelled to Edinburgh to join the theatre. Two years later he was back in the capital as a member of Henry Irving's Lyceum company.

He was never a great actor; more likely to be playing the comedy sidekick than the starring role. The great actress Ellen Terry damned him with faint praise: "He was always good in the 'silly ass' type of part, and no one could say of him he was playing himself."

In 1885, Pinero stopped acting and started writing. Over the next two decades his plays were a fixture in the West End, drawing huge audiences. His first play, *The Magistrate*, opened at the Court Theatre in March 1885 and ran for a year, to favourable reviews. Like most of his early work it was a bright, funny farce. His biggest hit, *Sweet Lavender*, opened three years later and ran for 684 consecutive performances: a hugely long run for the period. Pinero's usual comedy was layered with sentimentality: always a popular blend in the London theatre.

As he matured, Pinero's plays developed greater depth. While he remained a dab-hand at comedy (his *Trelawney of the 'Wells'*, a satire on the theatre world, is probably his most enduring work), the 1890s saw him morph into a writer of 'problem plays': the serious, socially-conscious dramas that captured the London stage in the wake of Ibsen's successes.

The Second Mrs Tanqueray was perhaps the finest of these, essaying the travails of a lower class woman with a colourful sexual history as she battles against middle class hypocrisy. As with a remarkable number of Pinero's plays, it centred upon a strong, intelligent female protagonist.

The best actresses of the day loved working with Pinero, with good reason.

Such was his status, in 1909 Pinero became only the second man after WS Gilbert to be knighted purely for services to the theatre. The same year he moved to 115A Harley Street, where he slipped gently into retirement, keeping himself busy with writing essays, chairing committees and generally being an all-round good egg.

Pinero's final public performance was played out through the letters page of the *Times*. In May 1915, after the horrific sinking of RMS Lusitania by a German u-boat, he wrote a thundering missive calling upon the many naturalised Germans in prominent positions in London society to "break silence and individually or collectively raise their voices against the infamous deeds which are being perpetrated by Germany". In doing so, he sparked a lengthy and sometimes angry public debate.

On 23 November 1934, Pinero died at Marylebone Nursing Home. He left behind an impressive body of work and one of the Journal's favourite ever lines of dialogue, from *Sweet Lavender*: "While there is tea, there is hope." That's something we can all get behind.

Profile: John Buchan (1875-1940)
Novelist and politician, lived at 76 Portland Place

There can have been few writers as prolific as John Buchan or as varied in their writings—from poetry to novels to biographies and other non-fiction works; a fact that is all the more outstanding when considering that writing was not Buchan's sole career.

At various times he was also a government administrator in South Africa, editor of *The Spectator*, a war correspondent for the *Times*, an MP, a soldier, a publisher, a director of Reuters, His Majesty's High Commissioner to the General Assembly of the Church of Scotland and Governor General of Canada. Buchan's feats are even more remarkable considering that he suffered from bouts of ill health throughout his lifetime.

Born in Perth in Scotland in 1875, John Buchan lived at 76 Portland Place during what might be considered the height of his literary success—1913-1919. *The Thirty-Nine Steps*, perhaps Buchan's most famous novel, was written there in 1914. It is no coincidence that the same area features as the location for Richard Hannay's London flat, where the initial intrigue takes place: "My flat was the first floor in a new block behind Langham Place. There was a common staircase, with a porter and a liftman at the entrance."

Such references to Marylebone occur to differing degrees in several of the fiction works written during and after his London sojourn, including *The Power-House* (1913) and *Mr Standfast* (1919). Despite being Buchan's 17th published work, *The Thirty-Nine Steps* is the novel which has most captured the public's imagination, due in part to the Hitchcock film version of the story. There have also been two further film versions, both even less loyal to the original novel than Hitchcock's.

The novel contains distilled versions of most of the themes which preoccupy Buchan's spy and thriller works—the protagonist being hunted by an enemy, familiar surroundings suddenly becoming strange, corruption at the highest level, a conspiracy to be thwarted. *The Thirty-Nine Steps* contains certain references which we now consider to be distasteful but were, when the novel was written, an unfortunate product of its time. Nonetheless, the novel remains a superior thriller, which accounts for a great part of its long-standing popularity. In the novel's protagonist, Richard Hannay, many see the blueprint for every action hero who followed him, be it on paper or on screen.

By today's standards, *The Thirty-Nine Steps* seems very short for a novel. Originally, it was published in a magazine, *Land and Water*, and was only published in book form after it had proved immeasurably popular in magazine format. This was the case with the majority of Buchan's writing until the 1930s. Many of his earlier works were only published as books after the success of *The Thirty-Nine Steps*.

In addition to fiction works, Buchan was also a prolific non-fiction writer, with subject matter so wide as to defy simple categorisation. Buchan seems to have been able to write about any subject in which he was interested. Being a Scot, Scottish history topics loom large in his bibliography. He originally studied Classics, and towards the end of his life, he wrote well-regarded biographies of Julius Caesar and Augustus. However, this is really the tip of the iceberg, where Buchan's non-fiction is concerned.

Outside of writing, Buchan was a politician and an administrator. He was made Baron Tweedsmuir in 1935 and appointed governor general of Canada the same year. He died of a brain haemorrhage in 1940, leaving a lasting literary legacy.

Profile: Douglas Jardine (1900-1958)

Cricketer, lived at 21 Bentinck Mews

Few sportsmen have excited as much passion and controversy as the former England cricket captain Douglas Jardine. Certainly very few others have managed to spark a major diplomatic incident.

Jardine was born in India in 1900, the son of a colonial lawyer. After graduating from Oxford, where he captained the cricket team, Jardine played for Surrey as an amateur while practicing commercial law.

After making his Test debut against the West Indies in 1928, Jardine was selected for his first Ashes series in Australia. Jardine was, it must be said, exceedingly posh and had a habit of wearing his Oxford harlequin cap whenever he played cricket.

Such ostentation, coupled with a stiff-backed haughtiness and barely hidden contempt for the unwashed masses, triggered a wave of vitriol from the Australian public who saw the aloof, patrician cricketer as a symbol of everything they loathed about British imperialism. The fact that he hit the Aussie bowlers all over the park probably didn't help.

By the time Jardine returned to Australia to contest the 1933-4 Ashes he had risen to captain the England side. During the 1930 series in England, which Jardine had missed through work commitments, Australian batsman Donald Bradman had scored 974 runs at a staggering average of 139.14. He appeared unstoppable. But the England captain was convinced that Bradman had a weakness—a susceptibility to genuine pace—and he set about devising a plan to exploit it. Jardine called his new tactic fast leg theory. It would become famous under the name coined for it by the Australian press: bodyline.

Leg theory involved peppering the batsman with fast, short-pitched bowling aimed in at the body, with a packed leg-side field waiting to snaffle any nicks played in self-defence. While such aggressive tactics were not strictly against the laws of the game, they were far from gentlemanly.

The Australians reacted in horror. After the third test, when captain Bert Oldfield was struck above the heart by a Harold Larwood snorter and seriously injured, Australian distaste exploded into anger. The Australian cricket authorities wired the MCC in horror, and the government in Canberra made frenzied representations. Crowds became increasingly hostile, and the Australian press stirred up a storm. Jardine became a hate figure. As the England captain tried to brush a fly away from his face at the next Test, one spectator was heard to shout: "Leave our flies alone Jardine, they're the only flamin' friends you've got!"

Jardine stuck to his guns and refused to bow to what he considered to be intolerable provocation. England destroyed a previously dominant Australia 4-1, and limited Bradman to an average of 'only' 56 runs. The England captain faced leg theory himself during a bruising tour of the West Indies in 1933. Facing the bouncers of the fierce West Indies' pace attack, Jardine scored a battling 127—his only Test century. This success left him more convinced than ever of the legitimacy of his tactics. The MCC disagreed. Success against bodyline was, he believed, purely a matter of technique. In 1934 the laws of the game were redrawn by the MCC to outlaw leg theory bowling. Jardine, piqued at the lack of support offered by the committee, stepped down as England captain.

Douglas Jardine played in 22 Test matches for England, scoring 1,296 runs at an average of 48.00. In his 15 matches as captain, England lost only once—a statistic that puts most of his successors to shame.

Former England captain Sir Pelham Warner said of Jardine: "If ever there was a cricket match between England and the rest of the world, and the fate of England depended upon its result, I would pick Jardine as England captain every time."

Profile: Edward R Murrow (1908-1965)

Broadcaster, lived on Hallam Street

Edward R Murrow was born Egbert Roscoe Murrow in Guilford County, North Carolina to Quaker parents, the youngest of three brothers. Home was a log cabin without electricity or plumbing on a farm that brought in only a few hundred dollars a year. When Murrow was six, the family moved to Blanchard, Washington, where he later attended high school. It was during his second year at Washington State College in Pullman that he changed his name to Edward.

In 1935 Murrow took a job at the broadcaster CBS and on 12 March of that same year he married Janet Huntington Brewster. In 1937 Murrow came to London to serve as director of CBS's European operations. His position did not initially involve any on air reporting—his job was to persuade newsworthy European figures to appear on CBS broadcasts.

During the March 1938 Anschluss, in which Adolf Hitler annexed Austria to Nazi Germany, Murrow himself reported live from Vienna in the first on the scene news report of his career. He began his narrative: "This is Edward Murrow speaking from Vienna... it's now nearly 2:30 in the morning, and Herr Hitler has not yet arrived." His live broadcast from the heart of the crisis broke the mould for news reporting.

After the outbreak of the Second World War, Murrow stayed in London, providing live radio broadcasts during the Blitz. It was during these reports that two of his most famous phrases were born—his signature opening of "this is London", with the emphasis on "this", and his closing "goodnight and good luck". Murrow also flew on 25 allied bombing raids in Europe and his vivid descriptions of what was going on around and below him had audiences back home enthralled. Murrow's reports would sometimes cause a great deal of controversy, especially his uncompromising report from the liberation of the Buchenwald concentration camp in Germany, in which his vivid description of haggard survivors and the piles of corpses upset some listeners. He made no apologies for the strength of his words: "I pray you to believe what I have said about Buchenwald. I have reported what I saw and heard, but only part of it. For most of it I have no words. If I've offended you by this rather mild account of Buchenwald, I'm not in the least sorry."

After the war, Murrow's radio career went from strength to strength. After a brief and fractious period off-air as one of the network's vice presidents, he took over the nightly CBS newscast. He later presented a regular programme called *This I Believe*, as well as narrating various radio documentaries and hosting the weekly CBS radio current affairs show *Hear It Now*.

With the dawn of the 1950s, Murrow began to appear on CBS television despite his own misgivings about the new medium, which he felt placed too much emphasis on pictures rather than ideas. His *Hear It Now* radio show was transferred to TV as *See It Now*. The show will probably be best remembered for an incendiary episode that dared to criticise the activities of Senator McCarthy and his anti-Communist witch hunt. The show consisted mainly of footage of McCarthy's own speeches, linked to emphasise their inconsistencies and extremism.

Murrow concluded: "We must remember always that accusation is not proof and that conviction depends upon evidence and due process of law. We will not walk in fear, one of another. We will not be driven by fear into an age of unreason, if we dig deep in our history and our doctrine, and remember that we are not descended from fearful men."

This 30 minute episode ignited a nationwide backlash against McCarthy and the Red Scare. Despite a furious reaction from McCarthy, the letters, telegrams and phone calls which flooded into the CBS headquarters were 15 to one in favour of Murrow. McCarthy's personal attacks on the popular newsman only decreased his own fading popularity.

Murrow retired from CBS in 1961 after a career which had revolutionised news broadcasting. He died at his home on 27 April 1965, two years after losing a lung to cancer.

Profile: Victor Weisz (1913-1966)

Cartoonist, lived at 35 Welbeck Street

'Vicky' Weisz, who went on to become one of Britain's finest political cartoonists, was born Victor Weisz in Berlin in 1913. He studied at the

Berlin School of Art, but had to leave after his father Dezso Weisz, a Hungarian Jewish jeweller and goldsmith, committed suicide in 1928. It was then that Vicky began drawing caricatures. He made his first sale the same year, aged just 15. He later joined the graphics department of the radical anti-Hitler journal *12 Uhr Blatt*, and by 1929 was the paper's sports and theatre cartoonist. In 1933 the paper was taken over by the Nazis, and by 1935 Weisz, a committed socialist, had fled to Britain.

In London, Weisz returned to drawing freelance caricatures for publications including the *Evening Standard*, *Daily Telegraph*, *Punch*, *Sunday Dispatch*, *New Statesman*, and *Daily Express*. In 1939 Weisz began working for the pro-Liberal *News Chronicle* and in 1941 became the paper's political cartoonist. The editor Gerald Barry was a great supporter of Weisz, but things changed when Robert Cruickshank took over in 1947. Cruickshank was not fond of cartoons and disliked Weisz's left-wing politics. This led to clashes, with Cruickshank frequently rejecting Weisz's images.

In 1954 Weisz, who had become a British citizen, was offered jobs on both the *Daily Mirror* and the *Evening Standard*. His friends advised him to go to the Standard, but he objected to it as "a Tory paper", and went instead to the Mirror. He soon regretted the decision, feeling that his cartoons did not fit in among the glaring headlines, and that in political circles "nobody reads the Daily Mirror". When his contract ended in 1958 he moved to the Evening Standard, where he was to really make his name.

Weisz was now an integral part of the British political scene, although his socialism was at odds with the politics of the Standard. During the 1959 General Election he received hundreds of letters from readers protesting about his left wing views. But the paper's editor James Cameron believed that this socialism was largely theoretical, saying Weisz "would have been rather horrified to meet a cloth-capped worker face to face".

Weisz's most memorable creation was the character Supermac—a parody of the Prime Minister, Harold Macmillan—which first appeared in the Evening Standard on 6 November 1958. It confirmed Weisz as one of the most influential political cartoonists, with Michael Foot calling him "the best cartoonist in the world". Ironically, Weisz had intended Supermac to be an attack on Macmillan's "cult of personality" style of leadership, but the attack failed and the character actually worked in Macmillan's favour.

In 1960 Weisz was voted Cartoonist of the Year by Granada TV's *What the Papers Say*. Working mostly in ink and brush on board, Weisz sometimes included a small version of himself in his cartoons, commenting on the main character's actions. "I don't make fun of a face," he once said. "I make fun of what is behind that face."

But despite his success, things were not as happy as they might have seemed. "My work never leaves me and I worry about it," he said. "I find I have less and less time for leisure." Weisz was losing faith in his ability to maintain a high standard, and developed a terrible fear of losing his abilities. This feeling began to deteriorate into a serious mental condition. Fellow cartoonist Ralph Sallon, who admired Weisz's work, agreed that eventually "he took himself too seriously. Everything he drew had to be a touch of genius."

In 1965, in a sign of his deteriorating mental condition, he refused to accept the Cartoonists Club of Great Britain's Political Cartoonist of the Year Award. On 23 February 1966, in a tragic repetition of his father's fate, Victor Weisz committed suicide by an overdose of sleeping pills at his home in London. It was a sad end to the career of one of Britain's best loved and most influential political cartoonists.

Profile: Kenneth Williams (1926-88)
Actor, lived at 62 Farley Court, Allsop Place

Kenneth Williams will be remembered as one of the all-time greats of the British comedy. He first came to the nation's attention on Hancock's Half Hour, but it was the Carry On films that really cemented his place in the public's affections. The nasal voice, affected manner and often waspish delivery, were so uniquely Williams' that they remain instantly recognisable to this day. A talented artist, Williams could have had a successful career as a draughtsman, but from an early age, he seemed set on the path that would lead to stardom. Born Kenneth Charles Williams on 22 February 1926 to Charles and Louisa Williams at Bingfield Street N1 into a working class background, he never felt he belonged. When the family moved into accommodation above the hairdressers that his father owned, the idea of living above the shop appalled him, and he began to display the upper class affectations that he would put to such good use later in life.

Detesting all sports, one game Williams loved was "our game" which he played with his sister Pat, and involved him impersonating friends and relatives of the Williams household. It was clear from the very beginning where his real interests lie. However, he clashed with his father who considered the acting world to be awash with "poufs and tarts" and no place for a real man, or one of Christian principles.

As with millions of others, the Second World War transformed Williams' life. Aged 14 he was evacuated to Bicester. There he found himself in a comfortable book-lined house, owned by an educated and erudite man, Mr Chisholm. It was the middle class, educated life to which young Kenneth had always felt he belonged. He loved it there. Indeed he would later refer to this time as one of the happiest and most influential of his entire life. He returned to London a very different young man from the one who had left.

Williams' evacuation had interrupted his training as a lithographer, a course undertaken to placate his father as it held out the promise of a 'proper' job. After completing the course he was apprenticed to Stanford's the mapmakers as a trainee draughtsman. While here, Kenneth befriended a salesman named Valentine Orford. It is to Orford that the nation owes a vote of thanks, for it was he who introduced Williams to the world of theatre.

Aged 18, Williams was drafted into the army, where his mapmaking skills were put to use in a series of postings to survey stations. Most of his war had been spent in England, but in 1945, just three weeks before the end of the conflict, Williams was sent to help fight the Japanese.

Fighting off mosquitoes was the closest Williams got to combat, but his desire to perform never diminished. His first chance came when posted to Singapore, home of the Combined Services Entertainments. He immediately auditioned as an actor—and was rejected.

However his draughtman's skills came to his rescue as he was kept on to design the posters for the company's shows. It kept him involved; a move that paid off when on arrival at the Victoria Theatre for a poster commission, he learned that one of the actors had malaria. He instantly volunteered to take his place, and debuted as a detective in *The Seven Keys to Baldpate.* He was an instant success, securing his acceptance into the company proper as an actor. He was on his way; it would take time, but his success in the CSE finally started him on the path to fulfilling his comic destiny.

It was in 1963, when Williams was at the height of his fame, that he moved to Marylebone, taking a small flat in Farley Court, opposite Madame Tussauds. Despite his growing wealth, he lived a very simple, solitary existence—he didn't even own a TV. He remained in Farley Court until 1970, when the noise of the area got too much for him and he moved to live near his mother.

Profile: Jacqueline Du Pré (1945-1987)

Cellist, lived at 27 Upper Montague Street

To her friends she was 'Smiley'. Her playing often reached levels of exuberance that bordered on the uncontrolled and music critics were divided as to whether she was brilliant or just cavalier. To many, Jacqueline du Pré was the most gifted cello player they had ever heard.

Born in Oxford on 26 January 1945 to pianist Iris Du Pré and her husband Derek, an accountant, legend has it that on first hearing the sound of a cello on the radio, four-year-old Jacqueline looked at her mother and said she wanted "one of those". It was a bond that was as lasting as it was instant. From the moment she heard those first notes to her death in 1987 Jacqueline's love for the cello never wavered. At the age of five she enrolled in the London Violoncello School and it was soon obvious that she had a very rare talent. News of the gifted young cellist spread and in 1955 aged 10 Jacqueline began to study with William Pleeth—regarded as one of the great cellists, and music teachers of the 20th century.

The cello was everything and Jacqueline missed large periods of her formal education in order to focus on music. It was a decision that paid dividends in terms of her playing, but which would lead to self-esteem problems in later life.

In March 1961 she made her formal debut at Wigmore Hall, aged 16. The following year she was invited to make her concerto debut at the Royal Festival Hall. It was to be one of her defining moments. Jacqueline chose to play Elgar's 'Cello Concerto'. It seemed a strange choice as the music was known for an emotional depth that few thought a 17-year-old girl could appreciate. In the event, her performance that night has acquired near mythical status as she coaxed a level of melancholy from the music that belied her age.

In 1963 she performed at the Proms. Her appearance was another instant hit and she would return to the annual event every year until 1969. It was only a matter of time before her talents brought international recognition, and this duly arrived in 1965 when Jacqueline recorded the Elgar concerto with the London Symphony Orchestra, conducted by Sir John Barbirolli. The resulting record was a revelation—a flowering of all the promise contained in that first public performance three years previously. It has never been out of print and continues to sell well to this day. The recording has become the benchmark against which all other performances are measured. She had produced it at the age of 20.

Jacqueline's life was now a whirlwind of travel and music. On Christmas Eve 1966, she met Daniel Barenboim, who was on his way to becoming one of the world's most renowned conductors. The attraction was instant and the two were married in June 1967 after Jacqueline's conversion to Judaism. By 1970 Jacqueline was complaining of various ailments— sensations of numbness, sudden intense fatigue and weakness in her limbs. Several doctors dismissed her symptoms as psychosomatic, and she began to fear she was heading for a breakdown. In 1971 she cancelled her musical engagements and left Daniel in a trial separation.

In 1973 Jacqueline went back to Barenboim and tried to return to her musical career, but it was clear that something was amiss. Her fingers had lost sensation, forcing her to look at her hands to gauge finger position and pressure while playing. In February she cancelled the last of four concerts she was booked to play in New York. She would never play on stage again. In October of that year Jacqueline was finally diagnosed with Multiple Sclerosis. Her career as a cellist was over.

To this day, du Pré's recording of Elgar's concerto is among the most requested pieces on radio. She was not the most technically brilliant cellist, but she had an instinctive feel for the music she played. It takes courage to be so bold, and extravagant talent to pull it off. Luckily for the music world in general and lovers of the cello in particular Jacqueline du Pré was born with precisely these gifts.

LOVE & MARRIAGE

There aren't many London streets that have been name-checked in the title of an Oscar-nominated Hollywood romance, but one of Marylebone's has: *The Barretts of Wimpole Street*, the 1934 film adaptation of Rudolf Besier popular play, brought the story of the secret love between two of the 19th century's greatest poets, Elizabeth Barrett and Robert Browning, to a worldwide audience.

But Marylebone's link to affairs of the heart does not begin and end with this famous affair. Marylebone Registry Office has been the scene of several famous nuptials: Paul McCartney and Ringo Starr tied the knot there (not to each other) while in 1997 at the height of Britpop Liam Gallagher and Patsy Kensit married in secret having sent the slavering packs of paparazzi on a wild goose chase. The area's churches have also seen more than their fair share of celebrity weddings.

This chapter is somewhat misnamed though. While love does play its part, most of these stories are actually about infidelity, betrayal and divorce. Far more interesting.

The Barrett Browning story

By Todd Swift

MJ1.4, Winter 2005

Elizabeth Barrett Browning (1806-1861) is routinely referred to England's greatest (and most popular) woman poet, although she is far less widely read these days than either Wendy Cope or Carol Ann Duffy, and, eventually perhaps, this title may have to be retired.

She was home-schooled to a very high standard, and showed a prodigy's talent for poetry. She lived in great comfort when young, thanks to her father's slave-trade fortune, which declined with abolition, forcing the move to London. Elizabeth, likely suffering from tuberculosis, became a recluse of sorts, living famously on Wimpole Street, and becoming addicted to morphine, even as her poetic renown increased. She cut a strange, exotic figure with her dark beauty, and was the subject of much speculation.

Robert Browning (1812-1889), six years younger than her, and then a minor poet, fell in love with the idea of this closeted poetess, and wrote her hundreds of fawning fan letters. These gushing, epistolary love-darts eventually led to an invitation to the house, set for May 1845. According to the biographer Pamela Neville-Sington, Robert, a bumptious man, was led into Elizabeth's room, where she reclined on a divan with stunning ringlets and brown eyes. This first meeting went well enough, but too soon (almost immediately after) he proposed marriage, which she, at 38 and thinking of herself as a spinster, declined. But she wittily asked him to reshuffle the cards and "play the game again".

He did, and by the end of the summer they were engaged. As Neville-Sington notes, in *Robert Browning: A Life After Death*, "the engagement lasted a year during which time the visits, the letters, the lovemaking continued". Despite her age, Elizabeth's father forbade her to marry (he was obsessively controlling), so the love-mad poets planned to elope to Italy. When her father, on 10 September 1846, announced a sudden move from Wimpole Street, they rushed their plan into action. This they accomplished by secretly marrying in St Marylebone Parish Church two days later, witnessed only by "his cousin and her maid Wilson".

After being married, they left in separate cabs and spent the week apart, pretending nothing had happened, before a dramatic reunion on their way to the Continent. Making matters worse, Elizabeth's frail health at the time meant Robert half-expected his genius-bride to perish before reaching Italy's life affirming clime. Never before in the history of English letters had two great poets been so faithfully and passionately in love — and it is this, as much as their poems, engendered by each other, that has continued to inspire readers even to the present.

St Marylebone: for better, for worse

By Tom Hughes

MJ4.4, Aug-Sep 2008

Margaret Elsie Crowther Baillie-Saunders—an opinionated blue-stocking sort—once memorably declared: "Marylebone-ites know their own traditions so well—especially old Marylebone-ites—that they are quite cross if you allude to them, much less write about them."

Miss Crowther is now well past being rankled by such things, but I concede her point. Therefore, I will not vex the many Marylebone-ites among you with another re-telling of the tale of Robert Browning and Elizabeth Barrett and their fevered dash to St Marylebone Parish Church. The Brownings' wedding is probably the most chronicled non-Royal wedding in the history of the realm—or at least it was until the Beckhams came along. But St Marylebone was also the scene of several other notable nuptials.

Henry Irving & Florence O'Callaghan The courtship of the actor (and much later, Sir) Henry Irving and Miss Florence O'Callaghan, the daughter of a surgeon in the Indian Army, although clandestine, had none of the Mills & Boon drama of the Barret-Brownings. Unlike the glowering, possessive Mr Barrett just around the corner in Wimpole Street, Florence's father was in a cantonment half a world away in India. Still, he disapproved of his statuesque Irish daughter having anything to do with anyone so déclassé as an actor.

There was also the little problem of Henry's sometime partner, on and off stage, a young actress named Nellie Moore. In 1869, poor Nellie died and Florence's father gave in—although there is no known connection between the two developments. Henry and Florence were married at St Marylebone Parish Church on 15 July 1869.

Florence—though not as decided on the matter as her father—also had her misgivings about her new husband's career. Unluckily for her, but to the greater glory of the Victorian theatre, Irving's reputation blossomed in the years immediately following their marriage.

On 25 November 1871, at the Lyceum, he gave a life-changing

performance in the classic melodrama, *The Bells*. The reviews were ecstatic; the opening night party ran quite late. In a cab back to their home in West Brompton, Irving boasted to Florence, "Maybe now we can afford our own carriage." Florence, several months pregnant and no doubt tired, blurted out coldly, "Are you going to go on making a fool of yourself like this for the rest of your life?" Irving ordered the cabman to stop at Hyde Park Corner. The actor got out of the cab and walked off into the night. He never saw or spoke to his wife ever again.

William Montagu & Helena Zimmerman St Marylebone Parish Church will never rival St George's Hanover Square or St Peter's Eaton Square for the great weddings of the nobility. Dukes and earls and the like tended to tie the knot in Mayfair, Belgravia and Kensington; a few managed all three before they were done. But Marylebone did see the marriage of a duke and duchess in 1900. Well, few people actually saw it, as it was a rather hurried affair hardly befitting the rank of the groom, but then we are talking about a Duke of Manchester.

Canon William Barker was surprised one day when a bright young thing named Eddie Lambart came calling to ask if the old boy would be free to marry a duke that coming Wednesday. The Canon was a bit taken aback when informed that neither surviving parent—the groom's mother or the bride's father—had been informed or would even be invited. Eddie, living up to his role as best man, flashed a permission form signed by no less a dignitary of the church than the Archbishop of Canterbury and the thing was on for 14 November 1900.

William Angus Drogo Montagu was only 23 but had already answered to Your Grace for eight years, having succeeded his dead, dissolute daddy in 1892. He came near to marrying a French danseuse until his mother chased her off and promptly dispatched William to America—her homeland—to find a rich bride. To his credit (quite literally), he scored a great catch: Helena Zimmerman, the daughter of a ludicrously wealthy investor who controlled a great network of railroads in the American Midwest.

The "able and energetic" Rev Barker seemed to enjoy all the attention the ceremony attracted to St Marylebone Parish Church. He postponed a trip to the West Country to remain in London for the marriage, then hung about giving interviews to all the society papers keen for details. Barker revealed that the groom had requested that they be allowed to enter the church by a side door in Marylebone High Street as it might attract less notice. The Rev Barker, canonically speaking of course, thought the bride was one of the prettiest girls he had ever seen—quite an attractive American blonde. But he described the entire mood of the proceedings, with only the required two witnesses present, as melancholy.

The spare nature of the marriage might have been explained by the fact that the penurious Duke of Manchester was bankrupt—he couldn't have found a florist in Marylebone to float him an orchid. Only the previous week, the papers were full of nasty notices of the duke's debts that neared £40,000. The *Daily Mail* tried to put a romantic bow on the wedding day but most papers focused on the important detail that the bride's ludicrously wealthy father had pledged a rescue dowry of a reputed £400,000.

The wedding was so hasty that the groom's mother—the dowager duchess—issued a public denial that her son was even married. But after she bustled over to the church from her home on Portman Square to confront poor Rev Barker, she was shown the duly signed marriage register.

The duke and his new duchess went off on honeymoon to the US (and to pick up the dowry cheque, one suspects). The Manchesters fell out after a few years and legal measures had to be taken to keep the duke's sticky fingers off the Zimmerman fortune. Still, they didn't actually get divorced until 1931.

Judy Garland & Mickey Deans For the last of our Marylebone marriages, we jump from the fustian melancholy and fog of late Victorian London to the swinging sixties. In the early hours of the morning of 9 January 1969, who should come traipsing down the yellow brick, er, I'm sorry, the Marylebone Road, but Miss Judy Garland. With the divorce papers having just come through to legally jettison husband number four, Judy—at the age of 46—was coming to St Marylebone Parish Church to wed a 35-year old cove named Mickey Deans. Deans had managed a gay disco in New York owned by Richard Burton's ex-wife Sybil. Those were the days, my friends. We thought they'd never end.

Judy and Mickey had known each other all of a month. Still, arriving in London for a series of shows at Leicester Square's Talk of the Town, Judy told the papers, "I'm happier than I've ever been and the future promises that I will be happier still. I want to be loved by one man and Mickey is that man." The lovers later took care of the legal niceties of the marriage at the Chelsea registry office and Judy threw a champagne reception at Quaglino's in Mayfair. Though few of the invited guests bothered to show up, Miss Garland again told the press, "For the first time in my life, I am really, really, happy."

Less than six months later, the bride was dead. On a Sunday morning in June, Judy Garland was found on the floor of the bathroom of her flat at 4 Cadogan Lane, Belgravia. Mickey said that, at a house party the night before, Judy was "gay, laughing and joking". The cause of death was determined to be an "incautious overdose of the sleeping drug Seconal". There was no note and the coroner did not believe she had taken the overdose deliberately. The Rev Peter Delaney, who had married Judy and Mickey in the small hours of that Marylebone morning, flew to New York to conduct her funeral service in Manhattan.

The mismatches of St Mary's

By Tom Hughes

MJ3.2, Apr-May 2007

St Mary's Bryanston Square may be among the least well known of the churches in Central London. Tourists and shoppers rarely walk past. It's also a perverse bit north of Bryanston Square—enough to confuse those who might actually be looking for it. But despite its obscurity, a lot has happened at this little church including three of the most interesting— and tragic—weddings in Victorian England.

St Mary's was consecrated in 1824, designed by Sir Robert Smirke who would later build the British Museum. Smirke's portico and 'pepperpot' spire face south with a view through Bryanston Square, down Great Cumberland Place into Hyde Park. Unfortunately, poor St Mary's has been saddled with a snarky but oft-quoted comment made by the architecture critic Sir John Summerson, who opined that Smirke's spire "has nothing to say but goes to enormous lengths to say it".

Just over a decade after the consecration of St Mary's, the first of our three marriages of interest took place. The bride was Letitia Elizabeth Landon, one of the most popular writers of her day, thought by some to be a 'second Byron'—so famous in fact she was known generally only by her initials LEL, long before Eminem. Not altogether prepossessing in appearance, she remained single into her thirties, when her name was romantically linked with that of the literary lion and future Dickens biographer John Forster. Alas, the romance cooled rapidly when Forster heard and then repeated rumours that LEL may have misconducted herself with a married man.

The London literary salons of the day were abuzz. Miss Landon indignantly denied the rumours and lacerated Forster, writing to a friend: "I can't get over the entire want of delicacy to me which could repeat such a slander." Her heart broken, LEL threw herself into the arms of one Captain George MacLean, in London on leave from his post as governor of the African colony of Cape Coast (more or less modern Ghana.) MacLean was in his late thirties, a Scot, well-burned from a decade of African service. He admitted to having a native wife and family but explained it was no more than the custom of the country and vowed to have them packed off if the famous Miss LEL would become the queen of his grandly named Cape Coast Castle. On a June day in 1838, given away at St Mary's by the popular novelist Lord Edward Bulwer Lytton, LEL became Mrs George MacLean.

Sailing to Africa in high spirits, LEL wrote: "I dare say the blacks will think I am Queen Victoria." But arriving in Cape Coast, she soon found out that "this isn't Windsor". The climate was awful. Her husband, who spent most of his time drunk, demanded she stop her "scribbling". In one of her few surviving letters home, she called him "the most unliveable with person you can imagine". In mid-October, she was found dead in her bed, still clutching a vial.

Captain MacLean ordered the hastiest of inquests, which found that his wife had accidentally taken too many of the drops which she had occasion to use for her "spasms". The news of her death didn't even reach London until New Year's Day and LEL's stunned friends demanded a full investigation but Whitehall decreed such an inquiry unfeasible. LEL's remains were buried on the castle grounds, to be joined in 1848 by her husband's. As he lay dying, Captain MacLean ordered all mementoes of his brief and tragic marriage destroyed.

In April 1860 a carriage arrived at St Mary's Bryanston Square bearing Lady Susan Pelham-Clinton, only daughter of the Duke of Newcastle. In defiance of her father, Lady Susan had that day absquatulated from the family home in nearby Portman Square to marry the dissolute Lord Adolphus 'call me Dolly' Vane-Tempest. Newcastle had refused to even meet Dolly, so vile was the young man's reputation. Even the Queen weighed in, writing to her daughter in Prussia: "Only think, Lady Susan P Clinton has gone and married Lord Adolphus Vane who drinks and has been twice shut up for delirium tremens ... between drink and his natural tendency to madness there is a sad prospect for poor Susan." On this inauspicious wedding day, there were no family present, only the required witnesses, and it was said that Dolly trembled uncontrollably through the no doubt accelerated proceedings.

As the queen had predicted (proving it was ever true that the young won't listen) the marriage was a spectacular failure. The honeymoon had to be interrupted and Dolly hauled away by his keepers after he began chucking the cutlery and crockery at his young bride. In his later intermittent periods of sobriety, Dolly, joined by his doting mother, pitched into Susan demanding she shake her father down for the dowry he had refused to provide. When one of Susan's brothers got married, Dolly fell off the wagon at the reception and was later found drunk "in a house the nature of which you will understand". He took a trip to America, far from the allurements of London, but returned unchanged and unwell, acting "like a wild animal". In 1864, four years after the wedding, he died at a home in Chester Square aged 38. The queen wrote: "I believe [he died] in a struggle with four keepers when he burst a vein in his throat." HRH seemed to follow this tawdry story with unusual interest, and so it seems did her son. Soon, the young and pretty widow, 25-year-old Lady Susan, was being 'consoled' by the Prince of Wales. The notorious Bertie, a newlywed himself, made Lady Susan one of his very first extramarital conquests.

The last of this sad trifecta of weddings at St Mary's took place just a week before Christmas 1887, when the 2nd Earl of Cairns was married to Miss Olivia Berens. This wedding attracted more than its share of public interest not because of the bride—a mere vicar's daughter—but rather the groom, whose 'abortive matrimonial relations' had made him something of a laughing stock. Aged just 26 on his wedding day, the earl had only gained his title the year before. He'd previously been known to all London as the Viscount Garmoyle—a rather chinless booby. He had been a cadet at Sandhurst when he found himself engaged to Miss May Fortescue, a young actress with D'Oyly Carte's Gilbert & Sullivan company. This pleased Garmoyle's father not at all—the old earl was a dour Ulsterman who thought the theatre was the antechamber of Hell.

When Garmoyle caved to his father's wishes, Miss Fortescue cried on the shoulder of the famous Frank Harris of the *Evening News*. His furious articles created a great outcry and the result was a breach-of-promise suit for the vast sum of £30,000. After eight months of private wrangling, the Cairns clan agreed to pay the jilted ingénue £10,000 and publicly state their belief that Miss Fortescue had to them always been the very model of a "high-minded English gentlewoman". The Earl of Derby though, wrote in his diary: "The young lady's free and easy ways, & unrefined manners, were too much for their tolerance. They are well out of the scrape, even at the cost." The *Daily Telegraph* gagged over the sum. The paper had little respect for the man it called 'Gumboil' but, it pronounced, "an Earl's an Earl for all that".

Young Garmoyle blithely lurched on, becoming engaged to one of the ubiquitous rich young American beauties who came ashore in boatloads. It wasn't a good sign when the gossip papers thought Miss Adele looked "exceedingly bored" at Garmoyle's side at the tables in Monte Carlo. Days later it was announced that this engagement too was off. The Weekly Dispatch could hardly credit the story. 'An American girl has shown she will not sacrifice everything to be a Countess? This is an event in American history.' Garmoyle having lost two fiancées, now lost his father, but the new Earl of Cairns was to find true love at last. On 19 December 1887, Miss Berens took his hand at the altar at St Mary's. In 1889, the couple had a daughter. Before her first birthday, the Earl of Cairns died of the flu in Mayfair. He was 29.

The public undoing of Mrs Mary Evans

By Tom Hughes

MJ8.2, Feb-Mar 2012

The clamour over the recent phone hacking scandal is hardly new. There's a seamy tradition in the land of eavesdropping, bin-diving, letter-lifting, phone-tapping and other dark arts. While plainly everyone loves a good spy story about the derring-do of our 'spooks', it is certainly true that no one wants a nark for a neighbour. A man's privacy must be respected: his home is his castle and let him pull up the drawbridge against the world. One of the most flagrant cases of snooping took place at 2 Bryanston Street, Marylebone in 1854.

Prior to the establishment of a divorce court in 1857, sundering a fractured marriage was a lengthy and expensive chore. If it was a case of the wife's adultery, there was an alternative. The cuckolded husband could file an action for "criminal conversation" and milk the traducer of his happy home for damages. Lloyd Evans, a man of property from Cheltenham, had married Mary Carrington in 1850 but it had not gone well. He was addicted to field sports and preferred the country while his pretty wife missed the Big Smoke. She justifiably chafed at being kept in rustic isolation with her aged mother-in-law for a companion. After a few years of this, Mrs Evans wanted out. But misery was no grounds for divorce. Evans agreed to give her an allowance to live in London, chaperoned by his servants and her nephew, who was studying for the clergy. The spanner in the works was the nettlesome presence of Robert Robinson, an old friend of the bride's family. Though a married man himself, he had long showed unusual attention to Mrs Evans.

She refused her husband's commands to end this. He cut off her allowance. Robinson gallantly stepped in and rented a suite of rooms for Mrs Evans at 2 Bryanston Street, Portman Square, just where the Mostyn Hotel now stands. The rent was £3 a week, as befitted the address—and while Robinson couldn't properly live there he called daily. Mr Evans, meanwhile, learning of the new arrangement, was distracted with anger and sought the assistance of a professional.

Charles Frederick Field was a "late inspector of the metropolitan detective police". Inspector Field had no small reputation: he'd been one of Dickens' "night guides" on the author's peregrinations of the great city and is generally thought to be the inspiration for the immortal Inspector Bucket of *Bleak House*.

Field had given up the job and was now a "private inquiry agent". For his fee and expenses, the ex-Inspector Field was now employed to discreetly shadow Mrs Evans. He did this for several weeks, following her and Robinson to the Crystal Palace, padding noiselessly behind them while they walked in various parks, even spending an entertaining night or two at the theatre in their unknowing company. But alas, he had observed no "intimacies". He could only report that Robinson would contrive to spend several hours alone in Mrs Evans's room at Bryanston Street, the drapes drawn and the door locked. What to do?

Field approached the landlady to ask if she possibly knew what was taking place in her respectable lodgings. Mrs King refused to hear anything bad about Mrs Evans: Robinson was a family friend and a very proper gentleman. But for £25, she agreed to allow Field to place a new cook in her employ. Sarah Grocott came down from St Johns Wood and—in her free time out of the kitchen—spent her hours lurking outside that locked door. But she heard nothing. Field met her one day in Portman Square and presented her with a gimlet.

Now a gimlet—a hand tool used for drilling small holes—has its legitimate uses in any well run home but not many of them in the scullery. Unless, of course, there's a keg of lime juice in the larder, whence we get the eponymous gimlet cocktail. But Mrs Grocott was instructed to use her gimlet on m'lady's door. While Mrs Evans was out (and being tailed by the tireless Field), the "agent" drilled her first hole. The poor woman was a cook not a carpenter and the hole was useless as it afforded no clear view of the divan. Her second effort was spot on.

At the very next opportunity, with Mr Robinson closeted with Mrs Evans on the aforementioned divan, Mrs Grocott took up her position. Squinting through the gimlet hole she was greatly shocked by what she observed. She needed some backup. The landlady agreed to have a look and she too shuddered in horror. A third woman, a Mrs Price, was present and in her haste to take her turn at the peephole, she knocked a chair over. The crash brought Mrs Evans out to ask what was going on. She was apparently satisfied with the explanation that the three flustered women were simply "inventorying the furniture". Mr Evans, meantime, was to be even more satisfied with the gathering of the proof he needed.

Ex-Inspector Field and the three ladies were the key witnesses at the trial of *Evans v Robinson*. A wooden model of the ground floor of 2 Bryanston Street was brought into the courtroom for the assistance of the male jurors. The lawyer for the aggrieved husband declared that what the ladies would all swear to have seen would leave no doubt as to what Mrs Evans had been up to her with her old family friend.

Before the three witnesses could be heard however, Justice Crowder asked that all females withdraw from the public gallery. This disappointed the "numerous fashionably attired ladies" in attendance. All three witnesses then detailed seeing the gentleman in some way straddling Mrs Evans. The young woman was in a semi reclining position with her flounced muslin dress "greatly upraised". Mrs Grocott swore, "I were shocked by what I saw." Mrs King said it was all so very distressing that she wished she hadn't looked that second time.

Mr Walton QC, the lawyer for the defendant (and in effect Mrs Evans as well) denounced it all as a vile conspiracy of spies. When Inspector Field testified, "On my honour," Walton barked at him, "You have no honour, sir!" In his closing argument, Walton attacked Mr Evans for cruelly abandoning his young wife. Now, this loathsome husband was willing to stain the reputation of an innocent woman solely to be free from paying his agreed support package. The machinations of the trio of giggling Bryanston Street watchers taking turns at their gimlet hole were good for a jolly laugh but, Watson concluded, this was a serious matter. "If the jury will rely upon the evidence of the fat cook Grocott, upon the flippant lady who took the inventory of the goods and upon that of Mrs King, then no person in this country is safe."

The jury members were cautioned by the judge not to allow their indignation with the employment of such tactics to affect their judgment of the case. The jurymen took some time at their work but returned with a verdict of not guilty. It was quite the rebuke of such domestic espionage, a practice foreign to English soil. The *Daily News* hailed the verdict: "Who is safe if the myrmidons of Scotland Yard are to keep in pay cooks and other menials, to be sent into families, armed with gimlets?"

Mr Evans was not finished: he went on to appeal, and the verdict was in fact overturned on grounds that the jury had been unduly swayed by the eloquence of the defence counsel. Evans then pursued his wife into the newly established divorce court, where the cook et al reprised their evidence of the Bryanston Street leg over and new sordid claims were added to the "surfeit of filth". Evans got the verdict he had long sought, bringing to a close what the *Times* called a "thrice told abomination".

While snoopy servants were regularly to be relied on by Victorian divorce counsel, there seems to have been no other case in which a gimlet was employed in such a nefarious manner as in Bryanston Street. The tool has given rise to the well-known expression used to describe someone with an especially prying stare—most memorably, the "gimlet eyed Miss Marple". Which seems rather unfair to the dear old thing.

The Earl of Orkney and the burlesque dancer

By Tom Hughes
MJ7.3, Jun-Jul 2011

The beautiful Nash church of All Souls, Langham Place has seen many society weddings in its 186 years. Few have been quite such clandestine affairs as the nuptials of 19 July 1892, when the Earl of Orkney quietly married Miss Constance MacDonald. That was the bride's name on the register, but she was known behind the footlights as the "celebrated burlesque actress" Connie Gilchrist. For a time at least, she held the unenviable (but traditionally transitory) title of "the most notorious woman in London".

Adding to the sensational events of this summer Tuesday morning, the bride was given away by the Duke of Beaufort, a rakish octogenarian variously described as Connie's erstwhile lover, protector, or, whisper it, even her father. The wedding breakfast was held just a few steps away from the church, off Portland Place, at 4 Duchess Street, where Connie had resided in well-furnished Marylebone comfort for most of a decade, openly paid for by the duke, who was also a frequent visitor.

On her wedding day, Connie was 27, if one accepts that she was born in 1865. Her parentage was always a mystery. It was said her mother took in "theatrical laundry". Her father, if not the duke, was perhaps a civil engineer who rarely came around. As a little girl, Connie's cherubic beauty had attracted the interest of a popular designer of Christmas cards. Her face, surrounded by holly, bows and other holiday flummery, sold thousands of cards annually. Lewis Carroll, whose eye for a pretty little girl was quite well-developed, thought her "one of the most beautiful children in face and figure that I have ever seen".

When Connie outgrew the toddler phase (and Carroll's interest), her mother put her on the stage. She starred in children's entertainments and pantomimes. She also won acclaim for her facility in the greatly underestimated stage talent of rope skipping. So renowned had she become that she was asked to pose for Whistler. In 1877, he painted her (with her skipping rope) as *The Gold Girl—a Harmony in Yellow & White*. The theatrical press dubbed her "The Child."

Sadly, for a maturing actress, there were few parts in the West End that included a need to skip rope. But Connie could always rely on her beauty. She was possessed of what one of her numerous admirers described as "liquid blue eyes". John Hollingshead, legendary impresario of the Gaiety Theatre, soon employed Connie in his burlesque extravaganzas. The adorable ingénue would innocently deliver her lines—usually featuring the most ribald double-entendres. And did I mention her legs? The occasional flash of Connie's appendages was enough to fill the boxes every night with her gentleman devotees. Alas for Connie's long-term career, she had no voice. One of the few critics immune to her appeal thought her singing was shrill and her speech was shrewish. And so she mostly danced, behind those eyes and on those legs.

One of those stage-door admirers stood out. The Duke of Beaufort seems to have been a jolly old sort, if you like your peers with a little less of the noblesse oblige about them. His splendid home was at Badminton, Gloucestershire where he was known to all as, simply, 'the duke'. The duchess also kept her establishment at Badminton and rarely came to London. On one famous occasion, a portrait arrived at Badminton.

The duchess asked that it be brought to her—it was the painting of an actress (it may have been Connie). With that phlegm that only a duchess can display, she told the butler, "His Grace will want that placed in his room, perhaps."

The duke was a famous four-in-hand coachman in his day, a legendary supporter of hunting and field sports, and he keenly enjoyed the company of actresses. He lurked backstage at the Gaiety and elsewhere, taking his favourites to supper, gifting them with jewellery and maybe something nice from their corsetiere of choice.

The duke's fascination with Connie Gilchrist moved beyond the odd supper. When she was only in her late teens, he set her up at 4 Duchess Street. He furnished the house and superintended the domestic household. The arrangement excited a good deal of comment, almost all of it of the censorious kind. When she rode in Rotten Row, it was a scene not to be missed. The men ogled, the women tutted. Connie lived in Duchess Street for more than a decade, while the duke kept rooms nearby, generally a short walk away, often in Mortimer Street. As Connie's theatrical talents began to wane, her name became less common on the bill. She was now more likely to be seen riding with the hunt in Melton Mowbray. She thoughtfully eschewed pursuing the Badminton foxes, out of respect for the duchess.

In the duke's defence, he always observed all the proprieties of good conduct in public, as he understood them. Connie was always suitably chaperoned when on her hunting weekends. It was understood by any young swell who wished to be introduced to Connie that he must first approach the duke for permission. This brings the story back to All Souls, Langham Place, in the summer of 1892.

For some months that year, there had been talk in the clubs of a romance. While in Leicestershire, Connie had been seen more than once in the company of Edmond Walter Fitzmaurice, the 7th Earl of Orkney, a Scottish peer. Edmond was a year or two younger than Connie and—at least according to the London correspondent of the *New York Times*—he was a "flat-skulled, vacuous young noodle".

Regardless, the duke had not stood in Cupid's way. Some had whispered that perhaps the duke had wearied of the bills and thought it time for Connie to make a good marriage. The radical journal, *The Star*, put it plainly: "The heavy expense is more than a duke with one foot in the grave relishes in these days of agricultural depression."

The wedding had not been announced until the morning of the ceremony. The curate-in-charge, the Rev Mr Legge would officiate. All Souls was not overly crowded. The groom's parents were in attendance. The two official witnesses were the bride and groom's respective solicitors (a rather crass bit of business, one would suggest). Of course, the duke was there to walk the bride down the aisle. As mentioned, there had been whispered speculation that Connie was his daughter, as if perhaps that put a rosier tint on the duke's interest in her welfare. However, that morning, on the license, Connie swore to be the "daughter of David Gilchrist, civil engineer, deceased". These are not questions for a wedding day. A reporter from the *Penny Illustrated Paper* had dashed to the scene and wrote later that Connie looked "very well indeed" in a dress of blue bengaline with puffed velvet sleeves and a "very becoming straw hat". She also displayed a quite sizeable diamond brooch (said to be from the earl but possibly a parting gift from the duke?) It was a small but happy group that took the short walk to 4 Duchess Street for the wedding breakfast. The earl and his new countess would leave that night for Minehead and their honeymoon.

It's always preferable to end a romance "happily ever after" and, in this case, it seems to be an accurate statement. Her Duchess Street home was given up. The earl and countess settled in the Home Counties at Stewkley, their country house near Leighton Buzzard. Connie grew flowers and grew stout. The earl, presumably, became an older "vacuous noodle". They are remembered well in the area for their good works and long lives. Constance, Countess of Orkney died in 1946, the Earl lived until 1951. As for the Duke of Beaufort, he died (fittingly) before the end of the 19th century. The gout carried him off in 1899. One of the Gloucestershire papers acknowledged that Puritan sectors of the public may have found great fault with him, but "we do not think anything petty, mean or unsportsmanlike was ever alleged against him".

The shameless progress of Mary Anne Clarke

By Rupert Butler

MJ10.6, Dec-Jan 2014-15

Mary Anne Clarke, legendary beauty, royal mistress, shameless spendthrift and accomplished courtesan, had been on the way up from birth. Raised in a working class family on Chancery Lane in the 1770s, she ended up living a life of luxury that few could ever dream of. But she paid a heavy price in other ways.

Of her early life, separating fact from fiction is rendered almost impossible by the sheer volume of lurid, fantastical and largely contradictory biographical books that were dashed off at the height of her fame. Her father appears to have died when she was a child, but she enjoyed the backing of a stepfather, a proof reader at a Fleet Street printers, who taught her to read and write and helped her find work at the firm. Her role as a professional proof reader did not, however, fit with her loftier tastes and ambitions. "Her person and manners," it was said, "were infinitely above her condition."

Aged just 16, Mary Anne married Joseph Clarke, the son of a rich stonemason, and every bit as profligate a spender as his charismatic young bride. The couple were declared completely broke a few years later. The marriage produced two children, George and Ellen, but no money to provide for them.

After separating from her bankrupt husband, Clarke used her charm, good looks and relentless ambition to propel herself into the affections—and bedrooms—of a string of ever more wealthy and influential lovers.

"Though she is not a perfect beauty, she has many agreeable attractions; one in particular from a well-turned arm," wrote one observer. "Lively and gay in conversation. Her easy demeanour, upon the first acquaintance, is what the French call 'eminently prepossessing'. Her face is oval, but not long; small nose, dazzling dark eyes and captivating intelligence."

Mary Anne embraced a lifestyle no ordinary man could reasonably support. A vast distance from her old life on Chancery Lane, by 1803 the cheerfully impenitent Mary Anne was wallowing in the luxury of a mansion in the hugely fashionable Gloucester Place, Marylebone. Here she plunged into the wildest extravagances, keeping 10 horses and 20 servants, including three male cooks and wine glasses costed in guineas.

The man paying for all this was Prince Frederick, Duke of York, the second son of King George III and commander-in-chief of the army who set her up with a promised £1,000 a month. The fact that this money was only spasmodically paid did nothing to slow her spending, leaving her with volumes of unsettled tradesmen's bills. Unabashed as usual, Mary Anne turned elsewhere for the funds, touting her powerful influence over her lover and receiving various sums of money, most notably from army officers who were hungry for promotion at the duke's say-so and believed that his feisty mistress could help propel them up the career ladder. But the money she netted from these corrupt officers was by no means enough to stem Mary Anne's chronic overspending.

There seemed no reason why she should not have gone on indefinitely, but discretion had never been one of Mary Anne's virtues. In January 1809, Welsh MP and army veteran Colonel Gwyllym Lloyd Wardle learnt of her activities and prepared to turn them into a public scandal. The colonel alleged that the Duke of York not only knew about his mistress's actions, but was actually in on the deal.

After an undercover visit to Gloucester Place, Colonel Wardle, who had spotted a carriage with royal livery driving up to the front door, suggested that the commander in chief had authorised the sale of a commission. Mary Anne launched a personal attack on Colonel Wardle, revealing in print: "I have since understood that the name of Brown is very familiar to Colonel Wardle. Among the variety of his pursuits, I have been informed, that he once lived under this name at the Cadogan Coffee House, Sloane Street, with his favourite lady! Believe me, reader, I do not mean Mrs Wardle!"

The ensuing legal proceedings—a public sensation at which Mary Anne's shameless testimony was one of the highlights—forced the duke to resign his post as commander in chief, but he was re-instated two years later having insisted all along that he had known nothing about Mary Anne's activities and had derived no financial benefit.

The damage caused to the royal family brought into the affair Prince Frederick's private secretary and aide-de-camp Sir Herbert Taylor, a skilful diplomat given the delicate task of buying back the Duke of York's letters to his by then discarded mistress—communications in which he had been bluntly critical of fellow royals and sundry government officials.

An agreement was worked out that the amusingly remorseless Mary Anne would abandon the luxury of Gloucester Place and keep her mouth shut about the royals—particularly about the duke she had coyly called "that big baby". The result for her was a supremely satisfactory deal. She received a settlement of £7,000 and a large annuity, plus the costs of her son George's education and military commission—in return for the letters and the promise never to reveal anything about the royal family.

That agreement scarcely prevented her from collaborating on a blizzard of gossipy pamphlets deemed heavily libellous to numerous influential individuals. One of the most notorious was the brilliantly named *The Authentic and Impartial Life of Mrs Mary Anne Clarke, Including Numerous Royal and Original Letters and Anecdotes of Distinguished Persons, Which Have Escaped Suppression, with a Compendious View of the Whole Proceedings, Illustrative of the Late Important Investigation of the Conduct of His Royal Highness the Duke of York.*

The Rival Princes, a fierce defence published under her own name, freely discussed royal relationships as well as teared into Wardle in a quite brutal manner. She wrote: "Let it be remembered that I have never wantonly forced myself upon the public attention, and that it has only been when promises were made to me, and their performance afterwards neglected, that I have been heard to complain; and when pacific applications were unavailing, and I became goaded beyond all endurance, that I shook off the native gentleness of my sex, and assumed the heroine in defence of my claims, by taking arms against my enemy!"

These pamphlets frequently appeared at the same time as highly sensational portraits featuring Mary Anne and the duke. One of the most notorious portrayed the couple and a friend of Mary Anne's—titled *The Triumvirate of Gloucester Place*—seated at a circular table discussing the notorious lists of army promotions.

By 1813, Mary Anne's enemies had their revenge when she was convicted of libel and sentenced to nine months in jail. Her fame nevertheless remained notorious with many sketches, colour prints, etchings and a marble bust gaining eventual display at the National Portrait Gallery. All connections with the duke were terminated. She was obliged to quit the country and settle wherever she chose, at first opting for Brussels where knowledge of the more lurid details of her career was sketchy; not so when she moved to Paris, where she did not hesitate to build up a social circle including old friends from England whom she entertained with all the old lavishness accompanied inevitably with a string of the ripest anecdotes about the royal family. She died on 21 June 1852 aged 76.

Daphne Du Maurier, Mary Anne Clarke's great-great-granddaughter, would capture her ancestor's fascinating personality in her novel, Mary Anne: "The smile... was what they remembered in after years. The rest was forgotten. Forgotten the lies, the deceit, the sudden bursts of temper. Forgotten the wild extravagance, the absurd generosity, the vitriolic tongue. Only the warmth remained, and the love of living."

The old lady and her Buttons

By Tom Hughes
MJ9.5, Oct-Nov 2013

With reductions in staff so painfully common in today's economy, who among us can still afford to keep a page boy on the household pay roll? This was once a starter job for a lad interested in a career in service, usually hired at the age of 12. His duties included running errands, minding the open fires, answering the doorbell, cleaning boots and, in a pinch, serving as a tiny groom on the box seat of his employer's carriage.

Mrs Beeton, that Wikipedia of Victorian household management, thought six pounds a year was a good starting wage. Of course, the boy's livery was included—and what a spiffing suit it was. A page boy's coat was "fastened from top to bottom with metal buttons set as closely together as possible". In fact, so many were the buttons on display on chest and sleeves that the page boy in most homes was familiarly known, not by his name, but only as 'Buttons'.

Miss Jane Ann Warren was a Victorian spinster in her sixties and, as we all would wish for, she enjoyed a life of independent means. She moved in polite society. She lived in Marylebone—her home was at 5 Chandos Street, just north of Cavendish Square. It was a fine home—it subsequently served as an embassy and is the current home of the high commission for the Republic of Namibia. In her establishment, Mrs Warren kept a full complement of servants. This comfortable existence came a cropper in the summer of 1873. The roadway in front of poor Miss Warren's home was soon filled with laughing crowds, singing ribald songs, and sharing hastily printed broadsheets with "scurrilous woodcuts." The papers were filled with the details of "The Old Lady and her Buttons". It was all too awful.

Miss Warren employed a Buttons by the name of Walter Howard. Hired at 12, Walter was now 16. His older brother was her coachman. His mother was a part time nurse for the sometimes querulous mistress Warren. Young Walter, a good-looking cove, soon became Miss Warren's particular favourite. Small in stature, Walter was a familiar sight—in all his glorious buttons—riding behind Miss Warren in her carriage as she made her calls around Marylebone. At home, she coddled and petted the lad with various favours and freedoms. The other servants, resentful of course, thought that cheeky Walter had begun to fancy himself the master of the house. They spied on him and reported back to Miss Warren that Walter had been seen on his off-hours at a tobacconist's, playing the concertina with a few shop girls. She called him a naughty boy. He said the butler had first brought him to the shop. Miss Warren sacked the butler. Walter's influence grew. Miss Warren, who worried about burglars, thought she'd feel a wee bit safer with Walter's bedroom being brought down from the attic and he was installed in the dressing room adjacent to her boudoir.

In July 1873, Miss Warren suddenly dismissed Walter from her service. A few weeks later, she filed charges against the youth accusing him of taking from her through false pretences the sum of £303 9s 6d. She had given that sum to Walter, so she believed, to pay his medical bills and cab fare—he claimed the need to visit a doctor in Richmond weekly for a "painful ailment". But the lady's wary solicitor, a Mr Wright, sensed something wrong. He discovered that Walter was in fine health, there was no Dr Baker in Richmond and, rather, the lad was taking the money to spend at the music halls, treating the shop girls and living the life of what the papers called a "precocious and disgusting little roué".

Quite how Walter could have afforded him cannot be known for certain, but the page boy managed to employ a canny veteran of the criminal bar to defend his good name. Montagu Williams hammered the theme that "there's no fool like an old fool". Miss Warren, the barrister asserted, didn't have to be tricked into funding young Walter's capers—she gave him the money willingly. As much as a fiver a day. The poor woman, under cross-examination, conceded that she regularly called young Buttons her "Dear" or "Darling", and she was his "Pretty Jane". Yes, she had kissed and been kissed by the lad, she played the piano in her drawing room while he sang ribald songs and she permitted him to make "an indecent observation about her legs". Most embarrassing for her was the observation that she was seen paying nightly visits to Buttons' little bedsit. She insisted these nocturnal visits were for the sole purpose of tucking him in. All these admissions were made by her in a "most animated manner" that excited great amusement in the courtroom, alas, at her expense. Most important to Walter's defence, however, was her admission that she had kept him plentifully supplied with money.

The advocates for Miss Warren attempted to rescue their floundering client with the claim that, although now 16, Walter was a very small boy and he appeared much younger than his mature years—the age of consent in England in 1873 was 12. Nor could simple London jurymen perhaps understand "the habits of persons of the rank of life in which pages were kept". In such homes, "there is nothing to excite remark in a lady kissing and hugging her page, or putting him to bed".

After three days of such curious and, at times, mirthful discussions, the jury could not agree and the case was held over for a new trial. A few weeks later, Miss Warren dropped all charges. It was reported that her health had broken under a serious case of nervous prostration. She had never quite recovered from the "long and most cruel cross-examination, which harassed my feelings in a most painful degree". Since the first trial, crowds had gathered in Chandos Street singing bawdy songs. If she dared to go out, the raucous mob would follow her carriage. They shouted the most horrible and groundless imputations against her character. Though she was willing to withdraw from the case, "I also solemnly swear that there is not a word of truth in those insinuations conveyed in the questions put to me in cross-examination."

A not guilty verdict was entered for the defendant and so the case ended. A trivial domestic muddle, to be sure. With the lasting image of her "cuddling and slobbering her domestic," Mrs Warren was the loser. The Saturday Review found a cautionary message: "Elderly ladies who have no families to look after must, we suppose, have pets; but it is as well that they should confine themselves to the animal kingdom. Cats or parrots may be petted with impunity, but such a shameless young rip as Walter Howard is a social nuisance, and even a danger."

Mrs Warren sought to avoid the heckling throngs and, to the relief of her neighbours, she gave up 5 Chandos Street but did not move that far away. She remained in Marylebone, taking a new home near Portman Square. There, according to the next available census, by which time she had reached the grand old age of 71, Miss Warren still employed several servants, including a page-boy, aged 13.

The scandalous life of Lady Jane Digby

By Tom Hughes

MJ10.2, Apr-May 2014

Lord Byron—who certainly had the credentials to judge the contest—has declared that the most profligate women in England are those of high rank. Lady Jane Digby, like Byron, died in exile from scandal. Leaving the walled city of Damascus by the eastern Gate of the Sun, a short journey will bring the traveller to the Protestant Cemetery. The graveyard is locked and untended today in a region much affected by the recent Syrian violence. There, beneath a gaunt tree, lies the body of Lady Jane, whose story begins in an altogether different setting: Harley Street.

Jane was the daughter of an admiral and grandchild of the wealthy Cokes of Holkham Hall in Norfolk. As a teenager, her beauty was renowned. She was tall with large violet-blue eyes and blonde hair worn in "free-flowing ringlets". Jane was 17 in 1824 when she married Edward Law, Lord Ellenborough. His lordship was widowed and two decades older than his bride. Handsome and cultured, Edward was, in the parlance of the day, an "exquisite". In 1828, Wellington brought him into the cabinet, probably just to have him around. Ellenborough was named Lord Privy Seal, a sinecure described as having "no particular function".

The great hostess of the day, Lady Holland, thought the newlyweds were ill-matched. Jane, she feared, was "a poor girl who has not seen anything of the world". Edward, on the other hand, preferred his library and his club whilst satisfying his other needs with dalliances below stairs— curiously, he had little interest in his vivacious young wife and relations between them had ended. She moved out of Connaught Place and returned to her father at 78 Harley Street (now number 33).

Only a few doors down, at the corner of Queen Anne Street, were the first floor rooms of Prince Felix of Schwarzenberg, attache to the Austrian embassy and a protege of the great Metternich—the legendary diplomatic string-puller of his time. Young Felix, it seems, preferred pulling the strings on the stays of m'lady Jane. Theirs was a brazen affair. Lady Jane would call for her carriage (it was a "green phaeton" which sounds ever so much grander) and make her various calls. On the drive home, she would bid the coachman to let her out around the corner on Cavendish Square. She would prefer to walk but not directly home. Her daylight rendezvous with Prince Felix continued for weeks. But not unobserved. A very attentive and well-placed young man in rooms across the way from Felix's flat would later prove quite helpful when Lord Ellenborough sought his divorce.

In 1829, Lady Jane had confessed that she was pregnant. It could not have been her husband's. She and the prince left London "somewhat abruptly". Prior to her bolt, Jane wrote Edward a note thanking him for his "unbounded kindnesses". There was talk of a duel, but Schwarzenberg opted to keep the peace and paid Ellenborough £25,000 for his "criminal conversation".

A divorce in 1829 required a bill to pass through the House of Lords. The "exquisite" Ellenborough would have to suffer the indignity of having his dirty linen aired before his fellow peers.

The Argus-eyed man from over the road swore to watching Prince Felix, on many an afternoon, leaning out a window, scanning Harley Street for his lover's approach. Upon sight of her, Felix would scurry down to the door which he opened himself. Alone at last, the amorous pair didn't even draw the curtains. "They made no effort to conceal themselves." There was memorable evidence involving the prince's deft management of the many layers of dress which perforce had to be removed. Lord Ellenborough's agents also recruited the testimony of the coachman and the housemaid at 73 Harley Street. The latter menial reported that, after the lady visitor departed, she would restore order in the prince's suite, the bed being "very much tumbled".

The divorce bill was looking like a walkover in the Lords until the Earl of Radnor stood up. A biblical quote would not be out of place even in this unseemly discussion and Radnor quoted St Matthew — "He who putteth away his wife for any other cause than adultery, causeth her to commit adultery." Hadn't his Lordship's "neglect" driven his wife from his home? Did Lord Ellenborough "never trouble himself to inquire where she went, how she was spending the many hours of the day during which she absented herself?" Radnor admitted that he had never met the unhappy lady but he was well informed of her many attractions. "If a young and beautiful woman like this were allowed to go about the town totally unheeded [by Ellenborough], there were thousands who would be ready to take advantage of such negligence on the part of a husband."

Lord Ellenborough was not without allies in the chamber. "A more affectionate husband has never breathed," a friendly peer tottered to his feet to proclaim. Lord Wharncliffe asked, "Was there a single peer who did not know that their wives generally went out about two o'clock in the day, and returned at five?" Were they supposed to keep a minder at their heels? Such a practice would turn the loving trust of a true English marriage into something resembling the strictures of a Turkish harem. It was better for a husband to be a cuckold than a spy.

The newspapers denounced the "disgusting" details of the case, which, of course, they printed in columns of eye-wearying detail. The *Times* actually broke its long standing practice by putting it on the front page, normally reserved for advertisements. The phrase "sexual intercourse" made a rare appearance in the columns, amid the tawdry details of the Harley Street leg-overs.

In the great "public opinion", Lord Ellenborough—who laughed and sneered through much of the Lords debate—was found wanting as a husband and complicit in driving his beautiful young bride into the arms of her seducer. But fidelity and attentiveness were attributes not necessarily common amongst the husbands who sat in that ancient and honoured chamber (leaving aside, of course, the saintly bishops among them.) The Lords approved the divorce bill by a vote of 86 to 16.

Lord Ellenborough lived another 40 years and never remarried, capping his career as governor-general of India. Lady Jane never returned to London. Her affair with Schwarzenberg ended in Paris; they had two children. The romantic disappointment did not ruin her taste for Bavarians. In Munich, she ran with "the gayest of the gay". Her next lover was King Ludwig I. She also found the time to bear two children with another Bavarian diplomat. She dropped him for a Greek count whom she married and then jilted to begin an affair with King Otto of the Hellenes. Then she rewarded the king by running off with a Greek revolutionary, living the life of a brigand for a few turbulent years. In the 1850s, while traveling in the Middle East, Jane's caravan was escorted by

Sheikh Medjuel et Mezrabi, younger brother of the tribal leader in Damascus. Jane became fascinated with Medjuel and him with her. She "went native". They were married for 28 years, splitting their time between Damascus and the desert.

Jane Digby el Mezrab was carried off by dysentery in 1881. The London papers recalled the Harley Street scandal, deciding that "nothing can be more profligate" than her behaviour at the time. Lady Jane has been the subject of numerous books and Madonna has reportedly given some thought to making a movie of her life.

The Wallace Collection's dirty laundry

By Tom Hughes

MJ4.6, Dec-Jan 2008-9)

17 January was the coldest day yet in the winter of 1912. Winds howled across London—the maximum gust was clocked at 49mph at Kew. On that frigid morning, a doctor was called from his office in Manchester Street to come immediately to Hertford House, Manchester Square where the director of the Wallace Collection museum, 25-stone Sir John Murray Scott, had suffered what was later described as a "short heart attack". The efforts of the doctor were unavailing and Sir John was pronounced dead at the age of 67. He left behind a fortune worth an estimated £1,180,000.

Sir John was unmarried but, as his obituary noted: "He is survived by brothers and sisters." These siblings were not at all pleased when their brother's will was later opened—the bulk of the fortune, including two homes in France, one of them an art-stocked palace on the Rue Lafitte in Paris, and £150,000 cash were all being left to Sir John's dearest friend, Lady Victoria Sackville of Knole.

Sir John had earned his knighthood by advising the late Lady Wallace to leave her family's vast collection of paintings, porcelain and armour to the nation. Sir John's father had been a doctor who lived in Paris and served ex-pat patients. Among Dr Scott's clientele was the infamous 4th Marquis of Hertford, who had been driven from London by his profligacy. The Marquis, as well as amassing one of the worst reputations of all time, had assembled a magnificent art collection. When he died in 1870, he left it to his illegitimate son, Richard Wallace. During the old scoundrel's last illness, Dr Scott's own son, John, although training for the bar at the Sorbonne, had assisted his father.

Young John attracted the attention of Richard Wallace who promptly employed him as his personal secretary. Sir Richard and Lady Wallace had no children and Scott, a charming 23-year-old, soon made himself indispensable. The bulk of the family's art was moved back to Hertford House in 1871. After Sir Richard died in 1890, Scott remained as Lady Wallace's adviser. When she passed away in 1897, in addition to bequeathing Hertford House and its collection to the nation, she left all the rest—the homes in France and a million pounds—to her faithful assistant, John Murray Scott.

The Prince of Wales came to Marylebone to open the collection to the public in 1900. The *Times* exulted: "Henceforth Hertford House and the Wallace Collection, vaguely famous until now, among the experts and amateurs of Europe and America, will become a veritable place of pilgrimage for all who care for art."

While giving a private tour to some of the era's A-listers, Sir John was introduced to Lady Victoria Sackville (to be accurate, she was then Mrs Lionel Sackville-West. But, please, one romantic story at a time). Her Ladyship invited Sir John to visit her at her splendid if financially encumbered home at Knole. The friendship speedily blossomed. In his diary, Sir John wrote: "Sat under the tree with V till lunch. She told me all her trials and worries." In their correspondence, she was V or Vickey and he was 'Seery', a baby-talk derivative of monsieur.

With her husband otherwise engaged in his serial philandering, V was able to focus her considerable charms on Seery. She began to preside over his lavish home at 5 Connaught Place, just across the Edgware Road. She relegated his "stupid sisters" to their rooms upstairs. The sisters called Lady Sackville and her friends "the Locusts". The servants called her "the Earthquake" because every time she came, she would re-arrange the furniture and art. The prurient reader should be informed that there was never any suggestion of a physical intimacy between V and Seery, and Sir John's Falstaffian proportions certainly made him an unlikely romantic hero. Nonetheless, although he had known her for only two years, Sir John's will declared his wish to leave Lady Sackville "comfortable and independent in return for her goodness and sympathy". After Sir John's death, the brothers and sisters Scott angrily caucused and harrumphed: "We'll see about her goodness."

For eight days in June and July 1913, crowds packed the Probate Court on The Strand for the sensational Scott Will Trial. The best counsel had been employed by each side. FE Smith, for the Scotts, declared: "Until Lady Sackville entered into it, there was never a more affectionate family than the Scotts." This scheming woman, he said, "deliberately set herself to make mischief". She disparaged Alicia and Mary, the unmarried Scott sisters, saying that they did not have "the Knole manner". Sir John's aged mother became so upset over the impact Lady Sackville was having on her family she died of a stroke. Besmitten Sir John could not be stopped— he regularly wrote cheques, making gifts to Lady Sackville that Smith claimed "dropped like gentle rain from heaven". These gifts amounted to a cool £84,000.

The Scotts were, said Smith, greatly heartened when Sir John's ardour for his vexatious friend began to cool. In 1911 Sir John had written to Lady Sackville to tell her he had determined to make a codicil that would greatly reduce her expectations. He had decided that the valuable contents of the Rue Lafitte house should be brought to London and made part of the public collection at Hertford House.

But this codicil was never found. Did he ever actually make the codicil? Was it stolen? There were dark stories of Lady Sackville and her teenaged daughter (Vita Sackville West—later to become famous for both her novels and her colourful love life) skulking around the Connaught Place house during a party, trying to break into Sir John's desk. The Sackville ladies insisted they had alibis.

In that, as with the other charges, Lady Sackville was more than a match for her accusers and their dashing lawyer. She knew Smith quite well socially but by the trial's end she had dismissed him as a cad. On the stand, she gaily parried all his toughest questions. The *New York Times* thought "she spoke with as much ease as if in a drawing room". Her description of Walter Scott, Sir John's equally corpulent brother, crawling around her drawing room on his knees proposing that she become his mistress, was just one of many highlights.

Lady Sackville's lawyer Sir Edward Carson made the telling point that Sir John's legacy was his personal fortune—it was not Scott money, it had been left to him by the Wallaces. His siblings had been well cared for and had all enjoyed "the magnificent establishment" he kept for them in Connaught Place. He took country houses for them, paid all their travel expenses and his will provided them with the not inconsiderable 'residue' of the estate. Sir John was fully within his rights to pass his fabulous wealth on to whoever he wished. There was nothing beyond the wretched sisters' hurt feelings over their perceived 'belittling' to back up this entire case. Lady Sackville had been made subject to a "vitriolic black-washing" at the hands of the Scotts over what were mere trivialities. The presiding judge admitted to the jury that had Sir John made this bequest to a male artist friend, no one would have raised an eyebrow.

The jury—after eight gruelling days—took just 12 minutes to clear Lady Sackville of all aspersions of "undue influence". The *Times* opined that few would begrudge Lady Sackville her victory. "Into the somewhat vapid life of an old man, with no one about him to light it up, came a brilliant and imperious woman." It was his wish to reward her for having made his last years more pleasurable. So, let it be done.

Following her legal triumph, Lady Sackville rather rapidly—many thought with unseemly haste—sold the entire Rue Lafitte lot at auction for more than £250,000. The pain of losing dear old Seery was soon eased by new—and even wealthier—male admirers. Men like WW Astor and JP Morgan were soon to be drawn, just like Sir John Scott before them, to the "brilliant and imperious" charms of Lady Sackville.

The loveless marriage of Edward James

By Tom Hughes

MJ7.4, Aug-Sep 2011

In an interview shortly before his death in 1984, Edward James (born 1907) insisted, "I've tried to conform as much as possible. One is an eccentric against one's own will." Few will have believed him.

A controversial figure in 20th century art and upper crust society, Edward was rich as Croesus and spent it profligately. His critics say he was a dupe, that his friends, especially his wife, had used him as a cash point. His defenders hail him as one of the great art patrons of his day.

Edward was born in 1907. His parents had their town home in Marylebone at 38 Bryanston Square. William Dodge James, his father, was an American with an immense fortune from railway, timber and copper investments. Edward's mother was a Scot, Evelyn Forbes.

They moved in elite Edwardian circles. In fact, Edward was named after his godfather, King Edward VII. The legend is, and Edward James certainly believed it to be true, that the king was, in truth, his natural grandfather, having been a neighbour at Balmoral. Regardless, Edward James was a most fortunate boy; he was the fifth child but the only son and he stood to inherit the entire James fortune.

William James died in 1912 when Edward was just five. The boy's relationship with his mother was never good. If the gossip is true, she was not a warm figure. Edward claimed that she once asked the nursemaid to bring her one of her children, adding "Please pick one in an outfit that won't clash with what I'm wearing."

Edward's first brush with sensation came when he was a 15-year-old Eton schoolboy. He was quite a handsome, effete teen. He accused a well-known MP of groping him, and the scandal led to the old fellow shooting himself in Mayfair. Edward then went on to Oxford where he established himself as an aesthete with exquisitely decorated rooms. He began to write poetry, rejecting his mother's strict orders that he cease and desist. Edward's poetry was middling at best but his patronage helped to publish the first works of John Betjeman, Edward's classmate and friend.

Edward came into his fortune when he reached the age of 21. He really had no need to ever work but he tried the Foreign Office. It didn't go well. From his post in Rome, he sent word back to Whitehall that the Italians were building 300 warships. The Admiralty became frantic until it was learned that the Italians had plans for no more than three. Edward was recalled and sacked.

Back in London once more, he purchased 35 Wimpole Street and soon transformed this mid-Georgian home into one of the most remarkable residences in the city. The Tent Room was particularly celebrated. Amid white marble columns, Edward would entertain in a faux tent of billowing draperies, satin swags and exotic plants.

35 Wimpole Street would quickly become a notorious address following the arrival of Edward's wife. Edward's mother had strictly warned him against socialising with actresses or dancers, so it's not surprising that he married one. He had become infatuated with Ottilie 'Tilly' Losch, a quite attractive Viennese dancer and ballerina who had graced the West End in several productions. While Wimpole Street was being kitted out, they travelled together to Europe, America and as far away as Hawaii. The marriage was a disaster from the outset.

Not that Edward didn't try to provide every material comfort for his new wife. In Wimpole Street, the designer Paul Nash created "one of the most spectacular bathrooms of the era" for Tilly's private suite. Nash used smoked glass and chrome with the fixtures shaded in a mauve colour to highlight Tilly's fabled "ice-blue eyes". A nickel-plated barre was installed for her dance exercises. The bath itself was reached by a carpeted spiral staircase, and woven in to the carpet were images of Tilly's wet footprints.

Tilly, of course, could not spend her whole life in the loo, however splendid. In 1933, Edward financed Les Ballets, a new company in London to be managed by 29-year-old George Balanchine. That year, collaborating with Bertolt Brecht and Kurt Weill, Balanchine created one of his masterpieces, *The Seven Deadly Sins*. Tilly was in the production company along with the legendary Lotte Lenya. After only one season, however, Les Ballets was shutdown. Edward and Tilly were soon headed for the divorce court.

The trial lasted eight days. Edward had accused Tilly of adultery with a Tsarist expatriate nobleman, Prince Serge Obolensky. He could have named any of several lovers, among them Winston Churchill's son Randolph. But Obolensky served to prove the point. Edward's detectives claimed to have traced Tilly to a midnight tryst with the prince on the observation platform at the top of New York's Empire State Building, while Edward and Tilly were on their honeymoon. Tilly counter-sued, accusing Edward of "cruelty", suggesting that he was not interested in her as a woman and preferred male dancers and Hawaiian poolboys. The countersuit failed and Edward got his divorce.

Edward sought refuge from the scandal on the continent. There, he became immersed in the growing surrealist art movement. He renewed an acquaintance with Salvador Dali and the artist and his wife Gala came back with Edward to live at 35 Wimpole Street. Dali was employed to design the furnishings for Monkton, Edward's "cottage" in Sussex, near the family's 6,000 acre country seat at West Dean. For Wimpole Street, Dali designed a famous red sofa in the shape of Mae West's lips. This sensuous seating, which was built around the corner by the furniture makers Green & Abbott on Wigmore Street, recently sold at auction for over £60,000. Wimpole Street also featured several of Dali's lobster telephones, with papier-mache lobster shells fixed to the receivers.

Edward James's influence on 20th century art was undeniable. For an exhibition at the V&A in 2007, curator Ghislaine Wood stated: "We owe him a huge debt. Not just for encouraging and funding Dali, but for creating a climate in which the avant-garde could flourish. And he helped contribute to the cult of artist as personality."

Without Edward James there might not have been a Dali. In 1936, Dali spoke in London at the first International Surrealist Exhibition. At the New Burlington Gallery, Dali came out wearing a diving helmet and lead boots. His theme for the occasion was "diving into the subconscious", but the artist had a panic attack and couldn't get the helmet off. Edward James leapt from the crowd (with a screwdriver) to save Dali from suffocating.

Beyond Dali, James employed the Belgian surrealist Rene Magritte to paint several pieces of art for his various homes. The most famous painting is entitled Not to be Reproduced, (La reproduction interdite) which shows, from the rear, the back of a man's head (the head of Edward James) as he gazes into a mirror that reflects only the back of his head again. The painting hung in the ballroom at 35 Wimpole Street.

When the war came, Edward opted to leave England, spending most of his last 40-plus years abroad. He settled first in Taos, New Mexico, where he established a little art colony attracting among others, DH and Frieda Lawrence. He dabbled in Hollywood, again being used as an "angel" to finance various projects. In 1949, he crossed the border and, in the remote mountains of eastern Mexico, built Las Pozas, a compound of concrete villas and follies. There he died, a germaphobe recluse who loved animals and flowers.

Though it was said that he had the "money to indulge every fancy", Las Pozas nearly bankrupted him and he began to sell his art to pay for it. After his death, the collection was completely dispersed. 35 Wimpole Street was sold. Tilly's remarkable bathroom was ripped out and lives on only in architectural coffee table books. Her footprint carpet had long since been removed. Edward instead had a new carpet designed, made with the padded feet of his favourite—and much more faithful—wolfhound.

1. Tyburn Manor, c.1700

2. The view across Marylebone from Wigmore Street, c.1750

MARYLEBONE LIVES

3. Marylebone Gardens, 1780

4. A Rake's Progress, plate 2. James Figg holds a pair of quarterstaffs

5. Cavendish Square, 1820

6. Mrs Portman's House, Portman Square, c.1800

7. Nash's Park Crescent, 1822

8. The capture of the Cato Street conspirators, 1820

9. The Marylebone Workhouse, 1900

10. Anthony Trollope (1815-1882)

11. Wilkie Collins (1824-1889)

12. Edgar Wallace (1875-1932)

13. Sarah Siddons (1755-1831)

14. Mary Seacole (1805-1881)

15. Emily Faithfull (1835-1895)

16. The Victoria Press, founded by Emily Faithfull in 1860

CRIMES & MISDEMEANOURS

The Marylebone of today is, by historic standards, pretty light on criminal activity. There's the occasional shop-lifting incident, and probably the odd spot of low level white collar crime, but compared to yesteryear it is a veritable bastion of law and order.

This chapter begins with a fully-fledged attempt at violent insurrection and ends with a plane plunging from the sky—and remains pretty perfidious throughout. It is a veritable rogues' gallery. But who doesn't love reading about rogues?

The revolution at Cato Street

By Jean-Paul Aubin-Parvu

MJ1.1, Spring 2005

In the early morning of 1 May 1820, Arthur Thistlewood, William Davidson, John Brunt, James Ings and Richard Tidd stood upon the scaffold at Newgate. These five men had been found guilty of high treason and were awaiting their brutal fate. Their gang had been ambushed at its base on Cato Street, Marylebone. Their plot to massacre members of the Cabinet and spark a revolution had failed. At 7:45am, the executioner's axe fell on one of the most dramatic events witnessed in Georgian London.

Britain in 1820 was a country in some turmoil. The French Revolution of 1789 had generated a highly turbulent political, economic and social climate across Europe and had locked Britain into a virtually unbroken 25 years of warfare against France, fought out across the globe. Ironically, the situation in Britain deteriorated after the final defeat of Napoleon in 1815. The economy had been geared to the needs of wartime. When the war ceased it went into recession. Soldiers, sailors and munitions workers lost their jobs. Widespread unemployment, high prices and a bad harvest led to riots, demonstrations and a swell in popular support for radical political groups who demanded land redistribution and universal suffrage.

Arthur Thistlewood, the illegitimate son of a prosperous Lincolnshire farmer, had been in France during the revolution and had been a disciple of Maximillian Robespierre, who led the Terror of 1793. In 1811 he moved to London, where he joined a group of agitators known as the Spenceans after their leader, Thomas Spence. After Spence's death in 1814, Thistlewood became the movement's most militant influence.

In 1816, a spy reported that the Spenceans planned to overthrow the government by sparking a riot at a mass meeting and then leading a mob to seize the Portman Street barracks, the Tower of London and the Bank of England. The meeting was held on 2 December at Spa Fields, Islington. Magistrates decided to disperse the crowd, and violence erupted. A police officer, Joseph Rhodes, was stabbed. Thistlewood and three others were arrested and charged with high treason, but were acquitted after a government spy was proved to be an unreliable witness.

After a missile was thrown at the Prince Regent's coach in January 1817, the prime minister, Lord Liverpool, introduced several repressive measures designed to stamp out radicals. Then, at a public meeting at St Peter's Fields, Manchester, on 16 August 1819, tragedy struck. Local magistrates sent in troops to arrest the speakers and disperse the crowd. Eleven people were killed and hundreds injured. The incident became known as the Peterloo Massacre.

Thistlewood believed the time had come for a violent and bloody revolution. At one meeting he allegedly stated: "High treason was committed against the people at Manchester. I resolve that the lives of the instigators of massacre should atone for the souls of murdered innocents." He began to recruit desperate and militant radicals. Meetings were held in various locations, including the Horse and Groom pub in Marylebone.

George Edwards was an important recruit. He used all his powers of persuasion to convince others to join the revolution, even bribing destitute radicals with food, beer and money. He became Thistlewood's most trusted comrade.

The conspirators built up an impressive arsenal of grenades, swords, muskets and ammunition, then waited for the opportunity to strike. Finally it came. On 22 February 1820, Edwards showed Thistlewood a notice in the New Times. It stated that several members of the Cabinet were to attend a dinner the following evening at Lord Harrowby's house at 39 Grosvenor Square. The guests would include Liverpool himself; the Duke of Wellington, Lord Melville, and the two most despised ministers, Lord Castlereagh and Lord Sidmouth.

Thistlewood immediately hatched his plan. His gang would arm themselves, forcibly gain entry to the house, restrain the servants, and assassinate the dinner guests. By displaying the heads of Castlereagh and Sidmouth, they would then, he believed, incite a popular uprising.

The following afternoon, while Edwards kept watch on 39 Grosvenor Square, the other conspirators travelled to their meeting place: a stable loft in Cato Street. Though numbering just 27, they were confident of success. Surrounded by their weapons, they drank heartily to their cause. They even designed a bill which would inform Londoners of the new regime. It read: "Your tyrants are destroyed. The friends of liberty are called upon to come forward. The provisional government is now sitting."

Their confidence was wildly misplaced. The revolutionaries had been ensnared in an elaborate trap. There was no dinner planned at Grosvenor Square. The trusted George Edwards was actually an agent provocateur. Though he had been active in recruiting for and planning the conspiracy, he was also a paid spy.

The authorities had feared that without an opportunity arising, the conspirators would disband and melt away into the London underworld, free to strike without warning in the future. A decision was made to plant the notice of a dinner at Lord Harrowby's in the paper. Edwards brought the notice to the attention of Thistlewood. He took the bait.

Richard Birnie, a magistrate at Bow Street, was put in charge of the operation. He placed police officer George Ruthven at the Horse & Groom, which overlooked Cato Street. Ruthven watched and reported the arrival of the conspirators throughout the afternoon.

In the evening, under the cover of darkness, the authorities closed in on Cato Street. Ruthven positioned himself at one end with 12 officers. A contingent of the Coldstream Guards waited nearby.

On a signal, the police rushed the stable and climbed into the loft. Bedlam ensued. Police officer Richard Smithers sprang at Thistlewood, who lunged with his sword. Smithers cried out: "Oh my God; I am done!" He then fell, mortally wounded. The lights went out. Pistols fired. Chaos reigned in the darkness. The *Morning Chronicle* wrote that the police commander, in a bid to save his own life, was forced to join in the conspirators shouts of "Aye, kill them!"

Thistlewood managed to charge down the ladder. Police officer William Westcott later told the court: "Thistlewood presented a pistol at my head; I put up my hand to save myself, and he fired. I afterwards found that balls had gone through my hat. I made a rush towards him, and received a blow on the head, and fell."

The Coldstream Guards now joined the fray. Most of the conspirators either surrendered immediately or were taken after a struggle. A few managed to escape. Thistlewood was captured at a hideout the following morning. After extensive questioning, 11 men were charged with being involved in the Cato Street Conspiracy.

In the weeks leading up to the trial, public interest became insatiable. Several thousand people attended macabre tours of the loft at Cato Street to see the blood of officer Smithers still visible on the floor. On 3 March 1820, the *Sunday Observer* remarked: "Among others attracted to the spot, we remarked several of the fair sex, who braved the inconvenience of the difficult ascent to the loft for the gratification of their curiosity."

Vast crowds lined the streets to watch the prisoners being transported to and from court. The courtroom was packed. Special areas were railed off for the exclusive use of ladies, and extravagant prices were charged for people to witness the trial from the galleries and benches. Sir Walter Scott was reported to have been present at the second day of the trial.

The five principal defendants, including Thistlewood, were tried first. Richard Tidd claimed the conspiracy was the work of George Edwards, and demanded that he be brought to court for cross examination. However, Edwards had not been seen since the day of the Cato Street ambush. The authorities denied all knowledge of him. After the fiasco of the Spa Fields trial, the government was reluctant to expose to the court its own hand in the conspiracy. Instead, two of the conspirators, Robert Adams and John Monument, were persuaded to give evidence in return for their freedom.

The jury found each of the five guilty of high treason. On 28 April 1820, Lord Chief Justice Abbott put on his black velvet cap and pronounced sentence. Each man would be hung by the neck until dead, then decapitated and his body quartered.

The remaining six defendants were allowed to change their pleas to guilty. Their death sentences were subsequently commuted to transportation for life. On his last night on earth, John Brunt, sitting alone in his cell at Newgate prison, wrote a poem:

Though in a cell I'm close confined,
No fears alarm the noble mind;
Though death itself appear in view,
Daunts not the soul sincerely true!
Let Sidmouth and his base colleagues,
Cajole us with their dark intrigues;
Still each Briton's last words shall be,
Oh! Give me death or liberty!

On the morning of 1 May 1820, the condemned five were drawn on carts through the streets to the gallows. *The Traveller* captured the tense atmosphere: "The executioner, who trembled much, was a long time tying up the prisoners; while this operation was going on a dead silence prevailed among the crowd, but the moment the drop fell, the general feeling was manifested by deep sighs and groans."

The men acted bravely to the last. John Hobhouse, who witnessed the executions, wrote in his diary: "The men died like heroes. Ings, perhaps, was too obstreperous in singing Death or Liberty, and Thistlewood said, 'Be quiet, Ings; we can die without all this noise'. Once the five were dead, the executioner decapitated each corpse, displaying each head to the crowd. The bodies were later buried in Newgate prison."

The farcical uprising in a Marylebone hay loft marked the end of the Spenceans as a meaningful force. The conspirators lacked widespread support, and once their leaders were executed the rest simply faded into obscurity. No revenge was exacted upon George Edwards. Supported financially by the government, he disappeared to South Africa where he ended his days.

Posthumously, the conspirators scored one small victory. Lord Castlereagh was badly shaken by news of his attempted assassination, and became deeply depressed at his loss of popularity. Two years later, in 1822, he cut his own throat. A great many rejoiced at the news of his death.

The Great London Diamond Robbery of 1871

By Tom Hughes

MJ5.5, Oct-Nov 2009

For a few months in 1871, 4 Upper Berkeley Street, Portman Square, was one of the most famous addresses in England. Today it has gone, but it will be remembered as the scene of The Great London Diamond Robbery, an audacious crime that fascinated the entire country.

In January 1871, a well-dressed young man bearing a letter of reference from a respected gentlewoman of Bath let a suite of rooms at number four for a sum of six guineas a week (a sizeable sum). The new tenant gave the name of Mark Tyrell, and was accompanied by his wife. Soon after his arrival, Tyrell took a hansom into Mayfair to the New Bond Street premises of the jewellers Dudley & Ryder. He explained to Mr Ryder that he had recently come in to a sizeable inheritance and he wished to purchase some appropriate diamond jewellery for his wife. A sparkling array of expensive jewellery was presented to this most desirable customer, but Tyrell asked that, since his wife was unable to come to Mayfair, might someone bring the gems to Marylebone for her inspection? Certainly, squire. It was so arranged.

That afternoon, James Parkes, left New Bond Street with a satchel containing almost £5,000 in diamonds, rings and bracelets. Arriving at 4 Upper Berkeley Street, Parkes was greeted by Mr Tyrell who apologised for the servant having been called away. Mrs Tyrell was there and the three of them sat down to examine the merchandise. Parkes had displayed several items on a table, leaving the remainder in the bag at his feet. The Tyrells murmured their approval. Mr Tyrell asked his wife if she might want to consult her sister, who was in another room.

When the young woman returned, it was not with her sister but with a chloroform-soaked rag that she held across the face of the hapless Parkes. The doughty jeweller struggled but Tyrell had quickly pinned him to the ground and bound his legs and arms. The thief warned: "Don't move or I'll murder you." Parkes, who later testified to having been "perfectly stupefied", was left on a sofa for two hours. When he recovered, he was able to loosen his bonds, break a window and summon police.

The Tyrells, of course, had done a runner with the stones, though they unaccountably forgot to grab the bag on the floor. Value of the stolen gems was put at £2,500. While police were investigating the crime scene, a befuddled servant girl arrived. She said her new mistress had given her a letter to deliver to Tulse Hill but there had been no such address.

The police were baffled. Messrs Dudley & Ryder were embarrassed. Another Mayfair jeweller reported that "Mr Tyrell" had come to their shop that same day and tried the ruse, but when their salesman arrived accompanied by a "strongly built man", Tyrell had said his wife was too ill to see the gems at that moment.

A break in the case came very quickly. Mrs Pitt, a nosy landlady in Leamington—having seen a report of the robbery in the *Standard*—did some poking around the room of a young couple, Michael and Martha Torpey. They had been staying there after the wife's confinement—she had given birth only four weeks previous. The infant having been left with a relative, the Torpeys announced they had business in London. They were only gone a day and when they returned, the lady noticed that Torpey had shaved his beard. He asked for a timetable for the continental boat-train. He was carrying very closely a small parcel. Taking her opportunity, Mrs Pitt searched their rooms and found a bottle of chloroform. She alerted the police but they moved very slowly. "Really, madam? London jewel thieves, hiding out in Leamington Spa?" By the time the police could be cajoled into action, Michael Torpey and his bag of swag had fled to Europe. The police were left with Martha Torpey and her infant child.

The newspapers described Mrs Torpey as "ladylike". She was in her late 20s, slender and attractive. She appeared to have been well-educated. Her husband, still at large, was an Irishman by birth and had been in business in Leeds until he began to wager on "the Turf, with varying success." The police were publicly berated for having let Torpey escape. The only gems recovered were the bauble or two that Mrs Torpey had given her cousin for her child-minding while mother was out a-thieving.

As shocking as this well-planned scheme was to the law-abiding public, the ensuing court proceeding was even more remarkable. On 27 February 1871, Martha Torpey was tried at the Old Bailey for robbery with violence. Thanks to an indulgent warder, Mrs Torpey carried her infant child with her into the dock. It was a settled principle of English law that a wife, when committing a wrong in the presence of her husband, was presumed to have been acting under his instruction. It was no matter that Mrs Torpey was proven to have forged the letters of recommendation, that she sent the servant away on that fool's errand, and, of course, that she'd clamped the chloroform rag across the gasping maw of poor Parkes.

Montagu Williams QC, defending the young woman, told the all-male jury that, in effect, she merely did as she was bid. The wily barrister banged on about the absent spouse who had left his pretty young wife to face the might of British law, only weeks after delivering his child. In his memoirs, Williams recalled: "The more eloquent I grew, the louder the prisoner sobbed and cried." Of course, baby wailed too. One can imagine it was a most affecting scene. It was enough to soften the heart of even a London juryman. They let her walk, finding that Mr Torpey had planned it all and his wife had acted under his "coercion and control." The prosecutor blamed his defeat on "a little woman and her baby".

The verdict came at a time when the conversation about "the rights of women" was becoming louder and harder to ignore. Feminists could hardly claim Martha Torpey as their hero. She had only escaped the clutches of the law because of the "false and mischievous theory of the mental, moral and physical inferiority of women". Millicent Fawcett, a leader in the young movement, declared "the first article of the stock in trade of the female thief must henceforth be a husband".

Martha Torpey and her bairn were permitted to leave the Old Bailey. *The Pall Mall Gazette* wished her well: "It only remains for us to wish the young couple many years of unalloyed happiness in some sphere well suited to their anaesthetic tastes." Meanwhile, the beleaguered police had reported sightings of Michael Torpey in Antwerp and Rotterdam, attempting to sell his booty. Descriptions of the stolen pieces had been circulated across Europe but none of it had yet turned up.

Mrs Torpey had left the court but the police had kept her under constant observation. On 13 April of that year, she was tailed by detectives to an address on the Marylebone Road. Inspector Shore knocked at the door and with that classic phlegm of the CID announced: "Good Morning, Mr Torpey." Trapped in his bolt hole, the fugitive jewel thief put up no resistance. He was still carrying the gems, though many of the stones had been wrenched from their settings.

Montagu Williams returned to defend Michael Torpey but this time without a gender-driven argument to play on. Torpey could only plead guilty, claiming he had been driven to it by his gambling debts. Newly wed and with a child, he had been desperate. References to his previous character (presumably not forged by loyal Martha) were presented to the court. Still, he was sentenced to eight years penal servitude.

The Torpeys fade into historical oblivion. 4 Upper Berkeley Street was let again, ironically to Elizabeth Garrett Anderson, one of the pioneer female doctors of London. She moved later a few doors away to 20 Upper Berkeley Street where there has since been placed a blue plaque to mark her residence in the neighbourhood. The Torpey case had forced parliament to consider reform to the criminal laws as they applied to a married woman. It was a curious question. The editor of the *Bolton Evening News*, almost surely a good Lancashire husband, could only wonder: "The question about what a man may compel his wife to do is, no doubt, an important one—to married men especially, but particularly to those who find it difficult to compel them to do anything, unless the doing of it suits their humour."

The public destruction of Dr Stephen Ward

By Jean-Paul Aubin-Parvu
MJ1.3, Autumn 2005

During the summer of 1963, the nation was gripped by a story of sordid orgies, politicians, aristocrats, spies, harlots and horsewhips. At a time when the establishment and its morals were being challenged and subverted, the Profumo Affair helped rip open Britain's net curtains to the swinging sixties. The episode would all but bring down Harold Macmillan's government. It would end the glittering political career of one man, and cause the tragic death of another.

The scandal centred upon Dr Stephen Ward, a fashionable osteopath who lived and worked in Marylebone. At his Devonshire Street practice Ward fingered the spines of such illustrious names as Winston Churchill, Douglas Fairbanks and Elizabeth Taylor. He was also a talented portrait artist with a host of royals and politicians among his sitters.

Ward was a notorious name dropper, social butterfly and avowed libertine who loved carousing with high ranking and influential members of the establishment. He also had a penchant for beautiful young women who might indulge him and his well-heeled friends.

One of these girls was Christine Keeler. Keeler was a showgirl at Murray's cabaret club in Soho, where she was employed, in her own words, "to walk around naked". She had a passion for the high life and found it easy to attract wealthy men prepared to lavish her with money, presents and excitement.

Ward met Keeler at Murray's. They began a tempestuous yet entirely platonic relationship, with Christine eventually moving into his small flat at 17 Wimpole Mews. He would introduce her and fellow showgirl Mandy Rice-Davies to his titled friends. Ward leased a cottage from his patient and friend, Lord Astor on his Cliveden estate.

On 8 July 1961, John Profumo, a guest of Lord Astor, chanced upon a naked Keeler swimming in the pool with Ward. Profumo, secretary of state for war and a rising star in Harold Macmillan's Conservative government, was smitten by Keeler and they became lovers. But she was also sleeping with Yevgeny Ivanov, a Soviet naval attaché. MI5, believing Ivanov to be a spy, had him under investigation. Profumo was discreetly warned off. He finished his affair with Keeler, leaving her a note that would later prove his undoing. This might have been the end of the matter if it wasn't for a sudden burst of gunfire in Marylebone.

On 14 December 1962, Johnny Edgecombe turned up at Ward's Wimpole Mews flat in search of Keeler. Although she was no longer living there, she happened to be visiting her friend Mandy Rice-Davies, who was herself now staying with Ward. Keeler had used Edgecombe for protection after being attacked by a former boyfriend, Aloysius 'Lucky' Gordon. Edgecombe had gone on the run from the police after slashing Gordon's face with a knife in a confrontation at a Soho club. Wishing to give himself up, he asked Keeler for help in finding a solicitor but she had refused. He arrived at the flat wild with rage and fired several shots at the front door when refused entry. He fled but was soon arrested and later imprisoned for seven years.

The shooting brought Ward and Keeler to the attention of the press. Keeler's story of sexual and political intrigue poured forth to interested parties. She made sensational claims that she had been sleeping with both Profumo and Ivanov, and that the Russian had asked her to find out information from the minister about nuclear missiles in West Germany.

This was political dynamite. The Cold War was at its height. In parliament there were accusations that national security had been breached, and the opposition called for the rumours about a certain minister to be either denied or investigated.

On 22 March 1963, John Profumo committed political suicide by lying to the House of Commons, denying any impropriety with Keeler and threatening to sue if further allegations were made. The government, desperate to deflect attention away from a possible security breach, needed a smoke screen. From the highest levels came the decision that Stephen Ward was to be thrown to the wolves. The police began a vice investigation out of all proportion to his alleged offences. Ward's patients, friends and Marylebone neighbours were all visited repeatedly by detectives. Rumours began to spread and Ward's business and reputation began to suffer.

A desperate Ward wrote to the home secretary, his local MP and the leader of the opposition, Harold Wilson: "Obviously my efforts to conceal the fact that Mr Profumo had not told the truth in parliament have made it look as if I myself had something to hide. It is quite clear now that they must wish the facts to be known, and I shall see that they are."

Ward sent copies of some of these letters to the newspapers. The press, knowing that Profumo had lied, now moved in for the kill. Their stories led to further questions in the House. This was the end for Profumo. On 5 June, he admitted that he had lied about his relationship with Keeler, resigned from office and was allowed to slip quietly away from the glare of public scrutiny.

Ward was not so fortunate. Three days later he was arrested in Watford and taken to Marylebone Lane police station. The charge read: "That he, being a man, did on divers dates between January 1961 and 8 June 1963, knowingly live wholly or in part on the earnings of prostitution at 17 Wimpole Mews, contrary to section 30 of the Sexual Offences Act 1956."

The case against Ward became a tabloid sensation. He was the supposed ringmaster in a depraved circus involving peers and prostitutes. There were rumours of orgies and whipping parties, drug taking, sadomasochism, electrical stimulation, two-way mirrors and homosexuality. It was said that at one party a small grocer had suffered a heart attack and died.

The most infamous tale concerned the 'man in the mask', alleged to be a high ranking cabinet minister, who served guests at a dinner party attended by Ward, naked, except for a mask and who ate his dinner from a dog bowl. In the era when Britain had never had it so good, clearly some were having it even better.

By the time his trial began at the Old Bailey on 22 July, Ward had been widely condemned as an amoral, sexual deviant. Ludovic Kennedy, a journalist covering the case, summed up the situation, noting: "Rumour abounded, and none knew where fact began and fiction ended."

Vast crowds queued overnight, desperate for a place in the public gallery. Cameramen and reporters filled the pavements, hoping to catch sight of a celebrity witness or brazen tart. This was to be a show trial like no other.

Ward pleaded not guilty to each of the five counts. The first three related to living off the earnings of prostitutes. The last two, of procuring girls, now seem ludicrous. They made it an offence for a person to be introduced by a friend to a girl over the age of consent but below the age of 21 if they later had sex.

The police had interviewed nearly 140 potential witnesses. Usually only a tiny fraction of that number would be seen in connection with similar offences. Yet the prosecution could only offer a few witnesses. These included Christine Keeler, the demur yet saucy Mandy Rice-Davies and Vickie Barrett, described by one journalist as "a 10 bob knock in the Bayswater Road".

They even had a 'Miss X', a young Austrian shop assistant at a Marylebone High Street store who was introduced to Ward by Keeler. She alleged that Ward had made indecent proposals about a two-way mirror installed at his Bryanston Mews flat, where he had moved with Keeler after the shooting drama.

Ward told Miss X he could charge people to gaze through this mirror and watch others having sex. When Miss X told him that she had no interest in voyeurism, Ward had apparently replied: "I don't want you to watch, I want you to perform."

Vickie Barrett stated that Ward brought her to Bryanston Mews to have sex with paying punters, who enjoyed being caned and horsewhipped. And Rice-Davies told the court she regularly had sex for money at Wimpole Mews with an Indian doctor.

The evidence was deeply flawed. Several witnesses stated that the police had pressurised them to give damning statements. They had interviewed Keeler 24 times. Three female witnesses admitted they had told lies. Though it was clear that Ward had associated with prostitutes there was no real evidence that he had lived off their earnings. The prosecution had failed to prove that Ward had lived beyond his substantial means as an osteopath and portrait artist. In fact it appeared that he lent more money to the girls than he ever got back.

However, a hostile and one-sided summing up from the judge swung the case for the prosecution. The following morning the jury returned a verdict of guilty on the first two counts of living off the earnings of Christine Keeler and Mandy Rice-Davies. He was found not guilty on the other charges.

Stephen Ward never heard the verdict. Immediately after the judge's summing up, he returned to his flat in Chelsea, deeply depressed, abandoned by those he believed were his friends and believing that the judge had destroyed all hope. That night he penned a letter to the *Daily Telegraph* reporter, R Barry O'Brien. He wrote: "After the summing up I feel the day is lost. The ritual sacrifice is demanded and I cannot face it." Ward took a massive overdose of sleeping pills. He lay in a coma for three days at St Stephen's Hospital, Chelsea, and never regained consciousness.

Stephen Ward had a complex nature. On 1 August 1963, the *Daily Telegraph* wrote of him: "Ward's two biggest weaknesses were young women and a singular inability to handle money. He could do without neither but he was reckless with both. He was vain, egotistical and irresponsible, but he was also witty, resourceful and a man of immense charm."

Yes, he was foolish, vain and socially ambitious. By the standards of the day, he was probably even immoral. But he was no criminal. He introduced his upper crust friends to girls for fun and for social kudos, but not for profit. The establishment had chosen him as a scapegoat. And Stephen Ward paid the ultimate price.

Jacob Henriques and the body in the barrel

By Tom Hughes
MJ6.1, Feb-Mar 2010

In 1880, London was a smelly place. The recently finished Embankment scheme of buried sewers along the Thames had eliminated the conditions that had infamously created the Great Stink of 1858, but still there were odours. Tens of thousands of quadrupeds made their daily mess in the streets, and the air was rank with the smoke of countless fires, all of which helped to make a living for the flower girls peddling their nose-gays. That unchallenged authority on Victorian home-making Mrs Beeton had promulgated strict instructions for the proper airing of a well-run house. Fresh, clean air was vital for all. "Make it a rule," she wrote, "to neither sleep nor eat in a house where the drains are not in perfect order."

Jacob Henriques, a merchant banker, lived at 139 Harley Street. He travelled frequently and the house was left to a caretaker couple. When the master was at home, the Henriques' household was well-staffed. The previous year, Spendlove, the new butler, had complained of a bad smell in the cellar. A plumber was summoned and he dug about the stygian gloom but reported nothing amiss. Then on the morning of 3 June 1880, Spendlove disturbed his master at breakfast, whingeing on again about the below stairs stench. Mr Henriques was understandably vexed. "Not now, Spendlove," he said, turning back to his kippers. But the butler was insistent. It wasn't the drains, he told his employer. The source of the smell had been discovered at last. A body had been found, stuffed in a cask, in the innermost cellar. This was a matter even beyond Mrs Beeton's formidable domestic management skills. Instead, a footman was sent footing off to find a policeman.

We've all seen enough television to know what should happen next. Behind ribbons of yellow tape, teams of grim-faced forensics experts in white body suits comb the cramped cellar for any vital clue. But in 1880, the first plods on the scene said to each other, "Ello, ello! What 'ave we 'ere?", overturned the barrel and pulled the body out.

The coroner, Dr Hardwicke, did not approve of that at all. At the inquest, held at The Buffalo's Head pub on the Marylebone Road, Hardwicke chastised the hapless "first responders" before hearing from the police surgeons. The body was that of a woman, no more than four foot 10, and more or less 40 years of age. She had been dead for at least two years. She was most likely a poor woman—what little clothing was found was of a coarse nature. Her teeth were unusual—they were short and blunt and may have been sawed down. She had most likely been stabbed. There were signs that the body had been buried in some fashion before being "roughly thrust" into the cask where it was found.

The corpse had been bent backwards so that her heels were found resting on the back of her head. Mr Henriques told the coroner that he had lived in the home for 20 years but rarely went to the cellars. After the staff had complained the previous year, he'd had the drains checked and no fault had been found. Henriques said the awful discovery had greatly shocked him. He did not know of any woman matching the description of the victim who had come into his home with his knowledge. He had, he said, gone through servants in the previous two or three years, but he had no suspicions about any of them.

Spendlove, the olfactorily sensitive butler, reported that he had been keen to get to the source of the stench as he slept below stairs. He'd sniffed his way into a small back cellar that was rarely used. Here he found a cistern, on top of which rested an old barrel that seemed to contain some empty bottles. Thinking the cistern might be the problem, Spendlove, together with Kirkland the footman, moved it away. While doing so, they happened to look into the barrel. And there it was.

Both servants were new and hadn't been in Harley Street at the time of the victim's demise, so the coroner adjourned the inquest and police went in search of former denizens of the Henriques cellar. It was not a short list—there had been four butlers at 139 Harley Street in the previous three years.

The man most quickly in the frame was Henry Smith. When the proceedings resumed, Smith was brought forward. In 1878, he'd been fired as Mr Henriques' butler for being drunk. Smith insisted that he did not have any idea who the dead woman might be. He knew the lay of the basement very well but swore that he had never seen the barrel before. He admitted that in his days, he would leave the gate leading to the area steps unlocked so that other servants and their callers could come and go after hours. It seems clear that drinking was not his only employment liability.

The police had reported that some of the basement floor was paved with bricks and there were signs a few had been removed and then re-placed. Smith admitted he had dug up an area of bricks to bury some stale bread, lest "the guv'nor" discover his wastefulness. Smith was excused, with his hiring prospects surely limited. Spendlove, the new man, said most of the bricks had been moved by the plumber. Mr Goodley, the said plumber, came down from Kentish Town for the proceedings. He said he had been in the cellars and found nothing wrong with the drains. The coroner asked Goodley if he had noticed the smell. The tradesman declared, with full professional pride, "I did not, but plumbers do not notice them so much as other people."

After hearing from the caretakers, two more ex-butlers, a succession of footmen, and the cook, the coroner left it to the jury. They could do no more than find it was a case of "wilful murder by person or persons unknown". Dr Hardwicke thanked them for their service and said that he'd been assured that the police were "not without hopes" that the perpetrator of this horrid act would soon be in custody.

June passed into July and 1880 went on without any break in what newspapers across England dubbed "the Harley Street mystery". It was shocking to think that in such a respected neighbourhood, while "the tide of happy human life flowed gaily and unconsciously on", the victim of such a depraved act lay undiscovered below for so long. A reward of £100 was offered, but to no avail.

The *Standard* asked the question: "Is the CID a failure?" The paper wondered whether the police were too restricted in their interrogation techniques as compared with the laissez-faire "Secret Police bureaus" on the continent. The Marylebone tragedy had come at a time of several highly publicised and unsolved London murders. Only a few months before, a woman was found dead in the coal cellar of a house in Euston Square. The London correspondent for an Australian paper found all this cause for some macabre humour. "The more area cellars one has the more likely it is that one has a dead body in it. [City dwellers don't have a back garden.] The present system of murdering a person and putting them in the area is of course very reprehensible; but so far as the latter part of the proceedings is concerned, there is nowhere else to put them."

The Harley Street case was never solved. Mr Henriques remained at 139 Harley Street until his death in 1898. At the century's end, the author of a book about London's un-solved crimes highlighted the case of the woman in the cask and concluded. "No solitary ray of light has ever been thrown upon this black mystery."

The lady thief of Portman Square

By Tom Hughes
MJ7.1, Feb-Mar 2011

The theft of a good linen or silk pocket handkerchief was to the villains of Victorian London what the lifted laptop is today. Oliver Twist, you may recall, was introduced to his life of crime after seeing the many glorious "wipes" arrayed in Fagin's lair. "Ah, you're a-staring at the pocket-handkerchiefs, eh, my dear? There are a good many of 'em, ain't there?" But the temptation to purloin these colourful accessories was not confined to the light-fingered filchers from the East End. When a nice old lady from Portman Square was prosecuted for hoisting a handful from a Baker Street shop, it prompted a sensation.

Mary Ramsbotham was 50 and the wife of one of London's foremost obstetricians, Dr Francis Ramsbotham. In 1855, the Ramsbotham family resided at 7 Portman Square. Portman Square was then surrounded with the elegant homes of the wealthy and noble. Number 7 was on the east side and was long ago lost to the office block that now faces the square. From its doorway, it was but a step or two north to reach the milliners, wine merchants, tea & coffee dealers, and booksellers of Baker Street.

In 1855, the premises of John Moule, a fashionable linen-draper, were at 54 Baker Street, on the southwest corner of Dorset Street. Mr Moule employed several shop assistants, among them a young man named Samuel Welch, who was at his post on 27 March 1855 when Mrs Ramsbotham entered the establishment. It appears that some days previously, the clerk had reason to suspect that Mrs Ramsbotham had walked off with some fabric for which she had not paid. Welch had mentioned it to his employer and was told to keep a keen eye on her.

Watkins Moule, the owner's son, waited upon Mrs Ramsbotham. She purchased six yards of a lining material at four-pence a yard and arranged for it to be sent to Portman Square. After closing the sale, young Moule placed a small box of cambric handkerchiefs before Mrs Ramsbotham for her inspection. She did not think they were of the best quality. Moule quickly said he had better handkerchiefs, and turned his back to her to look in the stock case. In that moment of distraction, Mrs

Ramsbotham deftly picked up four handkerchiefs and slipped them into her coat pocket. The watchful Welch had seen it all. When the woman left, Welch was sent off in hot pursuit.

When Mrs Ramsbotham emerged from a nearby stationer's, Welch was there to greet her. He said that Mr Moule had requested that she return to the shop, to which she replied, quite freely: "Oh, I have the handkerchiefs in my pocket." Back at Moule's, Mrs Ramsbotham admitted swiping the handkerchiefs. Her husband would surely pay for them and if Mr Moule might, this one time, overlook the matter, she would be deeply grateful. But the merchant was adamant—the police would be summoned. Mrs Ramsbotham was rumbled off in a cab with the peelers for Marylebone Police Court.

Mrs Ramsbotham was not the first of her ilk. In 1843, in *The Mysteries of London*, the author declared: "The fact is that many ladies will go into a shop, purchase a hundred guinea shawl, and secrete an 18 penny pair of gloves." In the better families, m'lady's thievery was explained as an "amiable weakness". Mr Moule was not going to take it any longer. He found an ally in the formidable Marylebone magistrate Robert Broughton. Hearing the facts, he refused bail, telling the courtroom that the law must "rule irrespective of station or stage in life". Mrs Ramsbotham throughout was described as "calm and collected" and said nothing as she was led to the cells until her next court appearance.

Three days later she was brought forward, now represented by the Old Bailey legend Serjeant Ballentine. Press coverage had drawn a crowd that spilled out into Marylebone High Street. Ballentine said Mrs Ramsbotham had no interest in stealing such trumpery items (worth 9s 6d.) When the clerk returned with the superior handkerchiefs for her inspection, she "absently" put the others in her pocket. Mr Moule had her address. A gentleman would have sent a clerk to Dr Ramsbotham and the matter would have been "mercifully" handled. Broughton would not relent and sent the case for trial, although he permitted Mrs Ramsbotham bail of £2,000.

The *Times* pounced upon the magistrate: how could any man in his senses not see that Mrs Ramsbotham was out of hers? "Hers is an instance of that not very uncommon monomania which leads persons otherwise estimable and well-conducted to pilfer articles of trifling value in obedience to the impulses of a diseased imagination. Everyone could probably name a dozen ladies who have been notorious for abstracting articles of trifling value from the shops where they habitually dealt."

Whatever one thought of the theory, it was hard to justify mercy when poor men and women were being sentenced daily for "abstracting articles of trifling value" from shops far less grand than Mr Moule's emporium. Why should the wife of a Marylebone physician receive any more consideration?

Mrs Ramsbotham's trial was held at the Guildhall. The prosecution insisted that Mr Moule took no pleasure in bringing charges but acted in the interest of his "brother tradesmen". Young Watkins Moule had a very unpleasant time of it at the hands of the wily Ballentine. Wasn't it true that the original handkerchiefs shown to Mrs Ramsbotham were not "French cambric" but an inferior fabric? Did the clerk not know that Mrs Ramsbotham would likely reject them? He could then offer to show her something better and turn his back to her intentionally—all the while she was unknowingly under the observation of his lynx-eyed colleague Welch. It was a carefully baited trap.

Ballentine asked the jurymen to believe that Mrs Ramsbotham had suffered quite enough. The charge had brought shame to her distinguished husband and her blameless children. What possible reason had she to steal such "stuff"? In fact, she acted without reason: "She had reached that point in a woman's life when an important constitutional change took place." Hers was a life of constant nervous excitement, hallucinations, and delusions. She had no intent to steal at all. Ballentine, the hero of many life-or-death criminal trials, went so far as to say he never felt more anxiety about any person he had ever defended.

The presiding judge instructed the jury to dismiss all talk of a trap. Mr Moule was not on trial. The only question was: did Mrs Ramsbotham mean to steal the handkerchiefs? After four hours, the jury reported back a hopeless deadlock—six to six with no hope for resolution. The jurors were dismissed with thanks. Mrs Ramsbotham was released and left court with her husband, to be greeted with a somewhat mixed reaction from a "great concourse of persons".

The case of Mrs Ramsbotham and the Baker Street linen-draper generated a lively debate. The "exceptional leniency" granted to her was contrasted with the average barrow-thief who had no highly paid counsel and would likely have been given hard labour. One of the radical newspapers thought the "lady thief" would have benefited from "the curative process of incarceration and the treadmill".

Menopausal kleptomania (brought on by "the change of life") became a frequently employed defence. The pioneer English alienist Sir John Bucknill was not among the convinced: "Kleptomania is never urged as a defence for the delinquencies of the poor; but when ladies of respectable connection are detected in habits of shoplifting, the theory of kleptomania has been found exceedingly convenient."

Mr Moule's vigilance was applauded by his peers. The *Times*, however, reported: "We know many ladies who dread to enter any shop at this moment on the account of the state of mind prevalent among shopkeepers once the Ramsbotham story got wind." Any such "dread" was, to be sure, short-lived.

The memoirs of a Marylebone judge

By Tom Hughes

MJ8.5, Oct-Nov 2012

I will readily agree that an evening spent reading through a thumping thick volume of reminiscences cobbled together by some long forgotten Victorian worthy is not everyone's cup of Bovril. For me, the real enjoyment of the thing comes from what past generations were pleased to call "a book". The Victorians were masters at it. No dust-jackets required—covers of full burgundy morocco, titles etched in gilt on the spine, marbled endpapers, frontispieces and pages bound in the mysterious octavo format. Deckled edges optional.

Let me recommend one such gilded volume, published in 1903, entitled *Grain or Chaff: Memoirs of a Police Magistrate*. The author was Alfred Chichele Plowden who, for more than a decade, presided at the Marylebone Police Court in Seymour Place. Dispensing a remarkably summary brand of justice, Plowden was, quite simply, the law in Marylebone.

As for the memoir, and this is rather too commonly the case with the genre, the reader must first soldier through the potted details of the author's childhood and education. Plowden, from a good Shropshire family, was born in India and sent home for a Dotheboys Hall type of schooling at the hands of a cane-wielding vicar. Then came Westminster, Oxford, the Bar and a desultory circuit career. In 1888, Plowden was named Police Magistrate for West London, sitting in Hammersmith. In 1893, at age 49, at his request, he came to Marylebone.

Some 650,000 Londoners were on Plowden's new patch. "Marylebone covers a very large district, and the work is considerable. I doubt if there is any court in London which exceeds it. I am sure there is no court which offers a greater variety of cases or of human character. All classes are to be found in Marylebone, from the highest to the lowest, the richest to the poorest. And it is wonderful how in one way or the other representative specimens find their way into the police court. And those who have been there never forget it."

The police court was on the west side of the upper end of Seymour Place, a step or two south of Marylebone Road. It wasn't the most salubrious neighbourhood, but then police courts are rarely found in tonier purlieus. "For some reason or other they are hidden away in back streets, as if the country were ashamed of them," Plowden observed. The Marylebone court was a stolid two storeys of brick and Portland stone built in 1875 to replace the outdated facility on the high street. Plowden thought the interior was depressingly prosaic. "Anything less like a Temple of Justice can hardly be imagined. With its sickly blue tiles running round the walls and its hideous wooden fittings a stranger entering for the first time might feel puzzled to say whether he was in a lavatory or a conventicle."

Plowden regularly harassed his superiors for improvements—in 1903, the court remained bare of carpets, without electric lights or a telephone. A photograph of the courtroom shows Plowden sitting beneath "an alarmingly top heavy canopy, flanked by glazed bookcases full of weighty volumes". In a room lit by "lurid gas jets", Plowden heard 22,000 cases a year. He wrote that "it was like playing Hamlet in a barn".

Plowden could not understand why police magistrates received so little respect. The great Law Lords luxuriated in their magnificent Royal Courts and the assize judges travelled through the shires in splendid carriages and ate great dinners. But few Englishmen would ever appear before them. "A police court is the tribunal of all others which is most in touch with the people."

Yet it got the least attention. Plowden goes on for pages whingeing about not being allowed to wear a wig and red robe. Befuddled prisoners would gawp about looking for the "judge" and Plowden would rap the gavel, roaring, "I'm over here in the frock coat." The indignity of it all.

The settings of the place and trappings of the position notwithstanding, and in receipt of a salary of £1,500, Plowden enjoyed his work in Marylebone. "There is a perpetual conflict going on in the streets between the police and that portion of the public who are disposed to infringe the law in one direction or another, if they can do so without detection." Daily, he heard the cases of alleged burglars, bullies, furious drivers, anti-vaccinationists, food adulterers, deadbeat fathers and more. Off his own bat, he could levy fines and impose sentences of up to six months.

"It is one of the consolations of a police court that you never know what is going to happen," he writes. One day, a Marylebone woman complained she was being harassed by local street urchins. Plowden asked her why she thought that was happening. "Her reply was unexpected: 'I suppose it is because I have no husband.'" His advice, offered "cheeringly", was that she should "go and get one".

Plowden earned a reputation for flippant comments and his mailbag was frequently filled with critical notes. But in this case, Plowden got a letter from a Scottish address. The gentleman correspondent was willing to marry this poor harassed woman. Plowden made reference to the letter the following day and promptly got more mail from female suitors willing to gather their skirts and head north if the offer still stood.

Of course, domestic relations were a fruitful source of police court business. Plowden's laissez-faire approach to spousal abuse will jar with the modern reader. He was, in his way, understanding of the living conditions of the poorest Londoners. In cramped lodgings, even something as innocuous as whether to open or close the window could lead to a Punch and Judy affray. By the time the case was called the next morning, the brawlers would have repented and left arm in arm.

And then there was drink. A minimum 25 per cent of the cases before Plowden involved booze. "It is no exaggeration to say that you might close half the police courts if you could get rid of drunkenness. There is not a day of the week when I am not confronted with a more or less formidable list of drunks. On Monday mornings, the list swells to a procession," he writes.

There was a weariness to it all, but years of experience had taught him that "one drunken Englishman is very like another, and much practice in dealing with them tends to make perfect".

We can close, then, with a few more of Plowden's maxims:

"All that is best in the English character seems to find expression in a police constable—the sense of duty, a becoming modesty and respect for the truth. He is a typical Englishman."

"The hands of a liar are seldom at rest."

"I make a mental note if a prisoner has abnormal ears. They are often significant."

"The Irishman nearly always has something to say—generally a good deal and not infrequently spiced with humour. They almost make me feel I am wrong to punish them—they are so gay under adversity."

The last drunks were admonished in Seymour Place in 1961. The magistrates now have grand new digs on the Marylebone Road. The old Court House still stands, however, broken up into flats.

Plowden left Marylebone for the Police Court in Great Marlborough Street in 1910 and died just before the First World War. In Grain or Chaff, he proposed the epitaph for his tomb, from the book of Micah: "For what doth the Lord require of me? To do justice and to love mercy. Therein lies all my ambition."

Viscount Galway and the gambling den

By Tom Hughes
MJ10.3, Jun-Jul 2014

"Stately" is a word often associated with Marylebone's Portland Place. A late 18th century residential development by the Adam brothers, Portland Place was a wide boulevard lined with private palaces. So successful was the Adams' scheme that the great Regency architect John Nash simply included Portland Place in his planned "via triumphalis" leading from Piccadilly Circus to Regent's Park. Two centuries later, some of the original Georgian architecture has been replaced by more modern buildings, but several attractive original terraces remain. On the east side, between New Cavendish Street and Weymouth Street, is perhaps the most striking example. Pause before 46-48 Portland Place, built in 1774 and now Grade II listed. It is conspicuous by its unusual white stucco front, sparkling amid all that surrounding brick. The facing is "decorated with reliefs of urns, gryphons and paterae, with a similarly enriched frieze". A well-pleased observer has written: "The external plaster panels hint at the delights of the delicate decor within."

On a winter's night in 1922, another observer, who likely didn't know a frieze from a fresco, stood on the pavement opposite number 48. Hidden in the elm trees were Police Superintendant James Mackay and a handful of his burliest young plods. They stood stamping their boots in the cold wee hours of 17 January.

A steady procession of limousines and taxis had been disgorging young people in evening dress. A butler opened the large double oaken doors at number 48 to each arrival. From within, briefly, the tuneful sounds of a jazz combo could be heard. It was 1:20am when, at Mackay's silent signal, the raid was on. To the front went a pair of lads with axes. The Great West End Gaming Raid had begun. The newspapers rang with news of a scandal made all the more shocking by the fact that 48 Portland Place was the home of the Viscount Galway, an Irish peer and aide-de-camp to King George V.

The loud thump of the Old Bill's knock failed to produce the butler as quickly as he had responded to the previous guests. When the door finally creaked open, the servant in his most butlerish manner, attempted to determine the reason for this late night call. He was brushed aside. The officers scampered up the balustraded staircase of Carrara marble. The distant band now seemed to be playing with greatly renewed vigour and interest. The breathless policemen burst in upon a few couples pirouetting around the room doing the foxtrot. The others in attendance, all of them "bright young things", were arrayed in various languid poses smoking their "precocious cigarettes".

It was a studied picture of nonchalance and innocence. A gentleman who appeared to have some supervisory role in the proceedings demanded an explanation for this unwarranted intrusion into Lord Galway's home. He told the inspector that Mrs Brisley, "a well-known society figure", had rented number 48, which had been vacant. Lord Galway was in the country, while his soon to be married son had decamped to spend his last bachelor winter golfing on the Riviera. Mrs Brisley was unwell and had retired for the evening. "Now, would you please leave?"

The inspector was not to be put off. His men poked around the various rooms finding "nuffink" more suspicious than the remnants of a refreshment trolley. But a keen eyed constable noted a large Chinese screen rather suspiciously unfolded to block one corner. Just visible was the top of a door frame. The "dancing master" was asked: "Where does that door lead?" That was Lord Galway's private conservatory and his lordship had not deigned to leave a key. For such a purpose it had been thought that axes might be required. With a "splintering crash" the fine mahogany door was breached. The room was found to contain "paraphernalia of the most elaborate and modern gaming establishment." There were rakes, card shoes and other accessories to various games of chance. From the conservatory, another door was broken down revealing a secret stone flagged stairway. The lawmen hastened down into the darkness, their torches illuminating a staircase littered with cards and gambling chips. Ten men and three women were found in hiding. A cold breeze led the policemen on to a doorway opening into Hallam Mews. The smell of exhaust indicated that some of the punters had only just sped away. A touching detail in one of the news accounts was the discovery of an abandoned silver satin slipper whose wearer had hobbled her way to a waiting motor.

The majordomo gave his name as David Falcke and described himself as an estate agent. He gallantly urged the inspector to let all the others go; he would take full responsibility for the situation. The "palpitating flappers and their young squires" were allowed to leave amidst "a gust of giggles". The minstrels—no doubt shocked that there was gambling going on elsewhere in the building—quietly packed their kit and left. Falcke, the butler, a hapless waiter and Mrs Margaret Beryl Brisley, roused from her sick-bed, were taken to Great Marlborough Street nick.

A week later, the four were officially arraigned on charges of running a common gaming house. Falcke was no estate agent, the prosecutor declared, but rather one of the most inveterate gamesters in London. Mrs Brisley, who had posed as a society woman to rent the property, had no claim to any such standing.

A week in the cells had not suited her; the prosecutor informed the magistrate that "she is a physical wreck for what reason we are not here to inquire". The wretched woman had rented the place from Lord Galway's agent for six months, for the inclusive rental of £614 payable monthly in advance. Brisley and Falcke were living at number 48. No Mr Brisley seems to have been upon the scene.

Inspector Mackay told the court that the attention of the police had been called to the home by complaints from neighbours about the late hours and noise. Further, a peer had reported that his "chubby cheeked" young heir had lost rather a lot at the tables at number 48. He had been invited to a dance at the home of Lord Galway, expecting it to be a respectable proceeding. Once there, however, the young noodle was prevailed upon to play baccarat with predictable and lamentable results.

Magistrate Denman had heard more than enough. Young people were being lured to 48 Portland Place "under the pretence that it was open for bona fide dancing in a respectable house". Instead, the music was a mere blind for a "pestilential" gaming establishment. Not on his patch. The butler and valet were jailed for a month, Mrs Brisley for two. Falcke was given six months but he deftly skipped on his surety of £500 that been put up by a 'Lady X' who had met the gamester at one of his dance evenings. The fellow sent a charming apology from Paris, which was quite decent of him.

The public were alerted that "the most historic homes in London, including stately old mansions of the nobility, with secret passages and underground chambers dating back to the romantic era are today being used as secret gambling clubs by British society". Lord Galway did get his home back, the question of repairing the various splintered doors being left to settle between his Lordship and Scotland Yard. Portland Place returned to its quiet stateliness.

The US ambassador's deception

By Tom Hughes
MJ9.6, Dec-Jan 2013-14)

South of the river, at Nine Elms in Battersea, £600 million (or a billion dollars) give or take a ha'penny or two, is currently being spent on the construction of a new American Embassy. When it opens in 2017, the 'Glass Cube' will boast the utmost in modern security, quaintly enhanced by a medieval moat. The new building will replace the Cold War era concrete fortress that glowered for half a century across Grosvenor Square.

It is always pleasant to reflect on the fact that there was a happier time in world affairs when the American presence in the old mother country required no such embattlements. The American ministry could be located in whatever suitably posh house the envoy could afford to rent.

Thus it was in June 1871 in Marylebone when Major General Robert Schenck arrived as the new Envoy Extraordinary and Minister Plenipotentiary to the Court of St James. The stars and stripes soon flew proudly above the American legation in Lady Strangford's home at 58 Great Cumberland Place, on the east side of the street, just below Bryanston Square.

General Grant, Mr Lincoln's conqueror of the South in the recently concluded Civil War, had found this plum diplomatic post for his old colleague at arms. At 62, General Schenck was a widower but he was accompanied by the three "Misses Schenck" (sadly, their surname was diseuphoniously pronounced Skenk).

His first 'at home' in Great Cumberland Place was well-attended and Miss Julia Schenck was much admired by all. The general was exceedingly ambitious socially and quickly became a popular figure in his adopted city. An excellent poker player, it was said that he introduced the game to English society.

With the war over and reconstruction achieved, the Americans had turned back to the old Yankee drive for a dollar. The railroads were snaking west. New states were being carved. New mines were being dug to exploit the great mineral riches of the inner continent. Investors were needed and American company promoters had flooded London seeking financial angels. There was a lot of money flying around town and Schenck was not a man to miss such an opportunity. The biographer William McFeeley wrote: "There has never been a man more unabashed in his ability to exploit familiarity with government circles in his quest for a private dollar." Not to put too fine a point on it.

One of the most talked about ventures in 1871 was the Emma Silver Mine in Little Cottonwood Canyon, Utah. On 9 November, a gaudy prospectus was issued in the City—25,000 shares of stock were being offered at £20 each, with a promised annual dividend of 18 per cent.

The letterhead, as usual, listed among the company directors a few MPs, an available minor lord and a handy 'honourable' or two. What really caught the eye, however, was that one of the directors was none other than Major-General Robert C Schenck, United States minister, London. And if the American ambassador wanted in on this opportunity, say no more—this was a go-er. The share sales took off accordingly.

Even with the transatlantic cable, there was a time lag between London and the United States. When news of Schenck's role in this mine deal reached the American newspapers, there was a sensation. The Grant years were not a high water mark for probity and honesty in public service. The State Department cabled General Schenck, who was forced to sever all connection with the Emma Mine Company. Interestingly, while the order from Washington had arrived before Christmas, the announcement that Schenck was stepping down was not made until 12th January 1872, allowing favoured insiders time to sell. When the news did break, however tardily, investors were assured that the action was being taken solely to comply with diplomatic niceties. Shares wobbled but most investors opted to hang in.

This was to their ultimate regret, as by December 1872 the Emma Mine Company ceased to exist. Fact-finders returned glum-faced and sun-burnt and bearing the horrible news that there was no silver ore left in the ground. The mine that had been "so flamingly advertized" was, in reality, a worked out, abandoned dig. It didn't help soothe feelings to learn that the eponymous Emma had been a prostitute shared by the two prospectors who dug the original pit. The investors, almost all of them English, had lost every farthing. *The Nation*, an American weekly, suggested that the promoters knew very well that home grown investors could not have been suckered in and thus they took their worthless shares to London: "The mine must be sold where money is plentiful and the nature of canyons unfamiliar."

Of course, mining shares are notoriously volatile and more go bust than ever return on their investment. Caveat emptor. The Emma Mine folly might have been added to that sorry list but for the tireless efforts of a solicitor from Wandsworth. ST Pafford was the disgruntled owner of a single share of the Emma stock. For the next three years, he besieged General Schenck (and the newspapers) with letters. He accused the promoters of having given the general, outright, 5,000 shares of mine stock, simply for the use of his name to hype the sale of shares.

Pafford would not let it go: "Sir, there are ugly rumours about as to what induced the American minister to lend his name to the concern. I will not repeat them; but this I can unhesitatingly affirm that among all classes of Americans now in London, at the Langham Hotel and elsewhere, General Schenck's connection with this notorious mine is spoken of in terms of regret, and is looked upon almost as a national reproach and calamity."

Enduring Pafford's attacks in silence for some time, the general, at last, invited his persistent foe to a meeting one Sunday morning in Great Cumberland Place. The meeting was polite but Schenck stuck to his story that he had paid for the shares himself. Still, the "malignant and calumnious" attacks persisted. Angry investors began to loiter outside the legation with writs.

The situation had become embarrassing. In February 1876, the general quietly handed in his resignation to the Court of St James. He and the Misses Schenck slipped away from 58 Great Cumberland Place in a curtained cab for Euston Station, then a train to Liverpool and a Cunard liner, her steam up. Schenck may have been the only American ambassador to leave London while being pursued by bailiffs. (We cannot be entirely sure of that.) In parliament, questions were asked whether Schenck, who no longer had the cloak of diplomatic immunity, had been permitted to escape from Great Britain to avoid arrest.

In America, the general was greeted by headlines declaring that he had been "turned out" of his embassy owing to his connection with the Emma mine. Inevitable congressional hearings followed and Schenck, with no proof he had taken gifts, was acquitted of bribe-taking. He was censured for his ill-advised connection with the Emma Mine, an association "improper and incompatible" with his position. He was allowed to retire to his farm in Iowa where he wrote books about poker. He died in 1890.

Lady Strangford got her house back in Great Cumberland Place and no lasting stain of scandal seems to have attached to it. Schenck's successor opted to live elsewhere, letting a house in Stratton Street, off Piccadilly. Mr Pierrepoint's legation events were most delightful and the new man worked hard "to stem the flood of disgrace which that rascal Schenck has brought on the American name".

The suspicious death of Dr Gordon Ley

By Tom Hughes

MJ10.4, Oct-Nov 2014

Our fascination—and we might as well admit, our trepidation—with aeroplanes traversing wide expanses of water has, sadly, only been heightened by recent events. It may be helpful to recall that back in 1922, it was thought rather daring just to fly across the Channel. That year, on a sunny Saturday 3 June, a small French-built plane that had just left Croydon for Le Bourget near Paris suddenly seemed to nosedive into the sea, not two miles off Folkestone. The pilot and two passengers were killed. Among them was Dr Gordon Ley FRCS, LRCP, a renowned gynaecologist of 5 Wimpole Street. Was it an accident? Or was Dr Ley the dope-fiend, gun-mad stalker that some held responsible for "the first love tragedy in the sky?"

Dr Ley was only 36 and an extremely handsome fellow. He was a married man—his wife may have been an actress. In addition to his surgery in Wimpole Street, he had a grand flat in the Cumberland Mansions at Bryanston Square. Owing to a bad heart, he spent the war on the staff of Lady Howard de Walden's maternity hospital for officer's wives. Post-war, he had won plaudits for his research into various female maladies, including the dreaded eclampsia (which, you'll remember, carried off Lady Sybil in Downton Abbey). That said, Ley's friends described him as "peculiar".

The doctor had arrived at the Croydon aerodrome for the late morning flight to Le Bourget. The SPAD 27 bi-plane had room for two passengers in the open topped fuselage: Ley sat behind the pilot and a Parisian businessman, M Carroll filled the rear seat. Leon Morin, the young French pilot, had won the Croix de Guerre in the war.

The weather was ideal. Aeroplanes overhead in peacetime were still novel enough that many people reported seeing the plane as it left the Kent coast, heading towards Boulogne. Moments later, almost directly off the Victoria Pier, the plane simply nosedived and plunged from some 2,000 feet into the Channel. There was no sound of explosion. There was no visible fire. There was a tremendous splash.

The disaster was witnessed by weekend holiday-makers on the shingle and by hundreds more aboard a passing cross-Channel steamer, the Maid of Orleans, which quickly put one of its lifeboats in the water. By the time rescuers could reach the scene, only a few floating splinters remained. Two bodies were found "quite beyond human aid". The one wearing an airman's kit was obviously the pilot. His head had a terrible wound. The other victim, in civilian clothes, was Dr Ley, who was identified by another physician aboard the Maid who had served with him during the war. Carroll's body was never found.

There was an inquest three days later in Folkestone. Regular air service between the two great capital cities was in its infancy and competition between the British and French companies was fierce. It was suggested that many English travellers were hesitant to even board a French plane. The SPAD had been seen to circle Folkestone once, whether for sight-seeing or owing to some possible mechanical issue, before heading out over the waters.

The French manufacturers vowed to raise the wreckage (they never found it) but they believed it was not a mechanical problem—Morin was a capable pilot and he could have been expected to recover from any issue. At the least, he could have landed the plane safely. There were some questions raised about the pilot's injuries. One witness said his head was nearly decapitated. The coroner chose not to press that matter and accepted that the pilot had suffered some sudden illness, perhaps sunstroke, and collapsed on to the controls, sending the machine hurtling into the Channel. The pilot and Dr Ley had died from their "injuries accidentally received".

The rather perfunctory English verdict, and the muted aspersions on the French aircraft and the capabilities of the pilot, were not generally accepted across La Manche. The bolder Parisian newspapers began to make some rather serious allegations about "le docteur Anglais". Dr Ley, it was alleged, was addicted to narcotics. Also, Scotland Yard had permitted Dr Ley to carry a firearm. The French papers described him as "un dangereux maniaque du revolver". A British pilot reported that some weeks before the crash, he had flown Ley to Normandy.

At one point during the journey, Ley had produced a pistol and begun merrily firing shots in the air. The captain, rather sensibly, ordered him to stop. The journey ended uneventfully, but Captain Bernard made a note not to let the doctor back aboard his machine.

The French press, and the American papers joined in as well, reported that Dr Ley was obsessed with a Gaiety Girl actress named Eileen Reed. The willowy, blue-eyed beauty seems to have taken it all in a rather blasé manner: "There are so many men who look upon women of the stage as fair game." She had been recently (and scandalously) divorced from her first husband, Major Galloway, and was now living in Deauville with a gentleman named Harry Borradaile. Dr Ley had been storming about that posh French watering place vowing to shoot the both of them, and wrote to Borradaile threatening to shoot him on sight. Borradaile, a chap in his early fifties, who wore a monocle, answered the threat with sangfroid: "I sent him my Paris address and told him he could find me there at any time."

Thus, a theory was put forward that, on 3 June, Dr Ley had boarded the SPAD bound for Paris and his meeting with his rival, Harry Borradaile. During the flight, in some mad, likely drug-induced passion, the doctor began firing his revolver again and, accidentally, fatally wounded the pilot.

The more over-heated reports suggested that Dr Ley despised the French. But it would be most unwise, indeed fatal, to show that anti-Gallic spirit by murdering your pilot at 2000 feet. Nevertheless, the French papers were now satisfied that, even in Britain, the hypothesis that the pilot was assassinated by Dr Ley was "generally accepted". There is a small memorial in Paris to the pilot which insists that poor Morin was murdered by a demented passenger.

When Dr Ley's affairs were closed in Marylebone, it was revealed that despite his thriving practice and reputation, he was insolvent, and was overdrawn at the bank by more than £6000. He had been living far beyond his means. It should be said that Dr Ley was never formally accused of a crime. His medical reputation remains high: "He had concentrated into his short career a volume of work such as men, many years his senior, might well feel content to have achieved." The Royal College of Surgeons' biography of Ley states that he died while "travelling on professional business to Paris in a French aeroplane".

The unexplainable circumstances of the 3 June flight had proved unsettling for the fledgling passenger business. The investigation was followed with great interest. "The British seeking to make commercial capital out of the affair by insinuating that the French machines are not as good as the British, and the French insisting that Morin met a terrible end at the hands of Ley."

The British Air Ministry soon issued a notice that no one shall be allowed to sit beside the pilot. A similar order was issued in France. Still, the former Prime Minister, Mr Herbert Asquith, was not reassured. The tragedy had convinced old Squiffy: "That I shall continue to cross the channel neither under the sea nor in the air. But that is a personal idiosyncrasy."

SCIENCE & MEDICINE

Like Fleet Street and Savile Row, Harley Street has become more than just a street name. All three places are imbued with so much tradition and history that, to most British people, they've become synonyms for the trades that first defined them: Fleet Street still means the press, long after the newspapers upped sticks, and Savile Row means traditional tailoring, while Harley Street's status as a shorthand term for high quality private medicine is as valid now as it has ever been.

Harley Street, Wimpole Street and the cross streets that run between them have since the 19th century been home to the very finest medical and dental practitioners. But the Marylebone Journal, with a few notable exceptions, has generally chosen to overlook the pioneers, the brilliant minds, the life-saving virtuosos. Instead it prefers to colour its pages with the charlatans, the renegades and the loud-mouths.

A brief history of Harley Street

By Mark Riddaway
Harley Street brochure, Feb 2014

Harley Street began, as the name suggests, with a man called Harley—Edward Harley. Edward's father, Robert, was a politician who rose to be Chancellor of the Exchequer before surviving an assassination attempt in Whitehall at the hands of a knife-wielding Frenchman and being named Earl of Oxford and Mortimer by a grateful Queen Anne. When he died in 1724, Edward inherited the earldom.

Edward Harley was a man of considerable means, having in 1713 married Henrietta Cavendish Holles, daughter of the late Duke of Newcastle and heiress to an estate that included the quiet backwater of Marylebone. Marylebone was then a small village on the banks of the river Tyburn.

Edward and Henrietta Harley decided to invest their considerable fortune in turning this estate, which was then mostly fields, into a grand suburban district that would attract the great and the good. They commissioned John Prince to design a grid of attractive residential streets, anchored to the south by Cavendish Square. Development began in 1719, but was delayed by the economic shambles of the South Sea Bubble. By the time Edward died in 1741, work on the street that would bear his name had made very little progress. It slowly took shape over the following century. The estate meanwhile passed through Edward's daughter to the Portland family, into which she had married, and then later, again by marriage, to the Howard de Walden family, in whose ownership it remains.

While beautifully proportioned, Harley Street was by no means the grandest element of the new estate—Portland Place and New Cavendish Street, for example, boasted vast, spectacular buildings designed by the likes of the Adam brothers and John Nash, while Harley Street consisted of more modest townhouses. Its first residents were a blend of different professionals—scientists, politicians, military officers, artists. JMW Turner lived at number 64, the future Duke of Wellington at number 11, the geologist Charles Lyell at number 73.

Medical men began arriving in the mid-19th century. By the 1860s there were a dozen or so doctors. By 1873 there were 36. After that, the numbers increased rapidly. There was no single trigger for this growth — London's population was growing, and so was the science of medicine, so there were more and more doctors, but why they should choose to coalesce on Harley Street is hard to define. Marylebone certainly had an expanding and prosperous constituency of potential patients, and the building stock was ideal — attractive but not unaffordable, with ample space for a consulting room on the ground floor and a spacious family home upstairs.

As more doctors arrived, among them a number of highly regarded specialists, others saw the benefit of reflected glory and followed swiftly in their wake. Early medical residents included the anaesthetist Joseph Clover, the surgeon and syphilis specialist Sir Jonathan Hutchinson and the urologist Sir Henry Thompson, who rummaged in the bladders of Charles Dickens, William Makepeace Thackeray and even Emperor Napoleon III. The Harley Street laryngologist Sir Morell Mackenzie became infamous after misdiagnosing the German crown prince's terminal cancer as syphilis in 1887, much to Kaiser Wilhelm II's disgust — an incident which, though damaging in the short term, merely increased the area's fame.

Perhaps the most brilliant of the area's early doctors was Joseph Lister, whose pioneering work on combating wound infection made major surgical procedures a genuinely viable option for the first time. He spent 34 years living at 12 Park Crescent and his statue can be seen on Portland Place.

Others of note included Sir Frederick Treves, who treated the Elephant Man and whipped out Edward VII's appendix, Sir Victor Horsley, the first man to successfully remove a brain tumour, and Sir William Arbuthnot Lane, who revolutionised bone surgery.

In the early years of the 20th century, the area's profile began to change. As Marylebone became more urbanised and transport links more efficient, doctors chose to live in the leafier parts of town, such as Hampstead, and travel to their jobs each day, rather than setting up home above the surgery. This led to the development of multiple tenancies, with entire buildings being converted into consulting rooms, each of which was let to a different clinician. This meant an explosion in the number of doctors—there were around 200 doctors in 1914 and 1,500 by 1948.

More than 150 years after those first clinicians arrived in their frock coats, spats and top hats, much has changed in the Harley Street Medical Area. No longer confined to a small medical elite, it is now populated by thousands of clinicians, covering just about every specialism. A few of the Georgian buildings were damaged in the war and replaced by more modern clinics; those that remain are now packed with cutting edge equipment. The area's reputation remains intact though—a centre of medical excellence right in the heart of central London, with a history and standing that would have made Edward Harley a very proud man indeed.

Dr Allinson's big mouth

By Tom Hughes
MJ5.3, Jun-Jul 2009

On a warm, sunny late summer Saturday—12th September 1891—Dr Thomas Richard Allinson wearily trudged the last few paces to his home and surgery at 4 Spanish Place, Manchester Square. It was not for nothing that he was "freely perspiring", for on that day he had walked the 25 miles from Welwyn down the Great North Road to Marylebone. In fact, he had toddled off from the Edinburgh GPO on the 29 of August. It had taken him just a fortnight to walk all 426 miles to London. His goal was to prove what a persevering Englishman could accomplish "without beef or beer". It was the kind of one-off publicity stunt that made Allinson infamous within the stethoscope set.

Allinson was then 33. He had been born in Grange-over-Sands in Lancashire and educated in Edinburgh, where in 1879 he earned his LRCP (Licentiate of the Royal College of Physicians). He came to London, where in 1884 he opened his surgery in Spanish Place.

While doctors had long been thick on the ground in Marylebone, Allinson was alone in Spanish Place. However, it was more than urban geography that would separate him from the great medical mandarins who lined nearby Harley and Wimpole streets. He spent most of the last 30 years of his life in professional exile, all the while gleefully tilting at the "great temples of medical priestcraft".

Allinson had received quite an orthodox medical education in Scotland. Having set up in London, however, the fledgling medico found patients hard to come by. This was not uncommon. As with another Marylebone physician, the eye doctor, Arthur Conan Doyle, Allinson found the down time in his surgery ideal for writing. Instead of creating an immortal detective, Allinson would proclaim in *The System of Hygienic Medicine*. Published under that title in 1886, the book developed Allinson's theory of the "vital force" within us all. Civilized man (circa 1886), living in close confinement, did not have the exercise, the pure air, or the ability to keep his skin clean enough to maintain a healthy body. Nor did he eat the proper foods at proper intervals. Sparing my reader the metabolistic minutiae, Allinson decreed: no meat, no alcohol, no tobacco (it made him feel "queer about the head"), no coffee (it gave him wind), no tea and— above all—no white bread. Instead, he touted a vegetarian regimen of brown bread, nuts, fruits and vegetables.

He was ridiculed in the general medical press for suggesting that people return to eating like "beasts of the field". It was said that the Allinson diet would leave its adherents too weak for any serious labour for Queen and Empire. Hence, his great walk from Edinburgh to Marylebone was an effort "to prove the fallacy of these people". To modern readers, none of this sounds particularly radical.

We annually wade through a torrent of such diet and exercise twaddle churned out by well-meaning doctors, let alone soap stars, football heroes and their ilk. Such books strain the shelves and (eventually) glut the remainder bins of high street bookshops. But, in the 1890s world of High Victorian medicine, attention-seeking was quite déclassé. There was more, however, than simply Allinson's writings and the "hey, look at me" antics such as The Great Walk. Even more troubling to the profession was Allinson's increasingly vocal denunciation of many of the fervently held tenets of the Hippocratic arts. He thought most surgeries were unnecessary, most prescribed drugs were poisons, and he lent his name to the anti-vaccination crusaders.

The faculty at his old school eventually demanded he stop signing his name TR Allinson, LRCP Edinburgh, claiming that "he runs amok at the teachings of that college which he proclaims himself a licentiate".

He didn't look the part of anyone even nearly "amok". Short in stature, he was described as possessing a "lofty brow and twinkly bespectacled eyes above a full beard". In 1888, Allinson had married Anna Pulvermacher, related to the inventor of the infamous Pulvermacher Galvanic Belt, a contrivance worn against the male genitalia to control masturbation, another threat to the "vital force". From seed to grain—in 1893, Allinson founded the Natural Food Company with a bakery in Bethnal Green producing Dr Allinson's Brown Bread. The bread was sold under the slogan: "Health without Medicine." Among other benefits, it was promised that a slice or two per day would fend off the "menace of constipation", a much discussed malady of the period.

The upshot of such marketing was that in 1894 the General Medical Council voted to strike Allinson's name from the physician's register, accusing him of "infamous conduct in a professional sense". Specifically, he was found to have violated the medical canon precluding "advertising, canvassing or touting for patients". Allinson challenged the GMC in a series of legal actions that, in the end, proved unsuccessful. Resigned to his defeat, he hung a new shingle outside the doorway at Spanish Place, "Ex-Doctor TR Allinson" and informed the public that, while he may have lost a title, it was really no matter after all. "The orthodox member of the medical trades union would like it to be otherwise, and does his best to spread this false conception; but it is not so… my practice goes on the same and my patients are as numerous as ever."

Such controversy of course did nothing to slow sales of *The System of Hygienic Medicine*. He had also become active in a litany of fin-de-siecle causes, including vegetarianism, rational dress ("I am pleased to say that Mrs Allinson had given up wearing stays before I knew her, so we had no cross words on that score.") and birth control. In the latter area, he privately published *A Book for Married Women*.

Allinson declared that, "The information contained in this book ought to be known by every married woman, and it will not harm the unmarried to read." The most controversial section (chapter six, if you want to go there directly) dealt with birth control, or as he phrased it, "Mishaps and how to avoid them." He defended the frankness of the material: "Some may think too much is told, such can scarcely be the case, for knowledge is power and the means of attaining happiness."

Those women, married or otherwise, who wished to have "the knowledge" were instructed to send 1s, 2d to 4 Spanish Place, Manchester Square. For reasons of discretion, "the book can be had in an envelope". Allinson was soon again hauled before the courts and fined for sending indecent material through the mail. His advanced views on birth control also cost him his position on the board of The Vegetarian Society, despite the support of a fellow board member, a young Mahatma Gandhi.

Allinson continued his pamphleteering and his practice into the

Edwardian years. The battles went on as well. When one of his patients died of cancer, Allinson was censured by the Kingston coroner. "No treatment had been adopted and no operation advised." The local official suggested that the medical authorities needed to be informed; Allinson declared that he was "an authority in himself" and he had the "largest practice in the kingdom". In 1911, he was caricatured in Vanity Fair, with the caption, "Wholemeal Bread". He must have been pleased that the weekly identified him as Dr Thomas Richard Allinson. Allinson died of tuberculosis in Spanish Place late in the Armistice month of November 1918. He was cremated. Largely forgotten in the last 90 years, he received some recent attention when a collection of his essays and recipes (including Dyspeptic's Bread and a Poor Epicure's Pudding) was located and published. The name of Allinson has come and gone on various whole wheat and brown breads over the years—the bread "wi' nowt taken out". Not as enduringly successful was another of his concoctions—a beverage he had tried to launch under the jarringly un-euphonic name of BRUNAK. It was advertised as being "as refreshing as tea, as tasty as coffee, as comforting as cocoa, and as harmless as water. There is not a headache in a barrel of it, and no nervousness in a ton of it". Apparently, the ersatz stuff went over like Watney's Red Barrel.

Sydney Ringer's heartfelt solution

By Dr David Miller

MJ3.5, Oct-Nov 2007

Many excellent scientific researchers and medical practitioners have lived in Marylebone. Sydney Ringer (1836-1910) who lived in Cavendish Place was one of them. But Ringer is an undeservedly unsung hero. His discoveries were vital in helping to define the salty fluid contained in many clinical 'drip' bottles. Saline drips are commonly seen in hospital wards and operating theatres. Patients suffering from blood loss and shock can safely receive this simple mixture of a few salts which has saved literally millions of lives.

Although his work was critical in defining the composition of salines now universally used in medicine and biomedical research, Ringer's name remains rather obscure. Ringer's Lactate Solution, at least, is a phrase that most medical students recognise. That version of saline is widely used by anaesthetists during operations and post-operative recovery. Perhaps Ringer's relative obscurity came about because he retained a diffident, unpretentious air. Unlike so many eminent Victorians, and certainly his medical contemporaries, he didn't blow his own trumpet. His upbringing had been sternly non-conformist (wrongly described as 'Quaker' in many reports). This family background could explain his natural reserve and the self-effacing manner that many of his contemporaries remarked upon.

Ringer lived for over 40 years with his Yorkshire-born wife at number 15 Cavendish Place, the short road that runs between Cavendish Square and the top of Regent Street. His younger daughter, Hilda Sydney Ringer, was married just round the corner at All Souls, Langham Place. Number 15 was radically altered in about 1911, soon after Ringer's death. Regrettably those changes prevent the display of one of English Heritage's blue plaques there. Ringer died, and is buried, at the beautiful little village of Lastingham, near Pickering, North Yorkshire, where he had his holiday and weekend home.

Sydney Ringer was born in Norwich in March 1836 (though even his own gravestone reports this as 1835). He was the son of a wholesale grocer who died in 1843. An uncle, Samuel Browne, sponsored his studies in Norwich and later in London. One of his Norwich schoolteachers was the Rev Dr Ebenezer Cobham Brewer who later became famous as the author of the *Dictionary of Phrase & Fable*, still in print and widely known simply as 'Brewer's'. He had two brothers who made their careers and fortunes in the Far East—John in Shanghai and Canton, China and Frederick in Japan where he was known as the 'King of Nagasaki' because of his commercial dominance. Sydney himself was only to leave England once, making a brief trip to Paris in 1860.

Ringer started his medical training at the Norfolk & Norwich Hospital before enrolling at University College London (UCL) in 1854. UCL was then still a 'new university'. Critically, and unlike Oxford and Cambridge, it was open to non–Anglicans such as the staunchly non-conformist Ringer.

Ringer's first jobs as a newly qualified doctor were at University College Hospital (UCH) and Great Ormond Street Children's Hospital. He lived then at nearby Grenville Street. By the age of just 26 he became a clinical professor at UCL and the senior physician at UCH. He quickly established himself as one of the leading medical teachers and researchers of the day. Many of his pupils became very eminent in medicine, but they were all generous in their praise of him as their mentor. One student and colleague, Harrington Sainsbury, who lived at 52 Wimpole Street for many years, became physician to Queen Victoria. Sainsbury also found his name amongst those suspected of being Jack the Ripper. The perpetrator of the macabre east London killings of 1888 was widely believed to have had specialist medical knowledge and a connection with the royal family. Sainsbury satisfied both these conspiracy theories.

Ringer had a role in establishing an early convalescent home in Eastbourne. That project was largely driven by Harriet Brownlow Byron, whose religious and nursing foundation, All Saints' Sisters of the Poor, was based at Margaret Street, near Ringer's home.

Unusually for a Victorian doctor, Ringer devoted as much time as he could to laboratory research. He even clambered over UCL's Gower Street railings one evening when he found the main door locked. Among many topics, he studied the heart's pumping action. In the period 1880 to

1884, he made his major findings that revealed the vital role of calcium in the heart's contractions. It is now known that calcium is critical to all types of muscle contraction and many more body processes besides. Ringer also found that potassium at precise concentrations was essential for normal heart function. His findings turned out to apply to all the body's tissues, not just the heart—that is why saline can replace missing blood for many purposes.

A celebrated story of 'chance' explains how Ringer made his ground-breaking discovery about calcium. He had studied the actions of various salts in keeping the heart beating as near to normally as possible. (Frogs' hearts were used for this study, but the results are just as relevant to humans.) His technician had been mixing the salts for the experimental solutions in ordinary tap water rather than distilled water—either being lazy or perhaps, even then, cutting corners to save lab funds.

Ringer noted this and, being the scientist he was, checked whether it made a difference. Of course, London tap water is 'hard'—it contains dissolved salts, including almost the same concentration of calcium as is found in the blood. He had a chemical analysis of the tap water done and immediately understood calcium's critical importance. People like to believe that luck—serendipity—plays a role in scientific discovery and this is one example. But what it really proves is that it is the "prepared mind", in Louis Pasteur's phrase, that turns mere 'chance' into 'good luck' by spotting what so many others would completely overlook.

Like all leading medical practitioners of the day, Ringer had a thriving private practice, with consulting rooms at his Cavendish Place home. He numbered the Grenadier Guards' general and Crimean War hero Prince William of Saxe-Weimar among his patients.

Ringer's scientific excellence led to his election as a Fellow of the Royal Society. He wrote what is widely seen as one of the first modern textbooks of pharmacology, using his own research and patient records to inform it. This book ran through 13 editions and became an international standard text. Its form and style helped to define how such books have been set out ever since. He studied and wrote extensively on diverse topics including acupuncture, the use of cannabis for migraine and the suppression of the libido with bromide.

Ringer's otherwise successful life suffered a defining tragedy. His elder daughter Annie died on her seventh birthday in July 1875. A much-repeated story tells that she choked on a plum stone at her birthday party. The reality is more prosaic. She had suffered an intestinal blockage, just possibly provoked by the infamous plum stone. Despite being attended by the premier surgeon in England, her father's UCH companion Sir Eric Erichsen, Annie's mercifully brief illness proved fatal. She died at Cavendish Place, but her body was taken to Lastingham for burial. Ringer and his wife, Ann, spent a small fortune restoring the ancient pilgrimage church of St Mary's in memory of Annie. A mark of Ringer's avoidance of ostentation is that, until earlier this year his name was not permanently recorded in the church to acknowledge this benefaction. Lastingham had always known him simply as 'Dr Ringer' and known nothing of his international significance.

Sydney Ringer was one of the true greats of modern medicine and biomedical science and deserves to be better known. As your heart beats, calcium is moving in and out of every cell with every beat—modern knowledge that Ringer's careful experiments first began to reveal. If you are unfortunate enough to have needed it, thank him for defining the physiological saline that may well have saved your life during an operation. If you stroll through Cavendish Place, picture this Victorian gentleman with the silk top-hat and furled umbrella that he always sported, smoking enthusiastically as he made his brisk, daily walk along the same pavements to and from UCH and UCL.

Dr Hunter's miracle cure

By Tom Hughes
MJ7.5, Oct-Nov 2011

Twenty-five per cent of all deaths in Victorian Britain were caused by tuberculosis or, as it was better known, consumption, through which the lungs and the body wasted away to an inevitable gasping, emaciated end. Everyone feared it. Doctors fought it. Novelists exploited it—teary-eyed readers were ever moved by the "consumptive Victorian heroine".

Thus there was some hope in the summer of 1864 when a brash young American doctor came to Marylebone to establish a practice devoted "exclusively to the elucidation and treatment of pulmonary complaints". Dr Robert Hunter's surgery was at 14 Upper Seymour Street. The Edwardians later redid the numbering and seekers of Hunter's surgery will find it one door east of the present day Edward Lear Hotel on Seymour Street. The poet had lived there for a time, or as he put it, he had a "redboom near Squortman Pare".

Hunter advertised his presence in London, in the form of letters to the major newspapers. In *Dr Hunter's Letters on the Lungs*, he declared that a patient diagnosed with "tubercle" should not fear that he or she had been touched by "the hand of death". Away with dread and resignation, he cried. "The question is: can consumption be cured? My answer is unequivocally yes."

Dr Hunter's letters were published in book form and sold with "unexampled rapidity". The medical profession took umbrage at this interloper. The *Lancet* quickly dismissed Hunter as an unknown and mocked his medical degree. It was probably "the gift of some blushing university of America", it sneered. As for his touted cure, the Lancet demanded, unsuccessfully, that Hunter submit the details for what today we would call peer review. Wheezing Britons nevertheless panted their way to Upper Seymour Street in great numbers to receive Dr Hunter's proprietary secret "admixture of oxygen". He charged one guinea for the first visit and five guineas for a month of treatments. In September 1865 Hunter began seeing a new patient, Mrs Annie Merrick, whose husband was a tobacconist on Baker Street. A few weeks later, Samuel Merrick, accompanied by his brother-in-law, came to the surgery to give Dr Hunter a horse-whipping.

The "Extraordinary Medical Fracas" was soon the talk of London. Hunter told the police that the two men attacked him unprovoked. Merrick punched him and the brother-in-law, Frederick Jones of New Bond Street, "fastened his teeth" in Hunter's ear. Only the efforts of the doctor's attendants prevented further mayhem. Merrick insisted that Hunter deserved his beating for he had "grossly insulted" his dying wife. Two days later, having gone from accuser to accused, Dr Robert Hunter found himself in court charged with having "feloniously and carnally known and abused Mrs Annie Merrick".

Mrs Merrick was too ill to come to the magistrate's court on Marylebone High Street, so the court went to her. She was found propped up in her bed above the shop on Upper Baker Street. She was in her late 20s and bore the signs of having been a woman of prepossessing beauty but was now quite ill. She had seen Dr Hunter on several occasions; his methods were simple, she was told to sit and "inhale something". After a few sessions, she complained of continued pain in her lungs. The doctor then suggested a physical exam and asked her to strip down to her waist; however, being so thin from the effects of the disease, her clothes dropped entirely to the floor and she found herself naked in front of him and she fainted. When she awoke, she found the doctor "in an indecent position". She called him a brute and left immediately (presumably clothed). Dr Hunter, married and with family, denied all the charges but was remanded for trial.

At the Old Bailey, Mrs Merrick told a now greatly elaborated story. She claimed that whatever Dr Hunter had given her to inhale had left her with a "stupefying powerless feeling" and he took advantage of her. Told that she must give the exact nature of what took place, she described being overpowered by the doctor's passionate kisses before he eventually had his way.

Dr Hunter was defended by that legendary figure of the Victorian bar Serjeant William Ballentine, who showed no mercy cross examining Annie Merrick while she histrionically coughed and spat into her handkerchief. She hadn't screamed out for help even though 14 Upper

Seymour Street was crowded with patients and staff. When she left, rather than run straight home to her husband, she popped round the corner to the City of Quebec pub. Poor Mrs Merrick's dubious past was dragged up. As was the interesting fact that her husband was bankrupt and hadn't been paying Dr Hunter's fees.

The jury acquitted Dr Hunter and he left the court to be greeted by cheering (and hacking) patients and supporters. Samuel Merrick was later acquitted for his assault on the doctor because he had acted on false information from his perjurious wife. But the problems for Dr Hunter had only begun. The *Pall Mall Gazette* published a leader entitled "Impostors and Dupes". Whether Dr Hunter was guilty or not of the squalid charge brought by the discredited Mrs Merrick was beside the point.

The *Gazette* accused Hunter of falsely using the title of MD in England. He came to Britain and knowingly established himself "in that highly respectable part of London, Upper Seymour Street, Portman Square". By using the "pernicious puffery usually resorted to by quacks and charlatans", he was able to play upon the fears of the ignorant and to obtain enormous fees. The doctor sued the newspaper for libel.

Hunter defended his credentials, citing two degrees earned in New York and Canada. He accused the Harley Street clique of shutting him out because he brought a radical new theory to London, namely "the carbonaceous character of tubercle and the importance of an oxygenated mode of treatment". He was supported by several satisfied patients. A tailor from Holborn, for example, said he "found himself much better" after his course of inhalation.

The *Gazette's* editors brought forward a parade of respected physicians from the London Hospital for Diseases of the Chest and the Brompton Consumption Hospital. The mandarins dismissed Hunter's theories out of hand: his carbonaceous theory was not new, it had been studied and confined to a dustbin years ago. Hunter got his "cure rate", they testified, by frightening the nervous into fancying that the first sign of a sniffle, a cough or a sore throat was the warning sign of approaching consumption. These timid folk would hasten to Upper Seymour Street, pay their guineas and breathe in deeply that mysterious "admixture of oxygen". Then, as they most always do, the nose stops running, the throat stops rasping, and the happy patient would credit Dr Hunter with life-saving skills.

The jury took an hour to decide that Dr Hunter had been libelled by the *Gazette* but his reputation would have to be salved with the insulting damages of just one farthing. The *Lancet* offered the thanks of the entire profession for the exposure of such dubious practices.

Dr Hunter closed his surgery on Upper Seymour Street and spent several years on the continent. Despite the scandal, he reported that he was consulted by nobility and gentry from all parts of Europe. He eventually returned to New York where he was hailed as "the father of inhalation". He published a defence of his theories and denounced the London medical establishment for "what I cannot but regard as a conspiracy formed to destroy my reputation". But he would not fight them any longer: "If the public is satisfied to leave things as they are, and to place all its hopes on cod-liver oil, I am sure the Consumption Hospital doctors will have no objection. It will save trouble and kill competition!"

The US dentist and the British smile

By Tom Hughes
MJ8.6, Dec-Jan 2012-13

One of the lesser known museums of London can be found at 64 Wimpole Street. The Georgian building houses the British Dental Association, in whose museum visitors can view a collection of dental instruments going back to the Victorian years. Open wide for a hand-cranked drill! It is interesting, if not necessarily comforting, to realise that the various picks and probes employed in the dental arts have not really changed all that much. The museum also exhibits examples of the dental profession's tireless efforts to get the British public to take better care of their teeth. "Be true to your teeth and they won't be false to you," one poster reads.

So what is it about the British and their teeth? The subject has been a default laugh line for desperate stand-up comics for years. On the Simpsons, when Lisa wouldn't floss, her dentist brought out the terrifying Big Book of British Smiles. Austin Powers, the international man of mystery, famously displayed a motley mouthful of bucky chompers. When a US magazine recently needed a cover for its Decline of Britain issue, the editors photoshopped the Duchess of Cambridge and gave her a gap-toothed, stained smile. The meme lives. Could the painful root of this issue be found in Marylebone, only a few doors away from the BDA museum?

If there is any one person to blame for this persistent calumny, let the finger point to Harry Campbell MD BS FRCP of 23 Wimpole Street. The Essex-born son of a doctor wasn't even a dentist. He was what the Edwardians called a "nerve specialist". He wrote a book about "morbid blushing" which you should be ashamed not to have read. "Mouth breathers" from the shires wheezed and gasped to London for his advice. He was a long-serving president of the Society for the Study of Inebriety. But rather late in life, he became obsessed with British teeth.

Campbell had done some war work and was struck by the teeth of the American soldier; the Yanks, of course, were "over-sexed and over here" and these toothsome doughboys came with their perfect over-bites.

Campbell would not keep his mouth shut. In 1920, before a meeting of British dentists, he declared: "We have the worst teeth of any nation." There, he said it. "The state of our teeth beggars description. It is a national disgrace which should excite a feeling of shame and humiliation." He estimated there were 200 million bad teeth in the country, 200 million soft socket abscesses and 30 million root abscesses. And not enough dentists. And you thought the wait to see a NHS dentist was intolerable today.

It was not Dr Campbell's remit to drum up work for the dental profession or to add his voice to the chorus of well-meaning health advocates who hector the population into more frequent brushing, flossing and other ministrations of dental hygiene. Of course, that would be a start. Yet, in modern terminology, that is simply cosmetic dentistry. All the buffing and scrubbing will not improve your average ragged picket fence of teeth.

Campbell determined the real problem was the national diet. What is the purpose of our teeth? To chew and tear and crush our food. We who know our Shakespeare can quote the words of Henry VI to Richard III: "Teeth hadst thou in thy head when thou wast born, / To signify thou camest to bite the world." But Campbell asserted that modern Britons do not bite. They do not chew. They suck their food.

It starts, of course, in the nursery. Children are raised on pap: porridge, bread-and-milk, milk puddings, rice-puddings, buns, and cakes. "Down with pap, and porridge, and buns," he roared. "Give the children of a great people their proper crusts. The teeth are to chew with. For all the use we put them to, we might as well not have them." All that chewing, or as he put it, the "beneficent action of efficient mastication," produces abundant natural saliva and increases the blood flow to the region and helps build a healthier jaw line, and thereby keeps the teeth naturally clean and straight. Is that so hard? It may have been a small sample size, but Campbell observed his Wimpole Street patients closely: "When a man or woman comes in to me with a normal jaw, I say to myself, 'You're from abroad.'"

Campbell's forcible views found some support within the dental profession. Dr J Sim Wallace, a neighbour on Wimpole Street, had written the leading book on *The Cause and Prevention of Dental Caries*, still in print today more than a century later. Wallace agreed with the man from across the road: "Nature meant us to keep our teeth smooth and polished by the friction which they received in masticating our food."

Campbell's Worst Teeth in the World legend really took hold of the headlines, in newspapers at home and abroad, arising out of The National Conference on the Nation's Teeth held in Manchester in 1920. Speaker after speaker bad-mouthed (so to speak) the state of British teeth. Line up folks from Land's End to John o' Groats and you'll no doubt find a "perfectly ghastly series of decayed fangs".

Harsh words but it was Campbell's apocalyptic pronouncement that got the greatest attention and caused such gnashing of teeth. Could this charge be true? The *New Statesman*, certainly a sober minded journal, sent a reporter across the Atlantic in 1921. Caleb Saleeby reported back that he was amazed at the prevalence of fine, regular, clean teeth in the mouths of so many people. "We need a far higher standard of personal pride in our general and local cleanliness and appearance, and we need a campaign in the lines of Dr Harry Campbell's dreadful diatribe to arouse us to the shameful character of our national dentition, its deplorable consequences, and its preventable character."

Getting an Englishman to do something one way because Americans do it that way is always going to be a tough nut. In fact, some Brits have embraced (if not braced) their problem choppers as more evidence of the stolid, stubborn character of this island race. Musn't grumble. The stiff upper lip can hide a few bad teeth. Flash a smile, however snaggle-toothed. Professor Jimmy Steele of the School of Dental Science at Newcastle University told the BBC that the British traditionally prefer "nice natural smiles—natural in colour". Geordies, he insisted, have a more functional view of teeth and dentistry, whereas Americans have always seen teeth more aesthetically. This attitude persists—when Gordon Brown spent a few hundred quid in Harley Street for a super-whitening job, he was mocked for it. "Why'd he have to go changing his English teeth?" the Telegraph asked.

We can at least conclude with the happy news that pertinent contemporary statistics reveal that Australians have the most teeth pulled of any nation on earth and when it comes to cavities in children, the little Poles have the most holes. But the British still cannot brush off the obloquy of having the "worst teeth in the world". As for Dr Harry Campbell of Wimpole Street, having sullied the reputation of British teeth forevermore, he moved on to other concerns. He died in London in 1938, leaving unanswered his last great question—whether mankind would be better off by once again learning to walk on all fours.

The medical men of Wimpole Street

By Tom Hughes
MJ4.1, Feb-Mar 2008

Harley Street has long been recognised as a premier centre of medicine. For more than a century, a whisper in a darkened hallway that Sir 'This' or Lord 'That' was on his way from Harley Street was often enough to reassure everyone that 'the guvnor' might yet survive.

If, however, anxious relatives were told that someone from Wimpole Street had been summoned, they might justifiably respond: "What good is a bloody poetess going to do?"

Wimpole Street has been forever entwined in the oft-told tale of Elizabeth Barrett. But it also has a long and interesting medical pedigree of its own. And in the few minutes it takes to walk up and down the street, you'll find the former premises of—among others—a regicide, a snake-handler and the world's foremost syphilologist.

The stroll begins at 1 Wimpole Street, the imposing headquarters of the Royal Society of Medicine. Moving northwards, at number 6 you'll find a blue plaque for Sir Frederick Treves, the doctor who rescued—in a way—John Merrick, the Elephant Man. Sir Frederick also became something of a crank on the subject of women's clothing—he railed against high-heels, tight corsets and low cut-dresses.

Sir Thomas Barlow practised at number 10. He was among a platoon of physicians summoned to the final hours of Queen Victoria. He also treated a brace of dukes and at least one Archbishop of Canterbury. A teetotaler, Barlow married a nurse matron and lived to be nearly 100. Dr Augustus Pepper was at number 13. This pathologist was called in on a number of high profile murders including the case of Dr Crippen.

Just a few doors up at number 16 was another pathologist, Dr Thomas Horrocks Openshaw, a man known to all Ripperologists. In that terrible autumn of 1888, Openshaw was asked to examine a portion of kidney that had been posted to one of the investigators. In an accompanying note, 'Jack' claimed it was a souvenir from one of his victims, Catherine Eddowes. Openshaw confirmed that the slice came from a left human kidney, but could not say male or female. 'Jack' then sent a letter to Openshaw congratulating him—with atrocious spelling—on his findings and vowing: 'I will be on the job soon and send you another bit of innerds."

At number 19 you'll find the residence of the man usually credited with carrying out the first brain surgery. In 1884, Dr Rickman John Godlee operated on a tumour—the patient "having expressed a strong desire to have it removed". The unhappy patient survived 28 days.

The former occupants of number 30 are interesting, if not for their medical achievements. From all appearances, Dr George Vivian Poore and Dr Marcus Beck shared a partnership, both medical and personal. Dr Poore was a public health activist who authored monographs on writer's cramp. Dr Beck was a surgeon. In addition to 30 Wimpole Street the two shared a country house in Isleworth. Dr Barlow, from up the street, said that the happy bachelors were known to all as "David and Jonathan". That's a Biblical reference, not very much unlike "David and Elton".

Lord Dawson of Penn—one of the controversial giants of Edwardian medicine—lived and practised at number 32. Bertrand Edward Dawson received his peerage in 1920 from his patient, King George V. Dawson was credited with saving the king's life at least once. And when the end finally came in 1936, he issued the memorable press bulletin: "The King's life is moving peacefully towards its close." Dawson's secret diaries were opened many years later. Only then was it discovered that he'd decided to end the king's life himself. Since his nurse wouldn't do it, he injected 0.75g of morphine followed by a gram of cocaine into the patient's jugular vein. Dawson wrote that he did it—not for reasons of mercy—but so that the announcement of the king's passing would be in the morning Times and not, should the monarch linger, be left to the déclassé evening papers.

Next we come to number 35, the former residence of Sir Henry Thompson, who earned that delightful Victorian title of polymath. He was into everything, including treating kidney stones, and numbered among his patients the King of Belgium and the exiled Napoleon III. The latter survived the operation by just four days but—we are assured—for reasons unrelated to Sir Henry's ministrations. Sir Henry was a renowned host and invitations were eagerly sought for his 'Octaves'—eight people for an eight-course dinner, arriving promptly at eight.

Now cross the street and turn back south. Look for number 53, where Sir Joseph Fayrer once lived. A naval surgeon by training, he found himself in India where he took it upon himself to become an expert in poisonous snakes. His masterwork, *Thanatophidia*, complete with painstakingly drawn coloured plates, is said to have "made generations of British even more fearful of snakes".

Kraits to cobras, they scared not the doughty doctor—although he had one very close call while inspecting a cobra's tail. The snake's head was secured in a box. But the native assistant neglected to hold down the lid and "the cobra suddenly put his head out to see what Sir Joseph Fayrer was doing with his tail. Luckily it was more pleased than offended with the liberties which were being taken with its tail, but it was unpleasant for Sir Joseph Fayrer to find his face almost touching the cobra's mouth."

At number 57 was one Dr Alfred Wiltshire, a physician unremarkable but for his published belief that men experience "vicarious menstruation", citing one fellow surgeon (unidentified) who bled from his genitalia once every three weeks. While Dr Wiltshire's paper was generally ridiculed, one supporter said it was indeed true and he recommended that men who suffer from it should be bled regularly from their feet.

At number 69 we find the eye specialist Dr Robert Brudenell Carter. What was it with Victorian eye doctors? Did they not have enough to keep them busy? Conan Doyle was so bored he concocted Sherlock Holmes. But Carter decided to range far from his field to opine *On the Pathology and Treatment of Hysteria*. Therein he claimed that women had learned to fake hysteria or otherwise used it to get their way.

Carter even suggested that doctors were contributing to a growing "moral evil": "I have seen young unmarried women reduced by the constant use of the speculum to the mental and moral condition of prostitutes; seeking to give themselves the same indulgence by the practice of solitary vice; and asking every medical practitioner to institute an examination of the sexual organs."

Hasten along now to number 84 and Sir Frederick Mott, a man known to both peers and posterity as the world's foremost syphilologist. Mott was a tireless campaigner for sexual hygiene and sexual education. In the 1920s he claimed that the equivalent of two army corps were invalided during the Second World War because of VD, adding the question to anyone listening: "What do you have to say to that?"

The last stop is at number 85, the home and surgery of Dr Octavius Sturges, a physician known to countless lawyers, though not for any issues of malpractice. Dr Sturges was a plaintiff in a landmark 'party wall' case. He decided to build a new surgery in his back garden. One wall abutted against a wall of the property around the corner at 30 Wigmore Street. There, for the last 60 years, Frederick Horatio Bridgman, and his father before him, had operated a confectioners business. And against their back wall they'd been using three massive mortar & pestle contrivances to grind the ingredients.

Dr Sturges soon grew tired of what he called a "thunderous noise". He filed suit. And despite Bridgman's understandable protestation that they'd been crushing their nuts there for 60 years, his business was ruled a nuisance. The Bridgmans were forced to move on.

So after this exhausting walk you'll doubtless be seeking a quiet café for a coffee and a cake. Be thankful for Dr Sturges that there are no thundering mortars at work out in the back to disturb you—just the drone of half a dozen mobile phone conversations.

Dr Richardson and the awkward bequest

By Tom Hughes

MJ3.5, Oct-Nov 2007

Reporters from the London newspapers of 1879 beat a steady path to 25 Manchester Square, the corner home of Dr Benjamin Ward Richardson. As the recipient of one of the most curious bequests in memory, everyone was keen to know what he could possibly do with his inheritance. The inexplicable will had prompted unprecedented "conversation, speculation and amusement". There were wild rumours. The doctor received many unsolicited suggestions, a few of them even serious. For Dr Richardson, one of the leading teetotalers in Victorian England, had been left the entire contents of one of the finest wine cellars in the realm.

Dr Benjamin Ward Richardson FRS was 50, married with three children, and a total abstainer. He studied poisons, developed several new anaesthetics, became a public sanitation activist and—in 1870—gave and then published a series of lectures on alcohol. He rejected the accepted medical wisdom that a "tot of brandy" was good for what ails you. Instead, he argued that there is no benefit from alcohol and the social cost in death and disease is immeasurable.

Thumbing through his post on the morning of 1 April 1879, Richardson came to a letter sent by one of the executors of the late Sir Walter Trevelyan. The Northumberland magnifico had, by codicil, left the good doctor the contents of his wine cellar at the Trevelyan estate. The only stipulation was that the collection be used for "scientific purposes".

Richardson's first thought, given the date, was that this was someone's idea of a leg-puller. "Some pitiless wag had made up his mind to make me an April fool. It was a club-room joke." However a quick check determined the executor was a bona fide Newcastle solicitor. A telegram was dispatched confirming acceptance of the terms and requesting the keys to the cellar be sent by return registered mail. With that message still crackling north by wire, the first reporter arrived in Manchester Square. Word of Dr Richardson's "good fortune" had already reached Fleet Street. The reporter left disappointed as Dr Richardson sent him away, confessing, "I really know no more about it than you do."

The doctor was not being completely honest with the journalist, which, if not recommended, is surely forgivable. The previous year, Sir Walter had called on Richardson in Manchester Square. The two men shared strong temperance views; Sir Walter thought all booze was the "devil-in-solution". His late wife had only just prevented him from throwing all of his wines into a river. But, if barmy on the subject, Sir Walter was also worried about those who worked in the industry. Richardson recalled: "He asked me if I thought a way had yet been indicated by which that produce, and the industry under which it is now utilised, could be applied, should the trade in wine and alcohol become, as he believed it would become, seriously imperilled."

Trevelyan left that afternoon with no talk of a bequest but only an invitation for Richardson to visit Wallington. Richardson never took up the offer—perhaps deterred by the legend that a headless woman stalked the halls at night.

In October, with Sir Walter's cellar key in hand, Dr Richardson travelled to Northumberland as a guest of the new baronet. Sir Walter had died childless and his cousin, Sir Charles Trevelyan, inherited Wallington. Richardson was awed by the vast stone cellars. As for the wine, a faded handwritten list was the only inventory. The oldest of the wine dated from the mid-18th Century and much of it had gone off. In all, Richardson found "60 dozen bottles in a state of preservation". He made a short inventory of his new collection: "Port, claret, cyprus, hock, French, white port, pruniac, St George, sack-tokay, malmsey-sack, frontignac, placentine, madeira, sherry-sack, a white not named, a dark wine not named, arrack, brandy, gin, bottles containing beer and a 'few' bottles of champagne." Not what you'd find on today's supermarket shelves.

Surrounded by all this fine wine, Richardson found himself fighting a case of oenophilia: "For a teetotaler, I must have been getting rather too near the verge of enthusiasm over this ancient wine, and there is about it, no doubt, an antiquarian flavour which is apt to excite admiration. The admiration is quite pardonable."

Richardson—having managed to gather himself—was still at sixes and sevens as he pondered his "troublesome duty". The wine was valued at perhaps as much as £4,000; a buyer offered him eight times as much. He was told that a giant, public auction, taking advantage of the attention, could raise a fortune for science. This, he felt, was not in the spirit (sorry) of the bequest. "It certainly was never his wish or intention that the wine should be so applied as to exalt the praises of wine or lead to the encouragement of wine-drinking, even for the sake of the curious in drinking; and that feeling I also share."

Meanwhile, the public were having their snootful of fun. Self-proclaimed "experts" offered to taste the wine. Several "unfortunate widows" wrote to Manchester Square imploring the kind doctor to perhaps spare a bottle of port for their aches and pains. A rival temperance campaigner proposed hiring a boat and anchoring it in the Thames off the Houses of Parliament and throwing the bottles into the river one by one "to the tuneful measure of a minute gun". Fortunately, in a sober moment, that idea was scuttled.

The wine, in fact, was moved from Wallington to London with "scarcely an accident". Richardson—for the purposes of science, of course—opened some of the older claret to find the alcohol content much lower than contemporary bottles. This, he believed, shot holes in the theory that our ancestors drunk two or three bottles a day and survived, occasional gout notwithstanding. Richardson warned that anyone drinking a daily two bottles of claret in 1879 would go out like the "snuff of a candle".

Soon, Londoners—as they do—moved on to other diversions. The drinking classes went back to their drinking glasses. In the end, Richardson's decision as to "how one total abstainer can make use of wine which another total abstainer has left him" came as rather a disappointment. He decreed that the wines would be subjected to chemical analysis, "the object in view being to determine the exact nature of the substances on which the varying flavour of different wines is dependent". A laudable goal, I imagine, but aren't wine bores still banging on about that?

Something to consider next time you shove your nose into a nice glass of Chateau Marylebone.

The eccentric genius of Charles Babbage

By Louisa McKenzie

MJ5.4, Aug-Sep 2009

Charles Babbage is widely considered to have been the father of the computer—a technological pioneer whose ideas helped shape the modern world. Quite how influential he actually was has been a matter of lively debate, but even the most cursory glimpse into his life and work shows that Babbage was a complex, eccentric and original thinker.

Babbage was born in south London in 1791 or 1792, but his father's business connections soon took the young family to the West Country. Due to ill health as a child, Babbage's education was split between schools and private tutors. He had sufficient promise to gain entry to Trinity College Cambridge from 1810 before transferring to Peterhouse College. He graduated from here in 1814, with a master's degree following three years later. At that time, university students studied a wide range of subjects and Babbage became a lifelong polymath—mathematician, inventor, philosopher, engineer, code-breaker, political economist and writer.

After finishing his studies, Babbage married and moved to Marylebone. He and his family first lived at 5 Devonshire Street. In order to work on his inventions, he built a forge and workshops in the grounds of his house. In 1828, the family moved to 1 Dorset Street (at the top of Manchester Street), and he transferred his workshops here, demolishing the stable block to make way for them. The character of the area—genteel, but new money—may have allowed Babbage more leeway with the noise and smoke produced by his work than one of the more stately areas would have done.

During his lifetime Babbage was little known and was often ridiculed as an eccentric. When he died in 1871, The Royal Society didn't even publish an obituary. His funeral, in Kensal Green Cemetery, lacked the pomp which characterised the funerals of "great men". It would be many years after Babbage's death that he would finally be celebrated as a pioneer of the technology which we take for granted today.

Babbage is now most famous for two inventions: the Difference Engine and the Analytical Engine. There were, in fact, a number of attempts at the Difference Engine, as Babbage gradually refined his ideas and designs. Babbage commenced work on Difference Engine No 1 in around 1821, while living on Devonshire Street. He secured a large amount of government funding for the work—£17,500.

The Difference Engine was an attempt to mechanise calculation. In Babbage's time, many professions, such as navigation, engineering and accountancy, relied upon printed mathematical tables to perform complex calculations. As they had to be produced by hand, there was a high rate of error in these tables—errors in the original maths, errors in the transcription of the tables or errors in the printing process.

Babbage wanted to find a way of mechanising the entire process of producing these vast tables, thereby eliminating all three sources of error. His solution was called the Difference Engine because it used the mathematical principle, popular at the time, of "finite differences" to compute the tables.

The design for Difference Engine No 1 was vast: weighing 15 tonnes, standing eight feet high, and having a massive 25,000 working parts. Unfortunately, it turned out that the complex parts required for Babbage's invention could not really be made using the manufacturing and engineering techniques of the age. Babbage himself acknowledged this, and the majority of the machine went unmade. The only part to be manufactured was the actual engine—the part which would have "driven" the machine. Work on Difference Engine No 1 finally stopped in 1833 when Babbage's skilled workman did not want to move to the workshop in Dorset Street without compensation.

After the unsatisfactory conclusion of Difference Engine No 1, Babbage had an even more ground-breaking idea—the Analytical Engine. It is this machine which has led to Babbage being considered the father of the computer as, according to the Science Museum, it "bears all the essential logical features of the modern general purpose computer". It could be programmed; it had a "store" (memory) and "mill" (processor) which were separated; it could be "looped" (repeating the same operation multiple times according to a program); and it could take different actions depending on the result of a previous calculation.

Babbage started work on the Analytical Engine in 1834. Rather than just creating specific mathematical tables, this machine was designed to find the value of almost any algebraic function. Again, the Analytical Engine is not one machine, but a series of designs which were tweaked until their inventor's death in 1871. None were ever manufactured. However, the Analytical Engine caught the attention of the brightest mathematical minds in Europe. The Science Museum suggests that, if constructed, the Analytical Engine would have been so large that it would have required a steam engine to drive it.

At the same time as working on his Analytical Engine, Babbage started work on designs for Difference Engine No 2. This was a much more refined version of the first Difference Engine, weighing nearly three tonnes, standing seven feet high and having only 4,000 moving parts. Again, the machine went unfinished in Babbage's lifetime. For many years, it was presumed that this was again a result of the limitations of manufacturing methods at the time. However, we now know that the machine could have worked. In 1985 the Science Museum undertook a project to make Difference Engine No 2 using modern methods but limited to a level of precision available in the 1840s. Not only did they succeed in making the machine, but it worked.

Babbage never saw his designs fulfilled. Instead, he worked on many other projects. His ever-busy mind could always think of a new innovation, or a new theory. Among other items, Babbage has been credited with inventing the concept of black box recorders, but for newly invented trains rather than aeroplanes. He also pioneered lighthouse signalling and the use of tidal power as an energy source.

Many of his theories and inventions are detailed in his 1868 memoir *Passages From The Life Of A Philosopher*. The choice of this title illustrates how Babbage thought of himself — as a theoretical thinker, rather than an engineer or scientist. The book gives us an insight into Babbage's mind: highly organised, with a true love of putting everything possible into tabular form. Indeed, Babbage is supposed to have had a collection of 300 volumes of tables.

His memoir also gives us a glimpse into the character of 19th century Marylebone. Babbage included a chapter entitled Street Nuisances. Chief among these, he believes, are street musicians, such as organ grinders and brass bands. He writes: "It is difficult to estimate the misery inflicted upon multitudes of intellectual workers by the loss of their time, destroyed by organ grinders and other similar nuisances."

Babbage also complains about the arrival of a hackney cab stand. He reports that the stand was established despite complaints from the inhabitants of the area, and there already being a stand in nearby Paddington Street. "The neighbourhood became changed: coffee-shops, beer-shops and lodging-houses filled the small adjacent streets," he writes. "The character of the new population may be inferred from the taste they exhibit for the noisiest and most discordant music." Babbage seems to have made himself quite unpopular in the area. He reports being goaded by neighbours, being followed by mobs and receiving death threats. "I received constantly anonymous letters, advising, and even threatening me with all sorts of evils."

Babbage could not understand why everyone else did not think like him. But this was where his genius lay, in thinking differently. Without such a unique, highly functioning brain, he would never have thought out any of his inventions. And the world might be a very different place today.

Profile: Sir Francis Beaufort (1774-1857)

Admiral and hydrographer, lived at 51 Manchester Street

Francis Beaufort was born in 1774, in County Meath, Ireland. Aged 14, he voyaged across the globe aboard the East India Company's Vansittart. His subsequent maritime career is a salty tale worthy of the finest seafaring yarn, where talent, pluck and good fortune enabled him to rise up through the ranks. He was lucky to survive when the Vansittart was shipwrecked in the East Indies. On returning to Britain he joined the Royal Navy, nearly drowned, and then became embroiled in the wars with Revolutionary and Napoleonic France.

In 1800, Beaufort, a midshipman on the HMS Phaeton, led a successful boarding raid to capture an armed Spanish ship. As he clambered onto the deck he received two sabre cuts to the head and one to his shin, before being shot at point blank range from a blunderbuss. He fought on and survived with 19 wounds.

Five years later, he was given his first command, the HMS Woolwich. He began to commit an account of his wind force scale to the ship's journal. Influenced by the work of hydrographer Alexander Dalrymple, he devised a simple system for quantifying the wind's force, by relating it to the amount of sail a frigate could safely bear.

The Royal Navy formally adopted the Beaufort Scale in 1838. It proved so functional because it set out to measure the force rather than the speed of the wind, which was, at the time, virtually impossible to calculate with any degree of accuracy at sea. The system worked equally well for all types of sailing ships.

In 1812, Beaufort was combining the surveying of the south coast of Turkey with the suppression of piracy. Armed local pashas attacked his onshore survey party at the port of Ayas. Beaufort was shot in the groin. This wound effectively ended his active duty.

The publication of Karamania in 1817, an account of scientific community. In the following years he produced dozens of new maps and charts. At a time when, in war, more ships were lost to bad charts than to enemy fire, his work helped save thousands of lives.

His scientific expertise was officially recognised with his appointment as hydrographer to the Navy in 1829, a position he held until the age of 81. During his time in office, many voyages of discovery, charting and surveying were carried out under his direction. He made it possible for Charles Darwin to sail with Captain Robert Fitzroy on board the Beagle.

Beaufort was promoted to rear admiral in 1846 and received a knighthood two years later. His personal life was not without a splash of colour. When his wife Alicia died from breast cancer in 1834, he launched, according to ciphered entries in his private diary, into an incestuous relationship with his sister, Henrietta. Though consumed by guilt, Beaufort frequented her bed for the next three years. This affair ended once he married his second wife, Honora. He was both willing and able to commit adultery with other women until well into his seventies.

In retirement Beaumont maintained his compulsion to observe, measure and record. He kept a meticulous weather journal for his entire adult life and, during his final years, even recorded the size, shape, consistency and colour of his stools.

Admiral Sir Francis Beaufort died on 17 December 1857, aged 83. In life he was an expert seaman and naval officer, a scientist, an author and the navy's most important hydrographer. The sea north of Alaska is named the Beaufort Sea in his honour, but he is doubtless best remembered for the wind force scale that bears his name.

Profile: Charles Lyell (1797-1875)

Geologist, lived at 73 Harley Street

Charles Lyell was born in Kinnordy in Scotland. His father, also called Charles, was (rather uniquely) a respected expert on both the poet Dante and mosses, a variety of which—orthotricium lyelli—was named in his honour. The younger Charles was moved to the New Forest at an early age by his mother who thought that the Scots were a nation of drunks. In 1816 he entered Exeter College, Oxford, where he studied law. While there, he fell under the influence of the eccentric geologist Reverend William Buckland who was renowned for his knowledge of fossilised faeces and his apparent desire to eat every living creature on God's earth.

SCIENCE & MEDICINE

(He enjoyed hedgehogs and sea slugs, but found the garden mole pretty unappetizing.) Soon after touring Scotland with Buckland in 1824, Lyell abandoned his legal career and devoted himself to geology.

Lyell's defining work, *The Principles of Geology*, was published in three volumes between 1830 and 1833. Its great achievement was to clearly define the uniformitarian view of geology: the theory that changes on Earth are both uniform and extremely gradual. Lyell insisted that everything that happened in the past could be explained by geological phenomena that are still going on today: rivers depositing layers of silt, for example, or wind and rain eroding landscapes. This clashed violently with the prevailing theory that geological changes were sparked by sudden cataclysmic events, a view that allowed the biblical flood and other 'acts of God' to be incorporated into scientific discussions.

Lyell's influence was huge. *Principles* went through 12 editions in his lifetime, providing him with a handsome income. Charles Darwin took a copy of the first issue with him on the Beagle. He said of Lyell: "I really think my books come half out of Lyell's brain. I see through his eyes." Despite being such a great influence upon Darwin, as well as a close friend, Lyell never fully embraced the theory of natural selection. He also refused to accept the idea of ice ages and large scale extinctions.

Despite these oversights, Charles Lyell has remained hugely respected. Following on from *Principles, Elements of Geology* (1838), became a standard work on stratigraphical and paleontological geology, while *The Antiquity of Man* (1863) brilliantly demolished the standard Christian belief that human beings have been about for only a few thousand years.

In 1854, at the height of his fame, Lyell moved to Marylebone where his home at 73 Harley Street soon became a major social huh. He and his wife Mary loved hobnobbing with London's social elite, and Lyell was hugely proud of being made a knight (in 1848) and a baronet (in 1864). Darwin thought it ridiculous how the geologist would spend hours poring over dinner invitations to decide which to accept, instead of devoting his efforts to further ground-breaking scientific study. During his later years, Lyell's eyesight, always bad, failed him completely. He died in 1875 and was buried in Westminster Abbey. Craters on the moon and on Mars have since been named after him.

Profile: Mary Seacole (1805-1881)

Nurse and Crimean war hero, lived at 157 George Street

Born Mary Jane Grant in Kingston, Jamaica, in 1805, she was the daughter of a Scottish army officer and a free black Jamaican woman. From infancy she watched intrigued as her mother treated the sick amongst the British military stationed in the Caribbean.

Mary first practised the arts of Creole medicine on her doll and, aged 12, began helping her mother tend human patients. Mary was fired by her twin passions of medicine and travel. As a young woman she visited other Caribbean islands including Cuba, Haiti and the Bahamas. She learnt to care for people with many tropical diseases and developed her own herbal remedies.

In 1836, Mary married Edwin Horatio Hamilton Seacole, godson of Lord Nelson. Edwin died in 1844. Six years later, she visited her brother at a gold prospecting town in Panama and dealt single-handed with a cholera epidemic after the American doctor fled the scene. She performed an autopsy on a child to learn more about the disease and even found time to stitch a man's ear back on after it was cut off in a fight. Back in Jamaica, her expertise was again in demand during a yellow fever outbreak.

With the onset on the Crimean War in 1854, Mary, now almost 50, became concerned about the welfare of the British soldiers she had known in Jamaica who were now serving in Turkey. She crossed the ocean bound for the nurse recruitment offices in London. Despite providing glowing testimonials she was rejected four times.

Ignoring the official snub, Mary financed her own passage to Crimea. She went to the battle zone as a sutler—a person who follows the army selling provisions to the troops—but from the moment she arrived in Balaclava there were sick and wounded soldiers to attend to. Mary used her business proceeds to open the British Hotel at Spring Hill, near the besieged city of Sevastopol. Here she provided nourishment, medicine and care to her beloved soldiers. Soon the entire British army knew of 'Mother Seacole'.

Unlike Florence Nightingale, whose hospitals were three days' sailing from the Crimea, Mary did her work on the battlefield, tending to the wounded whilst hostilities were raging. On one occasion she was almost shot.

The *Times* newspaper and *Punch* magazine ran stories of her courage and nursing skills. Unlike most of her British counterparts, Mary had invaluable experience of tropical diseases and was able to tackle cases of dysentery, cholera and malaria. At the time, disease was by far the greatest threat to soldiers. Of the 21,000 soldiers who died in the war, only 3,000 died from injuries received in battle.

After the war Mary returned to England sick and destitute. The press highlighted her plight and her supporters, from ordinary soldiers to the Prince of Wales, rallied with fundraising events. Over 80,000 people attended a gala in her honour held over four nights at the Royal Surrey Gardens. She was awarded the Crimean Medal and the French Legion of Honour. In 1857, Mary published a best-selling autobiography entitled *The Wonderful Adventures of Mary Seacole in Many Lands*. She continued her medical work and in 1873, became masseuse to the Princess of Wales. Mary spent her final years in London and died in 1881, aged 76.

Unlike Florence Nightingale, Mary Seacole neither came from a wealthy middle class background nor had any formal training. And although both her sex and skin colour counted against her, she always managed to do precisely what she wanted to do. In her lifetime Mary was a traveller, businesswoman, writer, pioneering nurse and heroine of the Crimean War. In 2004 she was voted Greatest Black Briton in a major internet poll.

Profile: Florence Nightingale (1820-1910)

Nursing pioneer, worked at 90 Harley Street

Florence Nightingale, 'the lady of the lamp', did much to make nursing a respectable profession for women. Before her, the majority of army 'nurses' were camp followers—lower class women who followed the army around, fulfilling any functions required of them no matter how unsavoury. They certainly had no specific medical training. This was also the case in British hospitals. Nurses were little more than char women, except for those few who found themselves in positions of authority.

These were generally of higher social standing—perhaps they had once been housekeepers—but they still had no training.

Nightingale changed all that. She was born in May 1820 into a rich British family living in Italy—she was named Florence after the city of her birth. She was well-connected, well-educated and set to make a very good marriage. But that was not what she wanted. Instead she wished to take up a caring profession. The roots of this desire can be found in her childhood, during which a love of nature drove her to care for sick animals.

Certain other European countries were slightly more progressive in nursing matters than Britain at the time. Nightingale trained in two such pioneering institutions, firstly at one run by Lutheran deaconesses in Kaiserswerth, Germany and then in Paris at a hospital run by the Roman Catholic sisters of St Vincent de Paul. This training provided a solid foundation for her future reforms.

On her return to England in August 1853, Nightingale became superintendent at the Institute for the Care of Sick Gentlewomen at 90 Harley Street. By all accounts she excelled at this role.

By taking up this position, Nightingale was doing something unusual but by no means revolutionary. Positions of authority in hospitals were awarded as a matter of class rather than skill. The higher the position, the higher the class of the woman filling it. And Nightingale was of a higher class than most. She remained at the institution for just over a year, until she felt called upon to help with the situation developing in the Crimea.

In March 1854, Britain, France and Turkey declared war on Russia. When the allies defeated the Russians at the battle of the Alma in September, the *Times* criticised the British medical facilities available for the wounded. In response Sidney Herbert, the minister for war, who knew Nightingale both socially and through her Harley Street work, appointed her to oversee the introduction of female nurses into the military hospitals in Turkey.

On 4 November 1854, Nightingale arrived at the Barrack Hospital in Scutari with a party of 38 nurses. She discovered that while a great proportion of the men were dying from their wounds, many more were dying from diseases caused by the squalid conditions of the hospitals. At the time, disease was by far the greatest threat to soldiers. Of the 21,000 soldiers who died in the Crimean War, only 3,000 died from their injuries.

Nightingale recognised that cleanliness, ventilation and a regular regime of food and water would vastly improve the situation. The hospital was thoroughly cleaned and a commission sent from Britain flushed the sewers and improved ventilation. Matters began to slowly improve.

Nightingale remained in the Crimea for almost two years. During this time she met with some resistance from the doctors and army officers in charge of the hospitals. But she used her contacts—a product of her social standing—to encourage British newspapers to report the situation. *The Times* in particular provided much publicity. This led to public donations, which provided the funds to set up the Nightingale fund for the training of nurses. By the time of her return to Britain in 1857 Nightingale was a national heroine.

Florence Nightingale's contribution to the reform of nursing and hospitals was enormous. Taking advantage of her fame she set about improving standards of cleanliness and sanitation. Driven by experiences gained in both Harley Street and in the Crimea, she was convinced of the importance of providing nurses with appropriate training. In 1860 she established the Nightingale Training School at St Thomas' Hospital (now called the Florence Nightingale School of Nursing and Midwifery). The same year saw the publication of her *Notes on Nursing*, which expounded the theories about nursing which she had learnt from first-hand experience. Professional nurses who were trained under the Nightingale system would go on to permeate the medical profession both at home and abroad.

MAD, BAD &
DANGEROUS
TO KNOW

To many people, history is the study of the great men and women who, through talent and application, bent events to their will and stamped their names upon the world for all eternity. This chapter will make it clear that the publishers of the Journal do not count themselves among that number.

This is a collection of idiots, wastrels, lunatics and eccentrics. None of them left much of an impression, but without them Marylebone would have been a far greyer and less interesting place.

The death of St George Henry Lowther

By Tom Hughes
MJ3.6, Dec-Jan 2007-8)

In early February 1882, the streets of Marylebone were shrouded in the worst fog in memory. This isn't mere atmospheric Victorian flummery — it really happened. According to the *Times*, it got so bad that "street traffic was impeded and gradually suspended". On Wednesday 8 February, one of the few hansom cabs daring to move about in the murk, pulled up outside 30 Bryanston Street. Several gentlemen came out of the house carrying a shrouded body, which they placed inside the cab. The cabman chucked his horse to warily move on in the fog.

If anyone saw this solemn event unfold, they probably wouldn't have paid any particular attention. Another death in the Great Smoke. How sad indeed. *Popular Science Monthly* reported: "An extraordinarily high death rate which was recorded in London for the week ending 11th February was ascribed to the dense fog which had been prevailing."

The choking miasma was claiming victims, young and old, high and low in station. Among the most notable victims, at the tender age of 27, was St George Henry Lowther, the 4th Earl of Lonsdale.

It was announced that he had died in his splendid home in Carlton House Terrace. But that was, to put it bluntly, a barefaced lie. In fact the body quietly removed from Marylebone and borne discreetly to St James was that of the late — and largely unlamented — peer. The ruse apparently fooled few people and even fewer would mourn his passing: "All things considered, his death will not be a great loss to the English peerage."

Today, Bryanston Street sits in the shadows of the huge tourist hotels at the west end of Oxford Street. In 1882, it was a street of rooming houses and small 'hotels'. St John's Wood was the bosky retreat where a Victorian gentleman could house his "proper mistress". But if a more casual "bit of what you fancy" happened along, Marylebone would do quite nicely — and save in cab fares as well.

At 30 Bryanston Street, on the north-east corner at Old Quebec Street, stood Neumeister's Hotel, under the management of George Neumeister.

It is easy to imagine 'mein host' being intimately involved in the quiet removal of a lifeless aristocrat from his establishment. Fortunately, Herr Neumeister had the assistance of a future prime minister. The Earl of Rosebery recalled the evening in his diary: "To 30 Bryanston St, where Lonsdale is dying. He is dying in the house he took to give actresses supper in. His wife does not leave Monte Carlo till tomorrow night. His brother is here in the next room cheerfully smoking cigarettes till the end comes, passing away incognito as it were from a world which appeared to reserve every blessing to continue for him, and where he never spent a happy hour. It was a squalid end, to be sure."

St George—as the family knew him—had succeeded to his peerage in 1876, at the age of 21. He stood six foot three and even in his teens was renowned as a horseman, yachtsman, gambler and drinker. Upon his succession, he used his fortune lavishly in pursuit of all those interests. It was thought a good marriage would steady him, so the news of his betrothal should have been well received.

The young lady was of impeccable pedigree—at 19, Lady Gwladys Herbert was a striking beauty, equally tall (standing 6 feet) and sister of the earl of Pembroke. In the more knowing drawing rooms of London, however, the direst predictions were heard. Lady Gwladys was a rebellious and extravagant girl who delighted in being called 'the Gypsy', a soubriquet that hardly marked her out as the settling influence Lonsdale so badly needed. Her own family opposed the marriage, meaning that the wedding at St Paul's, Knightsbridge, in July 1878, was all the more remarkable for who did not attend.

In the weeks following the nuptials, the couple crossed Europe, ransacking galleries, auction houses and jewellers for paintings and bric-a-brac to adorn Carlton House Terrace and, of course, the new Countess of Lonsdale. Upon her return, Gwladys appeared in a satin dress costing over £100 (quite a lot, back in the day) and wearing what were described as "magnificent diamonds". It was whispered that the couple had spent £100,000 on jewels alone.

Carlton House Terrace may have been lavishly furnished, but the couple rarely lived there together. Other than a love of reckless spending and an ability to appear regularly in gossip columns, the couple had little in common. St George was written up for being among the gentlemen in heated pursuit of Lily Langtry. In his defence, such "gentlemen" were pretty thick on the ground for a season or two. But the town talked too about Lady Gwladys—her name being linked with that of John Lister-Kaye, a wealthy, but notorious young Yorkshire squire. The rumours of her misconduct became so open that her brother, the Earl of Pembroke, ordered her out of London and back to the family home at Wilton House.

St George was often away as well, most of the time aboard his newly purchased steam yacht Northumbria, which in sober moments he talked of sailing to the North Pole. The cost of any such expedition was out of the question as the honeymoon bills and ongoing expenses were "even more than the princely income of the Lowther estates could stand". It was considered very bad form when Lonsdale made a legal declaration that he was no longer responsible for his wife's debts. When Gwladys made a rare visit to Lowther Castle, St George absented himself and left word with his agent that the Countess would be billed for her visit: "If we pay she does not care. If she pays she will take care." And so life continued for St George and Gwladys. He was at sea and rarely sober, while she, eventually freed from Wilton, entertained and socialised in London. In the delicate phrasing of the family historian, the Countess "unexpectedly" gave birth to a daughter in 1881.

By now, St George's drinking and dissipation had all but destroyed his health. With no male heir likely, the earldom would pass to his next youngest brother Hugh. The present and future earl had a cordial disdain for each other. At the end, in Bryanston Street, Hugh was the chap mentioned in Rosebery's diary, "cheerfully smoking cigarettes" in the next room. Long live the 5th Earl of Lonsdale.

Typically, the English press refrained from too much censorious comment on the death of the 4th Earl of Lonsdale. When there is little to say, little is said. Harsher assessments reached foreign readers: "He deliberately elected to trample the purple under his feet. He besmirched the name of his family with a mire of worthless associations and coarse practices."

Gwladys did the right thing and returned from Monte Carlo for the funeral, however unwelcome she might have been. She was a dowager countess at 23—still young and pretty enough to get in a lot more trouble, which she did. The Lonsdales now rested the family hopes on the new earl: "Few people can regret, either in the interest of the protagonist himself, or of his friends, that the curtain has now fallen. His family may be congratulated that the title and estates devolve upon that one of his brothers who is best suited for the responsibility."

Well said, indeed. Unfortunately young Hugh would, in the next decade, eclipse even St George's record for scandal and disgrace. For the sake of the good and decent people of Marylebone, Hugh possessed the good breeding to misbehave elsewhere.

Lady Mary Jeune, the real Lady Bracknell

By Tom Hughes

MJ6.2, Apr-May 2010

Harley Street has long been one of the most agreeable in London. Ramrod straight, as any respectable street should be, and sheltered from Oxford Street's noise and uncouth commerce by Cavendish Square, Harley Street proceeds north, lined with Georgian brick terraces. The walker's eye follows the narrowing perspective to the green burst of trees ahead at Regent's Park. Though the brass plaques in today's Harley Street doorways identify public relations firms and chartered accountants as well as cardiologists or surgeons, the overwhelming feel of the street has not changed. It can be summed up in one word—discretion. With the reader's permission, we shall single out one such doorway in Harley Street. After all, it was once said that 79 Harley Street was "the acknowledged rendezvous" of London society.

The man of the house was Sir Francis Jeune, a successful barrister who rose to be president of the Court of Divorce, Probate and the Admiralty. All due respect and honour should be paid to this venerable jurist but, it must be said, the most famous occupant of 79 Harley Street was in fact his wife, the redoubtable Lady Mary Jeune. At her death, the claim was made that "in the last 30 years of the 19th century, few women were better known in London society than Lady Jeune, probably few women were better known in all England".

Mary Susan Elizabeth Mackenzie was a Scot, born in Seaforth into an ancient Highland family but raised "as a Spartan child in austerity and simplicity". Her first husband, one of the Stanleys of Alderly, had died quite young. She and Francis Jeune were married in 1881.

While her husband went off to the Royal Courts on the Strand each day to deal with fractured marriages and disputed wills, Lady Jeune sat at home and planned her weekly "evenings". Invitations were coveted. Trans-Atlantic visitors would arrive clutching their "letters of introduction". To 79 Harley Street came politicians, writers (Thomas Hardy kept a room there), artists, and notable visitors from the Continent or the States. Said one man who went everywhere: "I go to Lady Jeune's because I never know whom I shall meet, but I know there will always be somebody I shall like to meet." Lady Dorothy Nevill, Lady Jeune's Mayfair-based rival, could only but graciously declare: "As regards parties, no one who is in the habit of being asked to them will ever forget the delightful assemblages of interesting people collected together by clever Lady Jeune."

It was, therefore, quite a shock when Lady Jeune let loose with a furious screed denouncing fin-de-siecle London society. In May of 1892, an article written by Her Ladyship appeared in an American monthly, The North American Review. The 1890s were a difficult time for a society hostess who wished to maintain the proper tone to her gatherings.

Those who should be leading by example were failing. The titular leader of London society, the Prince of Wales was in bad odour over his involvement in a squalid baccarat scandal (Gasp, he travelled with his own deck of cards!) There was a spate of shocking incidents that could be loosely lumped under the category of "earls and girls". And, perhaps most troubling, pushy middle-class arrivistes seemed to be everywhere. Even, heaven forbid, in Harley Street.

Lady Jeune declared: "There never was an age where fame of any kind was more of a cult, or where notoriety was more of a passport to social eminence. Society now runs mad after anyone who can get himself talked of." All of this may seem familiar to a modern audience inured as we are to the "it" crowd of the month that steals the headlines, but in 1892, it was rather shocking. These nouveaux riches were everywhere, and Her Ladyship warned against relaxing one's guard. She saw nothing but trouble to come from "the easy going manner in which women of the highest rank and culture have allowed the old-fashioned rules and restraints which governed society to be relaxed".

To be sure, there's a touch of the rantings of Lady Bracknell in all this earnestness. Wilde's character, almost certainly inspired by Lady Jeune, bangs on about the decay of good society: "It seems to me to display a contempt for the ordinary decencies of family life which reminds one of the worst excesses of the French revolution." Another writer actually suggested that Lady Jeune would likely endorse a novel plan to cleanse society of such interlopers: "A boat should be started, say, every

Wednesday morning from Tilbury Dock, bearing one week its load of West End loungers, and the next a like load of East End loafers, the cargo to be discharged in mid-ocean." Others wrote her off as a Tory defender of the status quo, lost in the foggy depths of her fogeydom.

This blowback from her critics did not silence Lady Jeune. From her sitting room in Harley Street she sent forth many more articles, all more or less on the theme of "English Society As It Is". Nor was she without defenders, the London correspondent of the New York Times among them: "One who has watched what calls itself society here with observant eyes for any length of time cannot but rejoice that a serious and brave little woman has been impelled to give voice to the disgust with which the spectacle inspires in honest people."

All was not lost—the forces of good society rallied and held their square through the last years of Old Victoria. Even the randy prince comported himself with some discretion on his Edwardian throne. It took the horrors of the Great War to put an end to the halcyon days of Harley Street salons for London's better classes. Lady Jeune saw that all happen—she lived until 1931. At her death, by then little-remembered, readers were reminded of her legendary status as a Victorian hostess. The oft-told apocryphal story re-appeared about the explorer captured by cannibals. As the hapless prisoner was being trussed up for his roasting, the chieftain peered at him more closely. "I know your face," he said. "We have met at my friend Lady Jeune's, and so instead of dining off you, I shall you ask you to dine with me and tell me all the London news."

William Wellesley's final humiliation

By Tom Hughes

MJ6.6, Dec-Jan 2010-11)

Thayer Street is a curious affair. The up-market buzz of the high street has not quite seeped down to Thayer Street. It was much the same in 1857. The census for that period reveals a street peopled by shopkeepers, paper-hangers, ironmongers and their ilk, with the odd rooms to let "over the store". It was in one such room above number 16 that, on 1 July 1857, the Rt Hon William Pole Tylney Long Wellesley shuffled off this mortal coil. He was 69. The more respectful papers reported that the earl had died "at his residence" in London. The cheekier press said that Wellesley had breathed his last "in obscure lodgings".

In truth, the earl had been consigned to well-earned obscurity for three decades, all brought about by his own disgrace. He was a scion of the great Wellesley family of Ireland, and his uncle was no less a man than the Duke of Wellington. In 1812, at the tender age of 24 and with his family's fortunes at a low ebb, William did what all noble sprats must do in such a situation—he married a rich woman.

With creditable persistence, he proposed six times to Catherine Tylney-Long. She accepted him on the seventh plea. Her mistake. Catherine was an heiress from Wiltshire and it was said that she was the richest commoner in the kingdom. William, in gratitude for his great marital good fortune, added the Tylney-Long names to his own. He then began spending that fortune so wildly that those who supped and drank at his table quipped, "Long may Long-Tilney-Wellesley-Long-Pole live."

At his—or, rather, Catherine's—home at Wanstead Park in Essex, William threw lavish entertainments. His Waterloo victory party cost a pile. The Iron Duke, who rode up unescorted, went unrecognised by the drunken revelers and soon took his leave. The Tylney-Long money ran out (as money will when spent so thoughtlessly), and soon William was doing a runner himself. To escape the bailiffs, he fled to the continent, levanting in an open boat on the Thames. Wanstead Park and its contents were auctioned off before huge crowds of gawkers; the great hall went unsold and was then pulled down. Catherine and the couple's three children retreated to Wiltshire to take shelter with her family. William, it must be said, lived as he spent—profligately. Word would soon reach Catherine from Brussels that William was living flagrantly with the wife of an officer of the Coldstream Guards. Catherine's humiliation was to be brief, for she died in 1825 from "inflammation of the bowels". Even *Bell's Life*, the journal for the sporting set, took pity on her: "Let her fate be a warning to all of her sex, who, blessed with affluence, think the buzzing throng which surround them have hearts, when, in fact, they have none."

William dared not face his creditors by crossing the Channel for his wife's funeral, but sent peremptory word that his children must be surrendered to him at once. Catherine's dying wish had been that they never see their father again and they were placed under armed guard. So bad was the odour surrounding William that his suit to take custody was rejected— one of the very few times that a father's rights were set aside by an English court. William soon married his paramour, after her divorce from Captain Bligh (no, not that one). This second matrimonial venture went no better than the first—William and Helena lived what was known as a "cat and dog existence" for six years, and she bore him several children before they separated.

William did not return to England until the death of his father, the 3rd Earl, in 1845. Close on his heels was Helena, now entitled to call herself the Countess of Mornington. Her numerous appeals to the courts for support for herself and the children were a public scandal. The old duke, in his final years, intervened and paid her off to save the family name from further disgrace.

William was also placed on the duke's dole, taking monthly handouts, although he professed "great mortification" at having to submit to such charity. The Mornington's home in Grosvenor Square was sold off and William (it does not seem right to call him "the earl") moved from rooms to rooms, settling in the Thayer Street lodgings in 1853; the place where, four years later, he would meet his end.

Mrs Brooks was his landlady and Edward King, his loyal valet. At the inquest following the Wellesley's death — held at the Coachmakers Arms in Marylebone Lane — King said that his master had latterly been unwell, complaining of pains in the chest. On the night of the first of July,

William turned away Mrs Brooks's dinner of fowl. He suddenly cried out, "Good God, what can ail me?" At that, the valet continued, William collapsed and spoke no more. A doctor came round from Portland Place, but it was too late. Poor King burst into tears as he told the coroner that the earl had lived his last years in want and destitution. After the great duke's death in 1852, the 2nd Duke of Wellington had chosen to reduce William's allowance. The jury also heard some talk of the earl's drinking habits (greatly reduced in later years), and his love for life which made a suicide so unlikely. In the end, all agreed to a statement of "death due to heart disease".

Ducal carriages are not often seen in Thayer Street. The local residents stood silently on the morning of 9 June 1857, as the carriage of the Duke of Wellington led the procession from 16 Thayer Street "without pomp or ostentation." The earl was carted off to await the last trumpet in the catacombs at Kensal Green. Few mourned his death; a Major Richardson wrote to the papers decrying the generally censorious comments on the passing of his "lamented friend". The major's was a lone voice. The death of such a long-forgotten miscreant gave the press a new chance to rake up the muck and moralise. The *Morning Chronicle* was typical in its verdict: "This most unworthy representative of the honour of the elder branch of the House of Wellesley" was "redeemed by no single virtue, adorned by no single grace. His life has gone out, even without a flicker of repentance. His retirement was that of one who was deservedly avoided by all men."

The strange legacy of Joanna Southcott

By Jean-Paul Aubin-Parvu
MJ2.4, Aug-Sep 2006

On 19 October 1814, Joanna Southcott lay writhing around in her bedroom at 38 Manchester Street, ready to give birth to the Messiah.

Southcott was born in 1750 at Gittisham in Devon, where she spent her early years working as a farm labourer and a domestic servant. Then, in 1792, her mother died. Joanna became gripped by mystical fervour, claiming to be in direct communications with God. She started making daily prophecies that drew on millenarian themes of a New Jerusalem and the Second Coming.

The French Revolution of 1789 ushered in a long period of political and social turbulence in Britain. To the establishment, the cold steel of the guillotine symbolised the beginning of the end of Christian civilisation. Soon wars raged across Europe and Napoleon stood poised to conquer Britain. Yet, for many religious dissenters these events were a signal of the imminent return of Christ.

The visionaries were everywhere. As Joanna Southcott foretold how large proportions of the population would perish against Napoleon's invasion forces, the great William Blake saw "dark satanic mills" in his Jerusalem, while Richard Brothers overstepped the mark by prophesying the death of the king and the end of monarchy. This self-declared Prince of the Hebrews was arrested for treason and imprisoned. Strange days indeed.

In 1801, Joanna Southcott published a book, *The Strange Effects of Faith*, a mix of doggerel and prose relating to her alleged conversations with God. It became a bestseller. Joanna moved to 38 Manchester Street and became a national celebrity. Dozens of societies were set up throughout the country to discuss and interpret her works. Though often derided by both public and press, Southcott's following included members of the clergy, theologians, scholars and leading artists. Thousands bought signed letters bearing her red Celestial seal. Costing as much as a guinea each, these letters became known as 'passports to heaven'.

Joanna made an unabashed claim to be the woman spoken of in

Revelation (12:1-5): "And there appeared a great wonder in heaven; a woman clothed with the sun, and the moon under her feet, and upon her head a crown of 12 stars: And she being with child cried, travailing in birth and pained to be delivered... and she brought forth a man child, who was to rule all nations with a rod of iron."

And so, in 1814, the 64-year-old Joanna stated that she was pregnant with the Messiah. The baby was due on 19 October and would be called Shiloh, a name of an Old Testament city. It was, of course, an immaculate conception. She made it clear that no man had come anywhere near her. This was purely the work of God.

There was great excitement among her followers, marked by a major outbreak of praying. Many disciples sold businesses and uprooted to London to await the Messiah. Supported by donations, Southcott had moved into 38 Manchester Street in the plush suburb of Marylebone.

In preparation for the Second Coming, gifts began to arrive by mail coach. They included an elaborate silver-mounted cradle, a gold font and large sums of money. As the midwives of London fought for the honour of delivering the Messiah, shops were filled with Joanna Southcott paraphernalia, such as cradles containing Shiloh dolls. Even the great and the good became hooked. Both the Russian ambassador and the Tsar's aide-de-camp came to visit, as did more than 20 doctors, including both the French empress Josephine's own gynaecologist and the royal physician, Dr Richard Reece. Upon examining Joanna, the majority declared that despite her age she did appear to display all the normal signs of pregnancy.

The newspapers had a field day. The Napoleonic Wars were relegated to the inside pages of the *Times* and the *Daily Monitor* to make room for daily reports about Joanna and her Holy Shiloh. And according to one newspaper: "Excitement could not have been more intense if the dome of St Paul's had collapsed."

October came and went, yet no baby appeared. As Christmas approached, Dr Reece was called upon to examine Joanna. He was heard to mutter: "Damn me if the child has not gone."

Joanna was by now in great pain. On Christmas Day she stated that the pain was in her side and that the baby was attempting to enter the world. She soon fell into a coma and two days later took on what her followers called "the appearance of death". At 3am on 28 December this was confirmed by a doctor as actual death. A post-mortem examination resulted in the discovery that Joanna had dropsy. Internal flatulence and glandular enlargement of the breasts had given the appearance of pregnancy. Joanna Southcott was buried in St John's Wood churchyard on 1 January 1815.

Though many disciples became disillusioned, the inner core remained undaunted. They believed that Shiloh had been born on Christmas Day as Joanna had foreseen, but had been whisked straight up to the heavens to save him from the dragon. It was a wise precaution: this was the great red dragon "with seven heads and 10 horns and seven crowns upon his heads that would devour the child as soon as it was born" (Revelation 12:1-6). These disciples firmly believed that Joanna and Shiloh would return to lead them all into paradise.

One of these faithful followers was a farmer called John Wroe who had joined a Southcottian sect in Leeds in 1820. The previous year, Wroe had been struck down with a life-threatening illness but had made a miraculous recovery; after which he began to experience visions and trances. By December 1822, Prophet Wroe had become leader of a sect that became known as the Christian Israelites.

On 29 February 1824, at Apperley Bridge, north of Bradford, a crowd of 30,000 gathered on the banks of the River Aire eager to watch Wroe perform a miracle, although exactly what miracle he would perform was still being hotly debated. Most anticipated him parting the waters of the Aire and walking across the dry riverbed. Others expected him to literally walk on water. Alas, the prophet sank like a stone into the freezing depths. Large factions of the crowd erupted angrily. They gave Wroe another good ducking before setting about him with sticks, mud and stones.

A few months later, fresh controversy stuck to the prophet like Aire river mud. He and a girl named Sarah Lees found themselves "with child", causing more than a little eyebrow raising among the congregation. Wroe tried to calm things by claiming that this was all part of God's divine plan. It would in fact be the Second Coming of the boy Messiah. Again. On 17 July 1824 the big moment came. The congregation looked up to heaven and rejoiced. Yet, the midwife's cries of "It's a girl!" were not quite what they'd been expecting. The prophecy had failed. Wroe thought it prudent to skip town and crossed the Peak District to Ashton-under-Lyne near Manchester.

This town would, claimed Wroe, be the New Jerusalem where the 144,000 elect would gather at the time of the Apocalypse. And luckily Ashton had plenty of wealthy Chosen People to pay for the building of the Holy City. They built a gatehouse on each of the four corners of the town marking the Gates to the Temple of the Children of Israel. The central citadel of Wroe's New Jerusalem was known as The Sanctuary. This place of worship cost a fortune to build and was opened by Wroe and his followers on Christmas Day 1825. The church had an "unclean" pew where women accused of "unchastity" were made to sit during the service. They would then be taken to the "cleansing room", beneath the pulpit, to be stripped naked then whipped raw by the prophet with a birch rod.

Prophet Wroe received a command from God to take seven virgins to "cherish and comfort" him. The church elders stated that Wroe and the virgins would act in every way as husband and wife except that there would be no sexual intercourse. Perish the thought. The race was on to find seven virgins in Ashton. Virgins must have been a bit thin on the ground as a few married women were drafted in to make up the numbers.

And soon there were fewer virgins still. In 1827, 12-year-old Martha Whitley accused Wroe of sexual interference, and further allegations from other young girls began to reach the ears of the Society of Christian Israelites. They held an inquiry at which fighting broke out and "pandemonium reigned". John Wroe left Ashton under cover of darkness.

The prophet returned to Bradford and within a week had sparked a riot. He settled in Wrenthorpe near Wakefield, where he built himself a fabulous private mansion, Melbourne House, entirely paid for by his followers. During Wroe's lifetime he made many trips to Australia, building an impressive following. In the summer of 1862, he voyaged there for the last time. He died the following February at the Christian Israelites Sanctuary in Fitzroy, Melbourne.

But that wasn't the end of Joanna Southcott's legacy. On her deathbed, Joanna left behind a sealed box. She told the trusted custodians that it should only be opened in a time of national emergency when the contents would reveal the means of saving the country. Nobody knew what the box contained except that the contents must be important. Along with other conditions, Joanna stated that it should only be opened in the presence of 24 bishops of the Church of England.

There were repeated calls during both the Boer Wars and the First World War to have the vessel opened, but England's bishops always showed a marked reluctance to rummage in Joanna's box. There was also plenty of debate about who had taken possession of the actual box and where they might have put it.

In 1927, Harry Price of the National Laboratory of Psychical Research said that he had received the sealed box along with a letter stating its authenticity. He organised a public ceremony at the Hoare Memorial Hall, Westminster on 11 July to which he invited three archbishops and 80 bishops. Only the Bishop of Grantham attended. Instead, the hall was packed out with the press, psychic enthusiasts, mediums and a colourful assortment of crackpots. Followers from two Southcott societies caused a disturbance, declaring the event to be sacrilege.

Gasps rang out as Price went at the box enthusiastically with a pair of metal shears. After cutting the bands he prized the lid open with a jemmy. The 56 items inside were held up dramatically to the audience. They included a lottery ticket from 1796, religious pamphlets, a selection of racy novels, a woman's night cap, a dice box, a bone puzzle and a pair of gold earrings. The silence in the hall must have been deafening. The Panacea Society, based in Bedford, strongly deny that was this box was genuine, and claims to have the real Southcott box in its possession. The society won't reveal the exact location of the Ark of the Testament (said to weigh 156lb and the size of a small coffin) but says that it's being held for safe keeping in a secret location in the Bedford area.

The Panacea Society was formed just after the First World War by Mabel Barlthrop (known as Octavia), Helen Exeter, Rachael Fox and Kate Firth, who each felt that the world might be a better place if only the bishops would attend to Joanna's box. They soon discovered that Barlthrop, who a decade earlier had suffered a mental breakdown, was actually the reincarnation of Southcott's divine Shiloh child.

Since the 1920s the society has taken out regular advertisements in national newspapers and on billboards. They carry the chilling message: "Crime, Banditry, Distress of Nations and Perplexity will continue until the Bishops of the Church of England agree to open Joanna Southcott's Box of Prophecies." All warnings have been ignored.

The distinguished failure of Francis of Teck

By Tom Hughes
MJ10.5, Oct-Nov 2014

Marylebone's Welbeck Street can often be ignored. A block or so shorter than its grander parallel neighbours to the east, Harley and Wimpole, Welbeck Street's attractions for the historical wanderer are few. In fact, in the last century, Welbeck Street was rather cruelly known as "the street of distinguished failures". If so, it was a fine place for the last days of Prince Francis of Teck.

Frank, as he preferred to be known, was born at Kensington Palace in 1870, the third of four children of the Duke and Duchess of Teck. His father was a penniless German royal who out-punched his weight class by marrying a granddaughter of George III, albeit a young lady known as "Fat Mary". The Teck dynasty was an old one, based in Württemberg, but the family finances were notoriously shambolic. After the wedding, the Tecks settled in London. The Marquise de Fontenoy, an ever waspish observer, reported that the Tecks were "generally considered as the ne'er-do-wells of the Royal family...and treated very much in the manner of poor relations." As is too often the case with poor relations, they were also very numerous. It got to the point that Queen Victoria ordered the Tecks to clear off to the Continent, where they might live more cheaply.

Thus it was a happy day in the Teck ménage when their only daughter, Mary, became engaged to the eldest son of the Prince of Wales. Alas, that affianced young man died rather suddenly in the flu epidemic of 1892. But after a suitable period of grief, Mary, having really no other plans, quite charmingly agreed to engage herself to the next chap in line (the future George V). They were married in 1893 and their marriage was a stalwart success.

As in-laws now of rank, the Duke and Duchess of Teck were again in the ascendant. They were welcomed back to Blighty and lived in a great old place in Richmond Park. All was going well for the Teck family, but Frank remained a "source of considerable worry and anxiety to his family." His early schooling had produced dismal results. As a younger son, Frank had no obligations and thus would be expected to find something to do. The military was thought to be the answer. Somehow he made his way through Sandhurst and looked every bit the part of a dashing dragoon in his army kit. Good looks were never a problem; Frank stood six-foot-three and was "formed like an Apollo". Women, it was said, found him irresistible and the feeling was mutual.

At around the time his sister Mary was set to marry a future king, Frank was an embarrassing distraction in the gossip pages. He was publicly smitten with and attentive to the only daughter and heiress to a great brewing house on the Trent. With a fortune estimated at half a million pounds, the young lady had announced her arrival in London:

"I am Nellie Bass of Bass—the beer, you know! And jolly good beer it is, too." Alas, last orders were called on the relationship as the family thought a royal marriage into the 'beerage' was not on.

The usual Pomeranian palaces were diligently canvassed to find Frank a suitable mate, but without success. For a while, hearts fluttered at the prospect that Frank might be interested in Princess Maud, daughter of the Prince of Wales. But Frank could never muster the needed ardour to come up to scratch with the rather plain Maud.

The relationship ended badly. The princess was genuinely hurt and Frank had made no friends with her father, his future sovereign. Did we mention that Frank enjoyed the odd flutter? In 1897, he reportedly lost £10,000 in one bet on a horse race at the Curragh, near Dublin. He faced social disgrace as he certainly had no way to meet the debt. The exasperated royals cobbled together the funds to settle up but all were agreed, the wretched boy had to go. He was exiled to Africa. Frank spent the last years of the 19th century serving his Queen from Cairo, via Khartoum, to the Cape.

Following the Boer War, Frank returned to London having served honourably and restored his reputation. Needing to make some kind of an income, he thought he might try his hand in the City, and managed to get on with the old firm of Panmure Gordon & Co.

Again, there were problems—mostly generated by an embarrassing spate of press articles chuckling over the prospect of "a prince in trade". The uproar put paid to Frank's employment hopes. Frank was now settled in rooms at 36 Welbeck Street. His princely title was always coveted by charities for use on their letterhead and Frank found himself serving as patron and the honourary chairman of both Middlesex Hospital and the Royal Automobile Club. If he has a legacy, it is the RAC clubhouse in Pall Mall. He raised the funds and supervised the project to an early completion. His secret? "I sent to America for American foremen and put them in charge."

In his private life, Frank had found equal solace. He had taken as his mistress Ellen Constance, Countess of Kilmorey, the beautiful wife of an Irish peer. It was a very Edwardian affair. 'Frank and Nellie' were quite discrete. Still, everyone seemed to know. Frank even attended the Kilmorey daughters' wedding.

King Edward VII died in early May 1910; long live George V and his queen, Mary of Teck. A month later, Frank checked into a private hospital at 15 Welbeck Street for some minor nasal surgery. Following the procedure, he went to Balmoral where the royals were still grieving the old King. But whilst in Scotland, Frank contracted pneumonia. Once he was strong enough to return to London, he re-entered the Welbeck Street facility where his condition quickly worsened. His cause of death aged 40 was "acute pleurisy".

As Frank lay dying in Welbeck Street, the King and Queen visited him daily. It was these visits that gave rise to the legend of "the Cambridge emeralds". Frank's mother, the daughter of the Duke of Cambridge, had purchased the stones with her winnings from a lottery. True story. When she passed away, the duchess left the gems to Frank. In Frank's "embarrassingly generous" will, he was planning to bequeath the stones to Lady Kilmorey.

The idea that these royal family gems would grace the neck of an Irish mistress was a non-starter. The palace and the countess palavered at length. The Irishwoman drove a hard bargain. Money changed hands (there are estimates that, in today's money, it cost £800,000 to get the stones back). The public were unaware of this drama as Frank's will was ordered sealed. It set a precedent, establishing a tradition that controversially stands to this day, disappointing the curious any time a royal crosses the bar, specifically princesses Margaret and Diana.

The Welbeck Hospital matron, Miss Clara Nelson Smith, received the Royal Victorian Medal for her services to Frank and the royals. Queen Mary wore the emeralds she retrieved in Welbeck Street at her coronation in 1912. More recently, they were among Diana's favourite baubles; she delighted to wear them as a headband.

The horse banquet at the Langham Hotel

By Tom Hughes
MJ8.2, Apr-May 2012

When the Langham Hotel opened on Portland Place in 1865, it was proclaimed to be the largest and most modern establishment in London. The luxuries on offer were unheard of at the time. Nearly a century and a half later the Langham remains one of the truly iconic grand hotels in the city. The names on the hotel register read from King Edward VII to Princess Diana, Churchill to de Gaulle, Oscar Wilde to Noel Coward.

One of the more memorable evenings in the annals of the Langham Hotel was certainly 6 February 1868, when a select group of gentlemen sat down to the Banquet Hippophagique or, what the cynics insisted on calling the Great Horse Dinner. England had just come through another of those periodic outbreaks of foot-and-mouth disease, similar to that of 2001, and the beef industry had been badly affected. The wealthy were always able to find safe viands for their table but the supply of edible and affordable beef for the poor had nearly disappeared. This gave rise to a campaign for the English to set aside their prejudices and eat horse meat. What better way to educate the English palate to the delights of hippophagy than to put on a grand meal in the finest dining room in London?

The Langham's spectacular Salle à Manger was some 140 feet long by 40 feet wide, beneath a 24 foot ceiling, supported by faux Carrara marble columns that lined the room. The kitchen staff below moved plates to the dining room via a small tram that served several small lifts. The workings of the Langham kitchen produced "expressions of wonderment" to all who had the chance to visit. On this occasion, the noble room above was set for 150; the cost of the meal was a guinea-and-a-half. The guests included numerous MPs—they would need to be persuaded to change abattoir laws to allow the slaughter of horses—leading medical men, scientists, and journalists (who, of course, will never look a gift horse in the mouth).

The 'horse-play', if you will, enlivened the evening. When all had been seated, Algernon Sidney Bicknell, the principle organiser, cheerfully acknowledged the wags and punsters who were present. He had heard all the jokes before, he warned them ("Straight from the horse's mouth").

But Bicknell asserted there was a serious purpose for the gathering, albeit accompanied by an excellent meal. With so much poverty and hunger in London, Bicknell argued that it was simply wrong that 75,000 horses a year were knackered and all that good meat wasted. Prejudices were to blame. Pigs were vile creatures and England loved its pork. Horses, on the other hoof, were quite fastidious eaters. The point of the banquet was to make clear that horse meat tastes good and, at less than three-pence a pound, was quite affordable.

Enough talk, the diners were chomping at the bit. The menus were handed out. They'd been written almost entirely in French, so it helped to know that the French word for horse is 'cheval'. There were to be 10 courses in total, with several options available for each course. The soup was 'le consommé du cheval'. The hors d'oeuvres included "les saucisses de cheval aux Pistaches Syriaques". The main courses were carried into the room with great solemnity as a Beefeater (ironically) played the Roast Beef of Old England on his cornet.

Placed before the multitude were "le filet de Pegase roti aux pomme de terre a la crème", "la culotte de cheval draisee aux chevaux-des-frise" and, lastly, "kromeskya a la Gladiateur". (The latter was a croquette of horse meat that had been named for the reigning turf champion of the day. Happily for Gladiateur himself, the steed was still running at the time and later lived out a long and happy life in stud.) Those diners who had an appetite for afters were then tempted with such delights as "la gelee de pieds de cheval au marasquin" or "les zephirs sautes a l'huile chevaleresque".

Mr Bicknell graciously conceded that anything would taste good when prepared in a fine kitchen, served well-sauced and accompanied by excellent wines. But to prove that horse meat was also an affordable and practical meal for the poor, the gentlemen were urged to sample the buffet, where cheaper cuts of horse meat had been prepared without any fussy Gallic cooking techniques. There was plainly no need to Frenchify the buffet for the masses: the selection was limited to "collared horse head, a roast of Baron, and boiled withers".

You could not have held such a meal in London without the presence of Frank Buckland. One of those true Victorian oddballs, Buckland was trained as a doctor, but became England's foremost naturalist. Today he would most likely be starring in some kind of animal-based reality show on Channel 4. He was also a zoöphagist—an eater of exotic animals. His father, a country cleric, had fed the children battered mice and squirrel, and from those culinary beginnings Frank had set out to eat the entire animal kingdom. In his home near Regent's Park, he set up a test kitchen to feed his wary guests anything from eland to stewed mole.

Plainly, Buckland's verdict on horse meat was going to be vital to the effort and the hippophagists waited with as much trepidation as modern restaurateurs cross their ladles in the hope of a kind word from AA Gill or Fay Maschler. Alas, Buckland crushed them. Perhaps once you have enjoyed the ambrosia of a stewed mole, horse flesh seems rather a step down. But Buckland insisted that he had sampled everything on the menu and, with no offense meant to the efforts of the Langham's excellent kitchen, he couldn't abide any of it. "The meat is nasty," he wrote in a public letter, with "an unwanted and peculiar taste that could be disagreeably recognised".

The whole room smelled, he said, of a hard-ridden horse put up in a stall. During the dinner, he stood up to look around at his fellow diners. He thought most of them seemed to take their fork in hand with a shudder. Each bite was quickly washed down with a quaff of the plentiful champagne kindly made available by the Langham. Buckland noted that while all the bottles went back empty, very few of the plates were clean. He declared that horse meat should be left for starving travellers, hunters, and "cavalry troops separated from their commissariat".

Buckland was not alone. A writer who attended on behalf of an American publication disclosed that the after-effects of the dinner were most unpleasant, "I confess that I suffered tortures over which I will draw a veil." But, generally speaking, the reviews were at least polite. The reporter from the *Penny Illustrated Paper* informed his readers: "It is quite possible to dine off horse, even your first meal, without nausea."

The attendee from the *Medical Times* found everything served at the main table to be quite palatable. However, he sampled a cut of the "roast of

Baron" off the buffet and found that it "left a pungency on the palate that is not agreeable and stays with the diner for some time." Such neigh-sayers, if you'll pardon the expression, did not ruin the evening. The organisers had done their own sampling of opinions among the tables and boasted that the far more widely held opinion was that horseflesh is "fine in texture, tender in quality and unimpeachable in flavour".

The Hippophagic enthusiasm was soon an all but forgotten dietary crank. The English just never could get the taste for it. Some blamed the proponents for over-selling their case. They should have set out to prove only that horse meat is better than no meat at all, not that it rivals beef or pork. Horse meat found its way to very few English sideboards – knowingly, at least. Less scrupulous butchers were always out there and customers were warned to be wary of "sausage makers of hippophagic tendencies".

The green door of Reverend and Mrs Haweis

By Tom Hughes

MJ8.4, Aug-Sep 2012

The Georgian streets of Marylebone cannot be said to 'run' north from Oxford Street—rather they appear to march lockstep to the north. The 18th century planners who mapped out the terraces of the Harleys, Wimpoles, and Welbecks in this part of the Big Smoke were grimly wedded to their straight-edge. Let the Victorians come along and playfully dabble elsewhere in circles and crescents but such was never quite the done thing in Marylebone. The streetscape remained one of hard right angles and rows of houses in their regimental lines, which to the eye created a narrowing file of smoke-blackened brick. Doorway after doorway after doorway.

It was, therefore, almost with alarm that, in 1873, Londoners came to gawp at the goings on at number 16 Welbeck Street. Mary Haweis, the wife of a local clergyman, had got the madcap notion that she would splash a bit of colour into this drab picture. She decided that the facing of her home should be painted moss green, with the windows trimmed in red and black. And so it was done. By her. Of course, ladder-climbing women DIY painters were not thick on the ground in the Marylebone of 1873. The curious gathered to watch and to offer their cheeky encouragement. For the closer neighbours, however, there was probably less shock to all this. The likely reaction was, "Oh bother, it's just the Haweises up to their tricks."

Attention seeking came easily to Mary and her husband, the Reverend Hugh Reginald Haweis. All but forgotten today, Hugh and Mary were as influential a 'media couple' as one could find in late Victorian London.

Hugh was not much taller than five feet, had a club foot, and was given to a frenetic preaching style, which he enhanced by playing the violin in the pulpit. On Sundays, Hugh's church, the nearby St James' Chapel in Westmoreland Street was "crowded to suffocation". When in full flight, Rev Hugh must have been something to see. The society gadabout Augustus Hare described attending one of his sermons: "He begins without a text, acts, crouches, springs, walks about in the pulpit—which is fortunately large enough, and every now and then spreads out vast black wings like a bat, and looks as if he was about to descend upon his appalled congregation."

Hugh was a clergyman's son from Egham in Surrey. In 1867, a year after coming to the chapel in Marylebone, he married Mary Eliza Joy. At 19, she was much younger than her husband. The daughter of a struggling portrait painter, Mary had already had some of her artwork hung at the Royal Academy, so the paint roller came naturally.

Mary explained her daubs of colour as an "art protestation" against the "long, black, featureless ravines" of Marylebone. The newly vibrant front of Number 16, on the east side of Welbeck Street, a few steps below Queen Anne Street, became an overnight must-see. She recalled: "The shock was at first so great to the popular mind, that little groups would collect and stare opposite, as if expecting a rare-show to emerge." The reaction, she thought, was far from surprising: "We are the slaves of uniformity! It is endeared to us even by soot." To come upon a red door or a green cornice amidst rows and rows of smoke-stained stucco and brick, was—to Mrs Haweis anyway—a life-changing urban experience: "People who have not a real sense of colour cannot understand the joy in it of those who have. Fine colour comes like food, like joyful news, like fresh air to fainting lungs—it is invigorating."

It certainly created talk, which, of course, always delighted the Rev and Mrs Haweis. They were easily mocked; it was said that they were "amiably happy in the consciousness that whatever they do is right".

The idea of coloured houses did not catch on without debate. There was a reason why boring old white was the default paint for London. A freshly painted green house might look just lovely but the colours would fade and soon be stained with soot and need repainting. Whereas, the boring old white could be spiffed up with a little soap and sweat. Meanwhile, in the art world, critics were not overly pleased with the prospect of every fool with a paintbrush toddling off to the nearest hardware store for a bucket of mauve. The critics reminded the less cultured that how one chooses to decorate and adorn the inside of one's home is a matter of personal taste. You hope your friends can at least tolerate it. But, opined one critic, "the exterior of his habitation forms a part of the scenery of the world, and he has no right to make (as a few eccentric private individuals have the power to make) the metropolis of his country ridiculous, nor to inflict discords upon sensitive eyes".

As Mary Haweis intended (and some overwrought critics feared), the coloured front of 16 Welbeck Street was soon imitated. A few doors away, a neighbour did his Georgian home up in red. Over on Harley Street, the distinguished scientist Sir Charles Lyell daringly had his front door painted a rather shocking blue. It was not thought to be one of the great man's more successful experiments.

Rev Haweis remained at his Marylebone church until his death in 1901 but he and Mary left Welbeck Street in 1878. They relocated to a home near Regent's Park which they promptly covered in new paint and re-named Amber House.

The New York Times thought it was a "hideous glowing yellow". The Rev and Mrs Haweis were about to make an American tour at the time and the paper advised readers, "Mrs Haweis is not a noodle, and her husband, a clergyman of the Church of England, is a very able man; but they seem to think it necessary to do something outre and mad to attract attention."

While her husband preached and fiddled, Mary Haweis churned out books; an unfriendly reviewer thought she was a writer of "incontinent prolific variety". The sensation of Welbeck Street helped her peddle The Art of Decorating. She later turned her attention to other self-help tomes, such as The Art of Dress—think What Not to Wear, circa 1879. She shunned the corset and decried the "wasp-waisted" trend, favouring instead free-flowing dresses. A social acquaintance recalled her as a "funny little woman most queerly and pretentiously dressed".

The Haweis marriage ended badly. At her death, at the young age of 50, Mary cut Hugh out of her will. A biographer states that their last years were "disfigured by misunderstandings caused by egotism and eccentricity on both sides".

Mary Haweis now appears in books about "forgotten female aesthetes". But her Welbeck Street "protestation" remains one of her lasting legacies. By the turn of the century, coloured houses were not uncommon, if not all tastefully done. Greyness was in retreat. As Mary had hoped, Londoners had learned to conquer their "honest dread of bright colours". They would now heed "the kinder impulse to put a little of what pleases us in our homes, where the people can enjoy it—outside our houses". It was all about giving enjoyment to the eye, "which every house should do in this gloomy English climate".

The Baker Street mad dog

By Tom Hughes
MJ6.3, Jun-Jul 2010

The extraordinary success of the most recent TV incarnation of Mr Sherlock Holmes will no doubt draw even more visitors to Baker Street. It is always touching to watch a new generation of pilgrims seeking that fabled address 221B—but they will not find it. Some may blame it on a bureaucratic renumbering scheme implemented by the evil Moriarty. Few will continue their search north just across the Marylebone Road. Yet when Watson first mentioned the detective's abode, he placed it at 221B Upper Baker Street.

Sherlock Holmes never kept a dog in his rooms at 221B. Perhaps Mrs Hudson would not suffer pets on her premises, although she seems to have had an otherwise high tolerance for the eccentricities of her lodgers. Whenever the detective had need of canine assistance, he would just summon the redoubtable Toby and his olfactory powers to dog the steps of the latest malefactor to disturb London. "I would rather have Toby's help than that of the whole detective force of London," said Holmes to Watson. It can only be surmised that Holmes and Watson were out of town on Whit Monday 1886. For almost on their doorstep occurred an incident that would split London between dog-lovers and those who are not; between dog-lovers and men of science.

On that late spring day, 14th June, the peace and quiet of Upper Baker Street was disturbed by a frenzied, yelping spaniel. The despairing animal was being pursued by a truly terrifying spectre—a group of children with stones, and a few adults spreading the clamorous alarm, "Mad dog! Mad dog!" Drawn by the tumult, constables from Marylebone's D Division cornered the frightened animal in the doorway of 8 Upper Baker Street, just across from the present tube station.

Unable to safely approach the dog, and fearing it may be rabid, the constables summoned Inspector George Prendergast—Lestrade, it seems, was also away—and on his orders, Constable Norman gave the animal three lethal blows from his truncheon. A large crowd had by then gathered to witness the scene. Adding to the general chaos, from an upstairs window at 8 Upper Baker Street a woman emerged, shrieking for the police to stop: "You have no right to kill a dog on my doorstep!" Her pleas ignored, she returned with a bucketful of water and promptly doused the inspector.

The uproar can hardly be imagined. Whistles blowing, police rushing into number 8, the sombre removal of the body to Battersea crematorium and, lastly, Miss Fanny Ravell, marched out on a charge of assaulting a police inspector.

"The Baker Street Mad Dog" became the talk of London. Back then, as many as 50 Londoners a year were bitten by "mad dogs" and, with no cure for rabies, they were left to face an agonising death from hydrophobia. The previous December, the new police commissioner Sir Charles Warren had imposed a new law—all dogs in London must either be muzzled or under a lead at all times.

That June morning, Dash, a Norfolk spaniel owned by Miss Emily Clyde of Lodge Road had been let out by a servant, duly muzzled, for an "airing" in nearby Regent's Park. No dog enjoys a muzzle, and this liver-and-white spaniel was no exception. Dash shook his head every way, he dragged his muzzled snout along the ground, or rubbed it on the trees and bushes. The more he tried, the more frantic he became, and slobber began flying about. Children began to taunt the animal, their shouts attracted adults, and soon the halloo went up of "mad dog!" The merry throng pursued the animal out of the park, south-westerly into Upper Baker Street and, finally and fatally, to the doorway at number 8.

In the Marylebone Police Court, the magistrate, Walter Cooke, called before him Miss Fanny Ravell, the 49-year-old, bucket-wielding spinster soon heralded in the animal-loving press as a heroine. Complicating the case, Miss Emily Clyde, the dog's owner had also appeared in court to press charges against all the policemen involved for "unlawfully" killing her spaniel. Miss Clyde insisted that Dash had never demonstrated any signs of being rabid. The animal had only been frightened and become excited by the annoyances of children and "officious" adults. She claimed that witnesses had told her the dog was still wearing its muzzle when beaten to death and posed no threat to the police. The police had their own witnesses—the man who first summoned the plods said he'd seen the dog foaming from the mouth and snarling. Mr Poland, the prosecutor, insisted the dog had managed to partially remove the muzzle and could have bitten the constables. The police had only enforced the law. The dog could not have been otherwise subdued. It took two days of testimony before all the charges against all the parties were dismissed. Miss Ravell apologised to the bucketed inspector (she claimed she was actually aiming at the truncheon-wielding constable.)

The incident and attendant publicity focused the ongoing debate over Superintendent Warren's muzzling edict. George Sala, a prominent journalist, wondered whether hardened criminals were running amok in London while policemen were "too busily engaged in hammering out with their truncheons the brains of harmless little dogs."

Sir Charles did not shrink from the contest, contributing an article to one of the monthlies, defending the officers. "The sound view of the matter is, that the welfare of humanity is the first consideration," he wrote, "and that when human life is in danger from a dog, that dog must be rendered innocuous in the most expeditious manner practicable; at present no better weapon in an emergency than the truncheon is known." The leading medical journal *The Lancet* noted that while Mr Pasteur's ongoing testing of a vaccine for rabies held the hopes of all, in the meantime, "surely one human life is of more account than any number of dogs".

At Buckingham Palace, the Queen read of all this with great interest. As is true of the present monarch, Victoria loved her dogs. This case of a doomed spaniel named Dash must have engendered poignant memories. Dash was the very name of young Queen Victoria's own spaniel, "Dear Sweet Little Dash", whom she rushed home to bathe after her coronation, 48 years before. Soon the home secretary received a memo from the Queen regarding "Her dear poor friends, the dogs". Insisting that incidents such as the one in Upper Baker Street must never happen again, Her Majesty demanded:

1. No dogs should ever be killed by police unless the veterinary surgeon declared they were mad (the dogs, that is, not the police). Dogs who were close to their masters or mistresses or their house doors, poor quiet dogs, should be left alone and not molested.
2. The Dog's Home in Battersea should be enlarged (she was a frequent

contributor).

3. Muzzles, except for very savage dogs, should not be used, nor should dogs be run after and hunted to be caught.

The memo was duly passed along to Sir Charles Warren (as was the Queen's inclusive postscript: "Cats should likewise be well cared for." She wasn't a cat person.) The muzzle law was removed from the statute books in 1892, meaning that it outlasted its creator, Sir Charles. His failures to catch Jack the Ripper soon cost him his job.

As always, the wits at *Punch* came up with the appropriate, well, doggerel: "In darksome glens of Hampstead's Heath, the hunted mongrel lay! / He saw the flash of the bull's-eye lamp, and heard the stern Policeman's tramp, / Die fitfully away / So, crouched and trembling, there he lay, while all else things are free; / The odds were if he slank away, he'd end, if not his days, the day / At lethal Battersea."

Ye Ancient Order of Froth Blowers

By Donna Earrey

MJ4.5, Oct-Nov 2008

Marylebone's history is rich with societies, associations and committees—medical, scientific, artistic and political. But there is one that in the absence of blue plaques and memorials is rarely given the recognition it truly deserves: Ye Ancient Order of Froth Blowers. This distinctly British charitable organisation set about "fostering the noble art and gentle and healthy pastime of froth blowing amongst Gentlemen of leisure and ex-soldiers". Which, in layman's terms, meant raising money by spending an awful lot of time in the pub.

The two founder members of this unique organisation were Sir Alfred Downing Fripp and Bert (Herbert) Temple. Fripp was born 12th September 1865, the son of watercolourist Alfred Downing Fripp. Oils and palette knives were not Fripp junior's forte, but the surgeon's knife was. He became surgeon ordinary to King Edward VII between 1897 and 1910 and tended to King George V from 1910. He also served as chief medical officer of the Imperial Yeomanry Hospital in Deelfontein during the Boer War and was knighted for his services in 1903.

In contrast to Fripp's impressive record of achievement, Bert Temple, born September 1880, seems to have been a bit of a loveable rogue. After fighting in the trenches of the Western Front in the First World War, he resumed his trade as a silk agent, merchant and manufacturing agent, living an itinerant lifestyle around London's hotels and clubs.

The paths of these two men first crossed in the autumn of 1924 when Temple was operated on by Fripp who performed a life-saving stomach operation, the cause of which is unknown. After his surgery, Temple asked for an ale—a slightly unusual request for a man recovering from such serious surgery, but a request that was nonetheless granted. Fripp, who watched as Temple drank with apparent gusto, was himself not adverse to the medicinal properties of ale, which he saw as something of a general panacea. It was later, during a post-operative consultation which took place at Fripp's home at 19 Portland Place in November 1924, that the renowned surgeon told Temple that he had been "a bad lad who has taken the best out of life and put nothing back"—harsh words indeed. Temple steered the conversation away from this assault on his character by expressing an interest in the worthy causes with which Fripp was involved, including the Invalid Children's Aid Association. Either from an acute attack of conscience or a sense of indebtedness to Fripp for saving his life, Temple offered to raise the princely sum of £100 to aid Fripp's charities. His vehicle for doing so would be Ye Ancient Order of Froth Blowers, which was founded the following day at the Swan Inn, Fittleworth, West Sussex. Fripp was given the illustrious title of Froth Blower No 1 with Temple as the Honorary Secretary No 0.

Temple immediately began producing membership cards which he sold mainly to former members of his wartime regiment, the 1st Sportsman's Battalion. Membership came at the cost of 5 shillings, with each member also receiving a pair of silver enamelled cufflinks.

A vivid description of the Froth Blowers' creed was contained in the organisation's handbook: "A sociable and law abiding fraternity of absorptive Britons who sedately consume and quietly enjoy with commendable regularity and frequention the truly British malted beverage as did their forbears and as Britons ever will, and be damned to all pussyfoot hornswogglers from overseas and including low brows, teetotallers and MPs and not excluding nosey parkers, mock religious bodies and suburban fool hens all of which are structurally solid borne from the chin up."

All members were entitled to blow the froth off any member's beer, and even on occasions those beers belonging to non-members. It was however prudent to wait until they were not looking, or at least make sure they were of a very mild and peaceful disposition, for obvious reasons. As with any self-respecting organisation, a motto was most definitely needed. It was decided that "Lubrication in Moderation" fitted the bill nicely. Regular meetings took place in either pubs or clubs (known as 'vats') where members would enjoy the holy trinity of beer, beef and baccy.

These meetings were lively affairs which took the form of general business, gargling and mutual recriminations, followed by singing, fights and general diversions. A complex system of fines was devised for those committing the heinous sin of not wearing their cufflinks. All of the monies resulting from these fines, together with membership fees, were sent to Fripp and his wife for their Wee Waifs charities.

The organisation attracted new members at a steady pace, but in 1925 the membership exploded after the editor of *The Sporting Times* published a series of articles on the Order's gatherings. Sparked by this media interest, the idea took hold of the public's imagination. Fripp, now retired from his surgeon's duties, found himself travelling around the country founding vats and suddenly thousands were clamouring to join the organisation. There was no discrimination—it certainly didn't matter in the slightest what gender you were and there were even a number of canine members.

Male members were referred to as Blowers, female members were Fairy Belles, their children and dogs were Faithful Bow-Wows, all were enrolled. It is not clear how a dog would manage with the intricacies of blowing froth, but they somehow muddled through. It was reported that even a pet Brazilian monkey, who resided at the Bricklayers Arms in Cable Street, was registered as a Froth Blower, with his AOFB cufflinks worn on a collar around his neck. The monkey was apparently partial to a tot of Whitbread stout, which he was allowed in cold weather—purely for medicinal benefit of course.

Titles were awarded to members who successfully enrolled others— Blaster for 25 new members, Tornado for a 100, Monsoon for 500, Grand Typhoon for a 1,000 and finally the Cloud Burst for a magnificent 2,000 new enrolments.

For five glorious years the Froth Blowers extolled a unique, beery Britishness. Their motto and their anthem—*The More we are Together*, an adaptation of *Oh du lieber Augustin*—were heard everywhere. Temple explained that he first heard the song on a pearling schooner in the South Sea Islands many years previously. It went: "The more we are together, together, together / The more we are together / The merrier we'll be. / For your friends are my friends / And my friends are your friends, / And the more we are together / The merrier we'll be." Some of you may recognise the lyrics from a chewing gum commercial on TV. The Froth Blowers would have been mortified—chewing gum and beer really don't mix.

Toward the end of 1928 the order had an incredible 700,000 members—an amazing feat considering that many in society found the whole concept disdainful and anti-social to say the least. Their popularity was rather upsetting to temperance campaigners who firmly believed that it was alcohol that had caused the 'Wee Waifs' their suffering in the first place. They were completely unimpressed that a surgeon to the king should be sponsoring such an organisation. In 1927, Walter Greville of the Good Templars described the AOFB as "the latest recruited ally of the liquor trade", saying that "for ridiculous vulgarity and foolish methods it took the first prize". Sir George Hunter, speaking for the Fellowship of Freedom and Reform in 1929 called the Froth Blowers "a disgrace to the country".

These were strong words from upstanding members of society, but they did rather miss the point. The sums of money raised by the order were nothing short of staggering—over £100,000 in a just a few years. The funds were used for buying hospital cots and taking invalid children on outings to the country. In 1929 a roof garden was established for mothers and their children on the Marylebone Housing Association's first block of slum clearance flats. There were those that did see their humour and appreciate their ability to raise money for underprivileged children—the Lord Chancellor, Viscount Hailsham, described the Blowers as "a great charitable organisation".

A wry article that appeared in the *Henley Standard* reported a visit by the Blowers in July 1927 to a convalescent home housing 22 youngsters which was established by the order at Brightwell-cum-Sotwell in Oxfordshire. The party consisted of Fripp, Cloudburst Jack Haes, Blaster Fred Leftly of Henley and Blowers A Axtell and E Willis. The Blowers entertained the residents with a rendition of Onward Christian Soldiers followed by the Froth Blowers Anthem before sitting down to dine.

Temple's health during these intense years of fund raising and beer drinking was ailing quite considerably. He had not been in the best of health since 1927 and had even penned a comment on page seven of the membership handbook stating "Your Hon Sec No 0 nearly dead".

Temple's love of beer and tobacco probably contributed to his condition, and it is likely he was suffering from tuberculosis. Time spent in the trenches of Northern France would certainly not have helped him, although there does not seem to be any evidence in his military papers to suggest that he had this disease before he was de-mobbed. He was known to hope that the future would find a way to stamp out this 'white plague of the tubercle scourge'.

Even with his health in serious decline, Temple continued to promote the AOFB along with his fellow officers: Fripp, David Henry Cain (*Sporting Times*) and John Andrew 'Jack' Haes (London Stock Exchange). He attended as many functions and gatherings as he could manage, but in 1928 his health took a turn for the worse. Fripp ordered him to refrain from attending any further vat meetings and functions for a considerable length of time. Temple reportedly travelled to Devon in order to spend time recuperating, as well as lubricating in moderation. Later during that same year Temple went into a nursing home at 22a Devonshire Street.

Fripp was now dividing his time between his Portland Place home and his family home in Dorset. In 1930 he died at Lulworth and is buried in the family plot at Holy Trinity church. Two years after his death a fellowship was established at Guys Hospital in his name. His Times obituary said of the Froth Blowers: "These, by their innocent mirth, assisted by a catchy tune, have contributed largely to charities, and have entertained and brightened the lives of innumerable children."

The following year saw the death of Temple who died from respiratory failure. His death was certified by Fripp's son, Alfred Thomas, who had followed his father into the medical profession. A death notice appeared in the newspapers reporting simply: "Funeral service at St Marylebone Church, York Gate NW1, Monday 23 February at 12 noon, followed by a private cremation at Golders Green. No flowers."

With the death of its two founding members, Ye Ancient Order of Froth Blowers came to an inevitable end and in 1931 it sadly went into voluntary liquidation. It seems such a shame that this unique organisation with its emphasis on humour and its relentless fund raising antics is now forgotten. Perhaps after reading this piece you might attempt to resurrect, just for a moment, the traditions of this fine organisation yourself. The next time you are in one of Marylebone's many drinking establishments, purchase a pint (or a half for the ladies) and in memory of this illustrious organisation, or just for sheer devilment, raise your glass, blow a little froth and make a toast to Fripp, Temple and their fine "fraternity of absorbitive Britons".

The ladies of Lower Jerome Place

By Tom Hughes
MJ4.2, Apr-May 2008

There was a time when Lower Jerome Place was one of the most talked about addresses in Marylebone. Today, you'll get a blank stare from a cabbie if you shout that address in his window. And you won't find it in the back-shelf editions of the A-to-Z either. Nor is it one of those lost streets of London, re-named, re-developed or blitzed from our memory. For Lower Jerome Place never actually existed, but rather it was just the term late Victorian society wits gave to a block or two of Great Cumberland Place where lived the three famous Jerome sisters.

This trio of American beauties had burst upon the London scene in the 1870s, sallying forth in search of husbands worthy of the daughters of the wildly rich New York tycoon Leonard Jerome. The quest had been met with indifferent success. There was Clara, married to a frenetic and frequently nearly bankrupt chap named Moreton Frewen (aka Mortal Ruin). There was Leonie, married to Jack Leslie, an Irish aristocrat who was forced to live off his military pay. And there was the best known of the three, Jennie, married to Lord Randolph Churchill and father of Winston.

It was Leonie who first took up residence in Marylebone when she and her husband moved in to 10 Great Cumberland Place, on the east side of the street, just north of Bryanston Street. In 1896, the recently widowed Jennie, to be closer to her sister, took 35a Great Cumberland Place, nearly across the street. There, according to her most lubricious biographer, she entertained a series of new lovers. What must the neighbours have thought? For next door lived no less than the Bishop of Gloucester and his wife. Clara had a home in Belgravia in Chesham Place, but it was frequently let and, with her husband away, she was generally in residence with one or other sister in Lower Jerome Place. In 1902, she opted to save on cab fares and moved in to 32 Great Cumberland Place.

Though Lower Jerome Place was all the qui vive of society, the sisters lacked not for distinguished neighbours. A quick check of Webster's Royal Red Book for 1897, finds that in the space of just a few city blocks,

Great Cumberland Place boasted three earls, one dowager countess, two lords, two admirals, two baronets, two ladies and the aforementioned bishop.

It was therefore no surprise, with such wealthy pickings so close to the ground, that Lower Jerome Place drew the attention of the shady 'company promoters' who seemed to be behind every waxed moustache at the turn of the last century. Enter 'Captain' James Henry Irvine Cruickshank, a man who claimed to have the very connections required for these fashionable American ladies to make a quick fortune in a Yankee railway scheme, which would of course have warmed their patriotic and corseted bosoms. Cruickshank seemed a delightful young man and, beyond the railway, he also discussed future lucrative opportunities in Havana cigars, a "Sultana mining syndicate" and more.

Naturally, and much to their credit, these women were not fools and did not admit Cruickshank to their drawing rooms without first vetting his CV. The Captain came with the endorsement of none other than Arthur Cadogan—of the Chelsea Cadogans, don't you know. The Hon. Arthur Charles Lewin Cadogan was the brother of the 5th Earl Cadogan, but in Lower Jerome Place he was just "dear Arthur". Cruickshank was first introduced by 'dear Arthur' to Clara, Mrs Moreton Frewen. A wise choice given her husband's penchant for wild, doomed investments in Rocky Mountain cattle-ranching, ice-making and gold-crushing devices. Arthur told Clara that he knew a man who could triple her money in six weeks.

This happy news spread quickly along Lower Jerome Place—being a good sister, Clara speedily passed word to Leonie and Jennie. Cruickshank was brought round to unfurl a map or two for these fine ladies—who probably couldn't have found Regent's Park on a map. But the Captain had even more exciting intelligence to share—he was now promising quadruple returns.

On 15 February 1897, Lady Randolph wrote a cheque for £400 and was promised a sum of £1,600 by 26 March. Tormented by thoughts of timidity, no doubt, Lady Randolph quickly sent off a second cheque, adding £800 to her stake in the Captain's great flutter. Leonie, who was nowhere near as flush as her more famous sister, could only scrounge together £100. Clara, with the thanks no doubt from her sisters for bringing this wondrous opportunity to their doors, put up £250 of her own money. The cheques were sent to Arthur Cadogan who delivered them to the Captain. There was nothing to do now but wait for the dividends to begin rolling in from what the ladies of Lower Jerome Place called, their 'spec'.

Surprisingly, it just didn't work out. When the date for the four-fold return came and went unrequited, the Honourable Arthur and the now unseen 'Captain' were able to fob off their worried investors with a few timeworn clichés about patience and "difficulties in the field". Cadogan relayed word that Cruickshank had encountered additional expenses in traveling to the railway site and, though delayed, was still quite sanguine as to the promised returns. As is customary, that tepid advisory was enough to keep matters going for a short while.

But it soon became clear that there was no money coming back to the greatly disappointed ladies of Lower Jerome Place. Jennie stood to lose the most. Pestered by her son Winston—serving in India and pleading for some more dosh from mummy—she had to admit she had been swindled out of a huge sum. At first too embarrassed to bring any charges, Jennie was convinced by the ever-combative Winston to go to law and he urged her to employ the redoubtable solicitor Sir George Lewis. Good choice. There is not a late Victorian scandal or scheme in which the discreet footsteps of the legendary Lewis cannot be heard somewhere.

By September, Lewis had tracked down the elusive Cruickshank and had him arrested and brought to London where he was remanded without bail at the Bow Street Police Court. Cruickshank was not a captain at all, but a bankrupt, divorced American of no occupation who had been residing in a hotel in Sheffield. Sir George read for the magistrate a list of grandiloquently titled companies being promoted by Cruickshank, sadly "all of which are believed mythical". Other defrauded investors, who had licked their financial wounds in quiet, now came forward including the Viscount Pollington and Mrs Drake-Brockman.

Cruickshank was going down. It was only a case of for how long. He got some unexpected help from Clara, Mrs Frewen. She admitted in the witness box that she had once cheerfully told him: "You know all our family are great gamblers, and if the speculation comes off we shall be delighted, and if it does not, you will never hear an unkind word from us." Poor Clara also conceded she had no firm grasp of where the railway was supposed to have been built—in England or America. She also put the Honourable Arthur Cadogan in the frame and said she no longer had as much confidence in that gentleman's financial acumen.

On 25 November 1897, James Henry Irvine Cruickshank was sentenced to eight years in prison. He was denounced by the judge as a member of a 'large, growing and dangerous class of men who live and thrive on the follies of mankind.' Of course, the Honourable Arthur Cadogan walked away a free, though somewhat tarnished, adornment to the British peerage. In his defence, he was surely not the only toff to act as a well-paid 'greeter' opening drawing room doors to scoundrels like Cruickshank, Jabez Balfour and Ernest Terah Hooley. Other 'Honourables' were paid to lend their names to various 'company' letterheads helping to swindle country clergymen and wealthy spinsters. The English do (or did) 'love a Lord' and *The New York Times* decided that snobbery was at the root of all these frauds.

Meanwhile, the three American Jerome sisters retrenched in Great Cumberland Place to await the new century. Maybe young Winston would one day amount to something.

Debenham & Freebody v Alfred Mellon

By Tom Hughes
MJ5.1, Feb-Mar 2009

Here is the the story of one of history's sadly forgotten heroes, Alfred Mellon. One day in 1877, after "dear, dear, Marian" Mellon returned home to Bradford from a London shopping jaunt, Alfred decided he'd had enough. Mrs Mellon had strayed across some invisible line. He stared at the bill and declared: "I will not pay." And by doing so, cocked a snook at Debenham's—the great drapers of Wigmore Street.

Alfred and Marian Mellon were in their mid-30s and something of a rarity for their time—a two-income couple. Alfred was secretary and manager of the Victoria Hotel in Bradford (For Families & Gentlemen), while his wife was the assistant manageress.

Alfred pulled down £250 a year, out of which he paid his wife a salary of £50, plus an extra £10 for the bonnets and frocks required for the couple's three daughters, Marian, Frederica and Elberta. Arthur thought this was a more than generous arrangement and he had warned his dear wife not to spend a farthing more.

Marian, her husband's edict duly noted, happily set off by the Great Northern Railway for London. She brought her custom to the Messrs Debenham & Freebody's establishment on Wigmore Street, where the firm had had its shop since the 1770s. Marian had a grand time spending the cash but, as will so often happen, espied a few more unmissable bargains. With not a cashpoint in sight, the good woman made her additional purchases and asked the clerk to please post the bill to Alfred Mellon, care of the Victoria Hotel, Bridge Street, Bradford.

When the bill arrived at the hotel, Alfred was not happy. The bill was in the amount of £43 9s 6d, or almost Marian's entire salary for the year. Alfred promptly wired word from Yorkshire to Marylebone that he, with respect, would not be paying the Messrs Debenham one sixpence of their demands. "Nowt!" Mrs Mellon had no right to pledge his credit, and if they didn't like it they could sue him.

This single act of defiance on the part of a distant provincial hotelier against one of the West End's poshest merchants soon took on national significance. These were heady times for the ladies who shopped. It was the era of the new department store. Travel was more convenient—they came by carriage, by the underground, or by rail, even from as far away as Bradford. The streets were much safer; women could shop alone, although many preferred to go in packs, as is still the custom. While cash was greatly preferred, merchants were willing to extend credit to ladies of quality and, almost without exception, the paterfamilias—with whatever grumbled asides he cared to utter—would later foot the bill. Alfred Mellon was bidding to topple this whole profitable edifice.

Debenham's hauled Alfred Mellon into court in late 1879. The court found that the Mellons were an otherwise happily married couple living together in the ordinary way. For their level of income, Mr Mellon's allotted budget for his wife was certainly more than adequate. At that point in time, the law generally held that when a husband cohabitated with his wife, she was entitled to go shopping with her husband's credit while purchasing those "necessaries suitable to his degree and estate." Her purchases at Debenham's were appropriate for a lady of her station in life and the items were reasonably priced. However, in this instance she had been given explicit instructions by her husband that she had a limited purse, and she had exceeded the limit. Mr Mellon was found to be under no obligation to notify every merchant in the realm. Debenham's had taken a chance on Mrs Mellon and lost.

They had lost round one anyway. In 1880 the Marylebone drapers went up a step to the Court of Appeal in their second bid to raid the Mellon exchequer. Again, they would meet with disappointment. The ruling was written by Justice Bramwell—described as a straightforward, unpretentious chap and, most importantly, a married man. Bramwell believed any husband had the right to say to his wife: "Go and pledge my credit to any extent your love of finery may prompt you to do." However, "the guv'nor" had the equal right to set a limit. Likewise, every merchant had the right to say: "We are a ready-money establishment." If the shopkeeper cares to sell items on credit, he must ask the lady customers if they have the authority to pledge their husband's credit. "It is said that a tradesman will not like to ask this, as it would offend his customers. That, no doubt, is a strong consideration, and it is an excellent reason why he should not ask such questions; but it is no reason why he should make the husband liable because he does not do so." It was another legal victory for the doughty Alfred, who was probably feeling rather chuffed by now. Debenham's would carry their now well-tattered bill for the wretched £43 9s 6d into battle one last time, to the House of Lords. However, the Lord Chancellor saw no reason to overturn the lower courts and Alfred Mellon's triumph was complete.

The Lords decision came down on 27 November 1880, just in time for the Christmas shopping rush. *The Economist* decried the "vicious" practice of shopping on credit but thought the ruling would prove very burdensome for "innocent wives and innocent shopkeepers". The *Times* thought it was a good thing that this important mercantile question had been at last decided. But the writer added that ladies should not take alarm: "[We do not] imagine that husbands will ever be less tender-hearted as a class. They will not cease to pay extortionate bills when called upon."

As for Alfred and Marian, this sensational, law-making disagreement failed to disrupt their seemingly contented life. They continued to manage the Victoria Hotel in Bradford—which is still open and has gone quite up market. The top rooms today will cost you just about Alfred's entire salary in 1877. The Mellons relocated to London in the 1880s where they managed the Covent Garden Hotel.

BUILDINGS & PLACES

It's no surprise that the Royal Institute of British Architects (RIBA) has chosen to make its home on Portland Place: Marylebone contains some of London's most appealing architecture, created by some of its greatest architects. John Nash left his fingerprints all over the area in the early decades of its development, as did the peerless Adam brothers. Between them they helped create an area notable for its formal grid, wide streets, and beautifully proportioned townhouses. It's not all endless good taste though: later generations have punctuated the flow of Georgian elegance with bursts of Victorian flamboyance or concrete brutalism.

This chapter looks at the area's built environment, but it isn't all about buildings—it's also about the spaces in between them: the parks, gardens and streets. On top of that, it tells the stories of some of the characters whose vision helped create the distinctive look and feel of Marylebone. Some of them were geniuses. Others weren't.

The genius of John Nash

By Glyn Brown
MJ6.5, Oct-Nov 2010

Cycling up Regent Street recently, crossing Oxford Street and tootling into Portland Place I was struck, as I always am, by the airy way everything opens out the nearer you get to Regent's Park. This road—which runs from the Mall up through Waterloo Place, Lower Regent Street, via Piccadilly Circus and on to what was once known as Marylebone Park—and the design of the park itself, were the vision of one man. Architect John Nash was sociable, audacious and sometimes appallingly slapdash, but it was his creative genius and drive that gave this backbone of London, and its cartilage of Marylebone streets and squares, a lasting elegance. His life was complicated, he tried to do too much, his grand schemes sometimes went far too far. But if it weren't for him, Regent's Park and its stately surrounding crescents wouldn't exist at all.

Born in Lambeth in 1952, John Nash was the third son of struggling Kentish millwright William and his Welsh wife, Anne. John was eight when his father died, but William had managed to save funds for his son's continued education. Nash studied architecture for over 10 years with Sir Robert Taylor, from 1769 the Surveyor of the King's Works (the king at this time being the increasingly bonkers George III).

In 1778 John's uncle Thomas died, leaving £1,000 from his calico printing fortune to his promising nephew, then 26. John retired, speculated hopelessly on property and by 31 was bankrupt. There was nothing for it—moving in with his mother in Wales, he returned to architecture and began to turn out impressive work, including Carmarthen Gaol, a fine bridge at Aberystwyth and intricate repairs on St David's Cathedral.

Nash formed a partnership with Humphry Repton, the man who coined the phrase 'landscape garden'. Together they constructed highly praised country estates, carefully siting a Nash-designed house in a Repton-designed garden. In 1792, Nash returned to London, where he met the man who would be his occasionally irresponsible patron, George, Prince of Wales—'Prinny'.

The increasingly unstable King George III had raised his 13 children with miserly iron discipline. As his sons came of age, they exploded into lives of spendthrift scandal. George led the way, drinking and gambling himself into debt and proving to be a dedicated womaniser. The urbane, sophisticated Nash came to know him well.

In 1798, the 46-year-old architect suddenly became inexplicably wealthy at the same time that he married the ravishing, dark-eyed Mary Ann Bradley, the 24-year-old daughter of a penniless coal merchant and rumoured to be one of the prince's mistresses. Miss Bradley was pregnant at the time. Nash acknowledged no children of his own during his lifetime, but over the next 10 years Mary acquired five babies, officially distant relatives with the family name of Pennethorne. It was widely assumed they were among the prince's offspring, and no one said otherwise.

Nash's working relationship with the prince was cemented. He loved the children, too, calling James, the eldest, his "adopted son", his "favourite pupil", and training him to be an architect. And Nash was hardly a shy man himself. As he got richer one of his colleagues, Richard Finch, bitterly dismissed him as "a great coxcomb. He is very fond of women, attempted even Mrs Parke, his wife's sister. He lives in Dover Street [in a huge town house of his own design, now demolished], has a charming place on the Isle of Wight and drives four horses."

That place on the Isle of Wight hinted at the extremes of which Nash would be capable. East Cowes Castle had gothic battlements, square, round and octagonal towers, and pointed doors and windows. There was also a clean, simple Regency staircase, a billiard room in the style of Sir John Soane, and a white marble fireplace decorated with Egyptian figures.

Over the next few years, Nash designed a score of country houses in assorted styles, adding extra floors to the castle and buying more property with the proceeds. All this time he entertained enthusiastically. One guest at the castle, Mrs Arbuthnot, said her host was "a very clever, odd, amusing man with a face like a monkey's but civil and good-humoured to the greatest degree". Though no longer working with Repton, he'd kept what he learned from the gardener in his mind, and in

1806 accepted the job of Architect to the Woods and Forests. Another step toward what would be his greatest achievement.

In 1811, parliament accepted the King's permanent insanity and made young George Prince Regent. At the same time, leases on the Crown land of Marylebone Park expired. The prince had the idea of creating a spectacular road, Regent Street, sweeping down from Marylebone to his palace, Carlton House, which overlooked St James's Park. With this complete, his future subjects would surely grasp his glory.

So what would any town planner be working with? Not the easiest terrain. Much of the land in Marylebone had remained undeveloped because the surface was covered in deep clay, making it boggy and wet, while the lack of London clay below ground made it impossible to sink wells for fresh water, but if anyone could deal with this, it was Nash.

Meanwhile, the park—originally known as the Forest of Middlesex—was still isolated heathland, and had been split into three farms, which supplied London with milk and hay, two inns, and some cottages.

Plans had been submitted to develop the park in a similar way to Bloomsbury, paving over the quagmire and creating well-ordered streets and squares. Nash, now 59, was having none of this. With input from Repton, he proposed to landscape the park and build a shimmering garden city. Twenty-six aristocratic villas and a central terraced circus would appear out of the trees, there would be lakes and a canal, and a pleasure palace for the prince would sit in the middle. Framing the park at south, east and west would be white-walled neo-classical terraces, with their own shops, church, carriageways and stabling. St James's Park would also be developed, and the new road would link these two oases.

The Prince Regent was delighted. If Nash could pull it off, this would be the largest single piece of town planning London had ever known and, he crowed, "It will quite eclipse Napoleon". Building began in 1813. Work was still ongoing in 1825, when Nash was 73.

The creation of Regent Street (at first named New Street) caused chaos. After the Great Fire of London, Christopher Wren had tried and failed to inflict order on London's medieval street pattern. Now Nash again attempted to create broad, architecturally distinguished thoroughfares.

The problem was that he wanted a straight road, but a lot of people owned property right in the way. Work began with Park Crescent, in 1813, and Nash had to endure the complaints of architects he brought in, handle negotiations with builders and deal with owners of adjoining properties. Luckily he was not just pompous and flashy—he also had optimism, energy and formidable improvisation skills, and he needed it all to keep the project alive.

Having to adjust the line of the road to whatever property was owned by the Crown or could be acquired and demolished in fact led to inspired ideas. Attempting to hinge the awkward angle of Regent Street and Portland Place (built in the 1770s by Robert Adam), where the road had to veer abruptly west, he created the lovely circular portico of All Souls, Langham Place. Unfortunately, the building sparked a parliamentary debate, since it mixed a gothic spire, classical rounded shape and Corinthian columns with cherub heads. "One of the most miserable structures in the metropolis," claimed a reviewer. Further down, Piccadilly Circus and the quarter circle (the Quadrant) of road that joins it to Regent Street were the only way of taking the line through Crown land. When no builder would risk financing the Quadrant (and leasing it out), Nash paid for it himself and put up a series of colonnades (later demolished by the Victorians due to the unsavoury characters said to loiter there). Despite all this, few of Regent Street's original shopfronts remain.

But the handsome white terraces around the park, at the top of Portland Place, remain. It's a surprise in some ways. First because Nash's building techniques weren't all they might be. His flair was theatrical, and it's been said that behind the glittering frontage, many of his constructions were as flimsy as stage scenery—often, he just made a rough sketch and left his assistants to work out the details. It was Nash's innovation to cover brick with plaster stucco (render), painted to look like stone; a sumptuous finished look, and a cheap way to achieve all sorts of other ornamental effects. Which is another reason the Nash terraces may not have survived, since the Victorians found them deeply suspect. These were town houses, after all; how dare they, with their Palladian style, pediments and statues, look like country palaces? The magnificent facades of Hanover Terrace, Cumberland Terrace and Park Crescent annoyed them—but they left them alone, along with Cornwall Terrace (built by Decimus Burton, still in his twenties, under Nash's supervision), Chester Terrace, York Terrace and all the spacious Marylebone streets and crescents behind them.

And as for the park, it never did become a Fantasia-style garden suburb. Only eight of the 26 aristocratic villas were built, and projects for a royal pleasure palace and the inner ring of terraces fell by the wayside, too. But there is a lake with herons, ducks and geese and a boating area, there are sculpted water features, and the existing villas and lodges are breathtaking. The 410 acre park is now a place to get happily lost in, with gardens, the open air theatre and that huge, meadow-like expanse, where a whole zoo is easily tucked away.

Nash moved on to other things. He planned Trafalgar Square, though it wasn't finished in his lifetime. Then he rebuilt the now King George IV's Ocean Pavilion into an insane oriental dream palace, complete with domes, minarets and pagodas. As it rose above the fishermen's cottages of Brighton, the Austrian Ambassador's wife, Princess Lieven, wrote, "How can one describe such a piece of architecture? The style is a mixture of Moorish, Tartar, Gothic and Chinese. It has already cost £700,000, and is still not fit to live in."

As soon as it was finished George lost interest in the Pavilion, turning his attention to his residence at Carlton House. It was "antiquated, rundown and decrepit"; he'd rather rebuild Buckingham House as a palace. Nash was set to work on it, but he was 73 and not up to the complex job before him. It's no surprise that he misjudged the proportions of the wings, which he pulled down several times, or that the Marble Arch, the centrepiece between them, was too narrow for the royal coach to pass through (and later had to be relocated to its own traffic island). The King died before the Palace was complete, by which time the country had had enough of Nash, and he was dismissed on grounds of profligacy.

John Nash died at East Cowes Castle in 1835, aged 83. To pay his debts, almost all his property was sold, and his wife and the children went to live at his farm near Shalfleet. Despite his lifelong flair, Nash ended his days as a figure of no account—a view history would revise. He may have been controversial, but unlike his neurotic contemporary Sir John

Soane, Nash was positive, light-spirited, and inspired. From Trafalgar Square to Piccadilly Circus, he changed the way London was seen. Here's Theodore Hook, then editor of the magazine *John Bull*: "Let the reader recollect the huddled mass of wretched streets and Houses which 20 years ago covered the site of Regent Street, the Quadrant and Waterloo Place. Then let him turn his eyes to that magnificent adjunct of London, The Regent's Park—now one of the healthiest and gayest of public walks and drives, and a creation of the mind of Mr Nash."

The architects' architecture

By Oliver Bradbury

MJ3.1, Feb-Mar 2007

The national headquarters of the Royal Institute of British Architects (RIBA) stands at 66 Portland Place, at the junction of Portland Place and Weymouth Street. This popular 1930s building was opened on 8 November 1934 by King George V and Queen Mary and was designed by Grey Wornum (1888-1957), who won the commission in an open competition—open at least to members of RIBA—that attracted 284 entrants. In 1970 the building was listed by the Minister of Housing and local government as a Grade II building of architectural and historic importance, one of the first of 50 buildings dating from between the two world wars to be acknowledged as such.

It's a little known fact that at least eight Georgian buildings were destroyed for the current RIBA building. These were 62-68 Portland Place and 14-20 Weymouth Street. The extant 12 Weymouth Street gives us an indication as to what these now lost buildings might have looked like, at least along Weymouth Street. Intriguingly, 12 Weymouth Street is the only Georgian, hence original, survivor within a block, bound by Portland Place, Weymouth, Hallam and Devonshire streets, which has been completely redeveloped during the 20th century.

For a completely unfamiliar view of the RIBA building I would recommend a stroll into the obscure Bridford Mews. From here one can see the surprisingly utilitarian rear of Wornum's building and the graceful Georgian bow at the back of 12 Weymouth Street. 68 Portland Place was a grand four bay-wide Adamesque town house and was similar to the extant examples on this street. The building directly opposite RIBA was by Adam and was disgracefully demolished by the Chinese Embassy in 1980 and replaced with an unconvincing facsimile.

Having considered 48 sites for a new RIBA headquarters, the Premises Committee settled on the corner site at 62-68 Portland Place and 14-20 Weymouth Street on 31 January 1929. And by 13 March negotiations with The Howard de Walden Estate had been completed for the acquisition of a 999-year lease. In early May 1932 the winner of the competition was announced and the 3,600 competition designs were put on exhibition at Thames House, Milbank. In May 1933 the old buildings on the site were demolished. Lord Howard de Walden laid the foundation stone on 28 June 1933.

Although many agreed that Wornum's Portland Place elevation was not ideal—the scale of the central window and the quality of the as-executed ornamental sculpture (Man and Woman on the front pylons positioned as sentinels to flank the main entrance, and the somewhat rum sculpted relief figure of Architectural Aspiration above the giant window)—it was unanimously agreed that the winning architect had resolved the testing demands of the internal planning brief in a masterly fashion. Wornum had solved the problem of conveying 500 people either to the meeting room or to the exhibition gallery without resorting to the use of corridors and lifts.

In the Modernist architect Maxwell Fry's opinion the building's tour-de-force was the "imaginative handling of the staircase levels which command views both upward and downward of great richness and complexity". This is still undeniably true.

Despite an ever-shrinking budget (originally projected at £125,000 to include furniture, fittings and all the fees, but whittled down to £106,250 on tender), the building was able to utilise rich materials throughout: Portland stone for the elevations; cast bronze for the entrance doors; Perrycot limestone for the walls of the hall; figured teak, olive ash and black bean timber for the Henry Jarvis Hall and foyer; and dark blue Demara (African) marble treads for the main stair above risers of black Derbyshire marble.

In 1947 *Country Life* included it in Recent English Architecture 1920-1940, for it "can be judged to be [a] good building carried out by British architects during the last quarter of a century". Country Life illustrated the Weymouth Street elevation, captioning it thus: "The elevations, in which regard is given to classical precedent, are combined with an original and ingenious plan interrelating a series of spacious conference halls, committee rooms, offices, and library." There is a strong Swedish influence on the architecture of this building, a highly influential style on British architecture of the 1930s (the 1933-36 art deco interior portion of

Eltham Palace, London being a good example). Grey Wornum had led the Architectural Association excursion to Stockholm in 1930 and it has been said by Charles Reilly that "he must, I think, have been inspired in his methods of setting about his big job by Ragnar Ostberg, the famous architect of the Stockholm Town Hall".

This Swedish influence manifested itself particularly in an unmistakably 20th century reworking of Neo-Classicism, economical fenestration and sparing use of ornament, as well as the sumptuous use of rich materials — especially marbles and exotic timbers, internally. So much so that in 1934 a Swedish visitor commented that with this building "England has at last discovered Sweden". Inside, Country Life also illustrated the main stair: "The display of materials and craftsmanship, both in sculpture and applied design, joins with the feeling of light and space deriving from the plan to produce a whole singular and colourful distinction." But that was in 1947 and, unfortunately, the richly walnut and maple-wainscoted council chamber, which was the uppermost room in the building in 1934, was in 2002-3 "substantially altered ... to suit the very different needs of the 21st century".

Ironically, Alison Smithson, the distinguished New Brutalist architect, was responsible (with William Howell) in 1961-62 for redecorating the Members' Room and Bar (now the South Room) in dark purple and white, as a period reaction against the by-then-unfashionable work of the 1930s. And yet, despite having worked on the RIBA building, Smithson told the Evening Standard in 1970 that 66 Portland Place was lousy and should be dynamited. Indeed, the Listing of the building in 1970 took the RIBA Council by surprise and caused general hilarity. It's only since the late 70s onwards that the building has been appreciated for what it is — an exemplar of 1930s institutional architecture.

Marylebone's garden squares

By Glyn Brown
MJ7.3, Jun-Jul 2011

Georgian squares are a defining feature of London, and Marylebone has more than its fair share.

Bryanston Square The square was built in the early 19th century, named by owner Henry William Portman after his home village of Bryanston in Dorset, and the garden, long and narrow enough almost to belong to one house, feels intimate and charming. Follow the winding path past English country garden beds of scarlet camellias, pink roses and hydrangeas, check out the cast-iron water pump in the form of a Doric column or just recline with a book under the massive plane trees.

Dorset Square Dorset Square is set in a quiet enclave of Georgian terraces that have by some miracle survived intact, sitting peacefully, with their elegant yellow brickwork, fanlights and wrought iron balconies. The garden is prized for the fact that Thomas Lord's first cricket ground was here—including, allegedly, seeds of the very grass put down for it in 1787 (thus, to other gardens' chagrin, Dorset is allowed to water even during hosepipe bans). Perhaps more impressive is the fact that George Grossmith, author of *Diary of a Nobody*, lived at Dorset Square, as did Dodie Smith (both houses marked by blue plaques). It's possible Smith's *101 Dalmations* might even have been set here, since the location is, ahem, spot on and the buildings match the London town house design inhabited by the Dearlys, Pongo and Missis. Residents plan to lay on refreshments for visitors. Listen out at dusk for the Twilight Barking.

Manchester Square Gardens Named for the Duke of Manchester who, in 1777, attracted by the area's duck shooting, built a stately mansion. That's now home to the Wallace Collection, which overlooks the garden as a country house overlooks its park. I'm met by Ann-Marie Johnson, a trustee who clearly adores every blade and petal. On a drizzly day, the garden is a mass of misty colour, with lilac spilling over the railings and scarlet camellias shyly beckoning. Ringed by plane and cherry trees, shrubs and a profusion of ferns, bluebells and tulips, the central area is an open pasture where as we speak a toddler gamely tries to kick a ball as big as himself across the greensward. Circular wooden tables with benches are edged by herbal beds—"borage, mint, Russian and bronze fennel, lovely as you brush against them." It's a happy bunch who use the place, according to Ann-Marie: "Office workers come for lunch or meetings, residents turn up with the Sunday papers, a bottle of wine and a rug." Trustees allow the occasional function—Hendrick's gin had a launch on a 19th century theme, with a roll-top bath full of booze and rose petals, and prizes for inventive Victoriana. "A local surgeon brought a jar of leeches, and a wonderful girl turned up in full riding habit, with a stuffed fox. Oh, and a Victorian train carriage was winched in on a low-loader." Thanks to Ann-Marie's care, you'd never know a train had been in here at all.

Montagu Square Plain, attractive brick houses: not, you'd think, too remarkable. But Montagu Square is actually the very definition of remarkable. Laid out in 1800, it was first leased to the man who built it, David Porter, who named the square after Elizabeth Montagu, his mistress when he was a child chimney sweep. Social reformer, patron of the arts, literary critic and writer, Montagu had a home nearby on Portman Square, where every May Day she held a party for chimney-climbing boys, handing out roast beef, plum pudding and a shilling to each. That house disappeared in the Blitz—but Montagu Square seems somehow more of a tribute. Notable in a different way is one of the houses. Number 34 was leased by Ringo Starr in the sixties, who leant it to Paul McCartney, and then to Jimi Hendrix. In 1968, John Lennon and Yoko Ono used the flat as a base during the making of the White Album—the nude cover shots for their Two Virgins album were also taken here. After a few months, the flat was busted by the drugs squad, who found hash on the premises and arrested the heroin-addicted pair. These days, the square is untroubled, the leafy garden a haven for families. An art exhibition and refreshments will be available as you marvel at the past.

Royal College of Physicians' Medicinal Garden, St Andrews Place, Regent's Park When Henry VIII founded the College in 1518, medicines prescribed by doctors were made up by apothecaries—but even after apothecaries were regulated, nothing was that certain. "If a plant looked like a part of the body, it was assumed God was telling us that that is what it dealt with," says learned garden fellow Henry Oakeley. "So the leaf of a pulmonaria, looking like the cut surface of a lung, must be for chest disorders. And if a plant had a strong, upright stem, it must obviously encourage lust." Over 1,000 medicinal plants are grown here now for reference, and to be taken on a tour of the garden is a salutary thing. "This is yew, from which we get taxol, synthesised to help cure ovarian cancer. Ephedra, a shrub that's a source of ephedrine for asthma. Then over here, echinacea, to prevent you getting colds—which, in my opinion, is cobblers." The plants are astounding, the stories quite riveting.

Park Square and Park Crescent Step into Park Square, and you step into a parallel universe somewhere in deepest Sussex. One of the largest private squares, it's a rambling garden with shingled paths winding away to hidden arbours, and benefits from its position on the edge of Regent's Park. Says head gardener Kevin Powell, "Did you notice, when you turned in the gate, how you felt relieved? The weight of traffic is taken away." Instead you hear birdsong, something Powell nurtures: the garden is home to blackbirds, greenfinches, woodpeckers and redwings; kestrels and peregrine falcons pay regular visits. Since it's not overlooked, the garden can bask in sun—a blue ceanothus drips powder puffs of blossom, canna lilies burst apricot and pink, and rosemary and honey spurge scent the air. Almost more fun is the nursemaids' tunnel, an early subway connecting the square to Park Crescent. You emerge as if from one field to another, unaware that you've passed under one of London's busiest roads. Shadier Park Crescent boasts woodland plants, from cow parsley to violet periwinkles; plane trees planted in 1817 to commemorate victory at Waterloo have real heft and presence. As we leave, passing the Coathanger Tree (there's a story: be sure to ask), we spot a fluffy fledgling mistlethrush, and Powell grins like a proud dad.

Portman Square Portman Square is not a deeply bucolic place, for one significant reason. "We're getting rid of a couple of lanes here," shouts Simon Loomes, chairman of the Portman Square Garden Committee, above the roar of traffic as we try to cross the street. (Loomes is also responsible for the area's public realm improvements.) Once Tudor farmland, Portman Square is now a small forest, with bluebell dells, ferns and hillocks. There's a lingering air of Victorian eccentricity, not just because of the 19th century-style gazebos. "A Turkish ambassador who lived on the square once had a portable summerhouse here," explains Loomes. "Rather like a small bandstand, with canvas shutters that could be pulled back, and it travelled round on casters." A rampant summerhouse meant you could take advantage of isolated spots of sunshine. "And in fact," says Loomes, "we're thinking of reinstating it."

The parks and gardens of Marylebone

By Richard Bowden

MJ1.2, Summer 2005)

"By the time the manor house was built near the top of the High Street in about 1250—its site now marked by a plaque—the Crusaders had brought back to England the full range of gardening traditions, classical and Arabic, then spreading across Europe. We can be sure that the manor house and the village that grew up around it included gardens in some form." This is the opening of a famous essay, Of Gardens, by Francis Bacon, philosopher and lord chancellor, who in 1606 came to Marylebone, then right on the edge of London, to be married. Was he perhaps inspired by its gardens?

The earliest surviving map of Marylebone shows each house with its own strip of garden. It dates from 1708 but we know from the oldest rate books that there were "French gardens" here before 1700 and probably much earlier, where the energetic and creative group of Huguenots who fled persecution in France after the Massacre of St Bartholomew in 1572 and the Revocation of the Edict of Nantes in 1685, grew flowers and vegetables commercially. The very first pub in the High Street, built probably around 1650 on the site of number 35, was called the Rose of Normandy. The pleasure gardens known as Marylebone Gardens also began in the 17th century, as a bowling green—no less than three bowling greens are shown on the 1708 map.

Domesday Book does not mention gardens but it does tell us that the woods of Tyburn manor supported "fifty swine", woods also being a feature of Marylebone's other manor. In 1312 this manor, Lilestone, belonged to the Knights of St John of Jerusalem, who gave their name to St John's Wood, where Anthony Babington hid after his plot to murder Queen Elizabeth I had been discovered. These woods disappeared long ago, some having been cleared to form Marylebone Park, Henry VIII's deer park, and the remainder—more than 16,000 trees—being cut down by Cromwell to build ships and swell the funds of the Commonwealth.

By the 18th century as Marylebone's streets began to be built a small garden had become established as one of the normal requirements of a

Georgian house. Just a few of these gardens have survived. The Tradescants' travels in the 17th century and the growing number of people doing the grand tour had led to there being many more plants available, popular books were written about gardening, notably Thomas Fairchild's *The City Gardener*, (1722, reprinted 1760), and nurseries and market gardens grew up all around London to keep pace with the demand for plants as well as fruit and vegetables. The 'nursery end' at Lord's, familiar to listeners to the Test match commentary, was originally one of these, first opened in 1793 by the Henderson family near the Edgware Road and known as the Pineapple Nursery. It later became famous for all sorts of flowers and rare bulbs, Lord's finally acquiring the site in 1887.

Marylebone's other nursery is now, appropriately, on the site of Queen Mary's Garden, the stunning rose garden in the middle of Regent's Park. Alexander Cunningham first leased land for a nursery near Lisson Grove in 1773, he and his son selling this to Thomas Jenkins in 1800. Jenkins then opened a second nursery in the newly built Inner Circle of Regent's Park in 1814, which was later taken over by the Royal Botanic Society. Its lease of the Inner Circle ended in 1932, and the rose garden was created there immediately afterwards.

The handful of drawings of private gardens in Marylebone—and London—that survive from around 1800 show luxuriant foliage, maturing from its earlier planting. As the 19th century progressed these small domestic gardens tended to be squeezed out as additions were made at the back of Georgian houses to accommodate larger families and more servants. Emphasis moved instead towards public gardens.

After Nash's plans for Regent's Park had been accepted in 1811 it took around 15 years for work to be completed, and much of it was closed to the public before 1841. The zoo—its full title the Zoological Gardens—had, however, been open in a limited way since 1828, and it was immensely popular. Engravings show that the gardens surrounding the animals and their cages were attractive and lavishly laid out, so much so in fact that they cannot fail to have influenced public taste.

As the Victorians introduced more public parks—Victoria Park in 1841, Kew in 1843, Battersea Park in the 1850s, Finsbury Park in 1869 and

Hampstead Heath in 1872—Regent's Park led the way with special features such as its bandstand, refreshment kiosks, drinking fountains and the opportunity for sports like archery. The two acres of herbaceous borders along the Broad Walk were laid out by WA Nesfield at the particular request of Prince Albert. After a period of neglect they were recently restored, using 19th century watercolour paintings as reference sources and some of the original designs, and they are once again a glorious sight.

The Royal Botanic Society, founded in 1838, rapidly established itself over an area of 18 acres in the Inner Circle, using the huge mound of earth thrown up to create the lake for special effects such as the waterfall. An enormous glass and iron conservatory, the earliest to be made of these materials, was built near the site of the Open Air Theatre. It is said to have had room for 2,000 people, the annual summer flower shows being extremely popular and attracting large crowds, including Queen Victoria, who came regularly with her family. The Royal Botanic Society came to an end when its lease finished in 1932 and its records, an interesting and rewarding collection, are now at the City of Westminster Archives Centre.

Paddington Street Gardens have a quite different origin, having first been acquired by the parish as a burial ground in 1730 when the churchyard was full. It continued in use as a burial ground for over a century until it too was full and the new St Marylebone cemetery was opened in East Finchley. By now people were starting to recognise the value of open space in central London and during the 1880s in an imaginative move many of these old burial grounds, including Paddington Street Gardens, were reopened by the Metropolitan Public Gardens Association as public recreation grounds.

Some of Marylebone's private gardens were also recorded by the many artists who lived here during the 19th century, among them the French painter, James Tissot, who lived at 44 Grove End Road in St John's Wood and used his own garden as the setting for many of his pictures.

Photographs of Marylebone Road of the 1950s show parts of it, almost unbelievably, still lined with gardens. Ten years later they had disappeared, victims of the intense pressure on space in central London.

Although it seems increasingly difficult to hold on to any form of garden in today's Marylebone we probably value gardens more than ever and brave attempts continue to be made.

Forty years ago a Marylebone lady made an unofficial count of the wild flowers still growing in crevices in the walls and pavements of Marylebone. Amazingly she found more than 150 species. Many of them are still to be seen, but there are now more hanging baskets and trees along the streets as well—nature seems more than able to put up with our carbon emissions, and London has now been free of its notorious fogs for nearly 50 years. The surviving older trees are carefully protected—Paul Akers, Westminster's arboriculturalist, identified the tall tree at the entrance to the old church garden in the high street as one of the very few Huntingdon elms still left in London, and listed it as one of the City of Westminster's 'great trees'.

And roof gardens of all sizes are becoming popular. The magnificent garden on the roof of Berkeley Court dates, like the block itself, from 1928. Was it the earliest in London to be laid out on this scale? It would appear to pre-date the famous one on the roof of Derry and Toms in Kensington High Street by almost 10 years.

Another Marylebone lady, Frances Hodgson Burnett, who lived at 63 Portland Place in 1893-98 and is recorded on a blue plaque on this house, did more than possibly any other single person to create the idea of enchantment that a garden still holds, in her children's book, *The Secret Garden*, published in 1911. And Marylebone does have its own secret garden, at St John's Lodge in Regent's Park. If you don't know it do go and find it—but don't tell anyone else...

The mystery of the Fitzpatrick Mausoleum

By Oliver Bradbury

MJ2.1, Feb-Mar 2006

Have you ever wondered about that mysterious little building in the middle of Paddington Street Gardens? Well, here is its story, or—more precisely—the little that I have been able to find out about it.

Paddington Street Gardens were formed in 1733 as an additional burial ground for the old St Marylebone Parish Church. It is sometimes referred to as St George's Burial Ground. In 1875-6, a mere 10 years before what was to be a wholesale clearance of the cemetery, Edward Walford wrote in his *Old and New London* (1875-6) that "it is computed that near 100,000 persons have been interred".

Now, if one stops to consider the size of the current Paddington Street Gardens—which are not especially large—this does seem to suggest that there had been a lot of burials within a relatively constricted area ("the monumental inscriptions are so numerous," according to an 1833 description). Moreover, this was just on the south side of the street—there is an adjacent burial ground on the north side of the street, too.

In 1885, the gardens became a recreation ground which was officially opened by HRH Princess Louise, daughter of Queen Victoria, on 6 July 1886. Most of the tombs were swept away but the Fitzpatrick Mausoleum was left because of its fine design.

The task of tracing the history of the mausoleum is not helped by the fact that the inscriptions that marked all four sides of the structure have been worn away by the elements.

As long ago as 1886 The *Marylebone Mercury* reported that "the inscriptions on the large mausoleum are now almost illegible". Although I have come across a published reference to the Fitzpatrick Mausoleum from 1811 (the earliest I have found so far), the most factually informative is to be found in Thomas Smith's *A Topographical and Historical Account of the Parish of St Mary-le-Bone* (1833). Smith's account is worth quoting in full: "Here is a splendid mausoleum, erected by the Hon Richard Fitzpatrick, to the memory of his beloved wife, the Hon Susanna

Fitzpatrick, who died on March 28, 1759 aged 30. The following inscriptions also appear on the west and north sides: The mortal remains of Anne, Baroness de Robeck, youngest daughter of the Hon Richard Fitzpatrick, who departed this life, Oct 22, 1829, aged 80 years, were deposited in this mausoleum, by her disconsolate Son, the Baron de Robeck, on the 13 Nov 1829. This Mausoleum was completely repaired by John Michael Henry Fock, Baron de Robeck, Grandson of the Hon Richard Fitzpatrick, An Dom 1830."

Unfortunately, I have been unable to discover much about the Fitzpatrick and Fock families, and, for that matter, we do not even know when the Paddington Street Garden mausoleum was erected. However, mausoleums were often built after the death of a spouse—possibly because they remind the living of their own mortality.

Architecturally, this is a classic mid-18th century sepulchral structure. This type of structure really came into its own during the 18th century, a golden age for mausoleum building. Aesthetically, the Portland stone tomb is a satisfyingly squat design, with its 'aprons' above the segmental arches, a graceful square dome, and—to top it all—a funeral urn with cherubs' heads. Nikolaus Pevsner and Bridget Cherry's *The Buildings of England, London 3: North West* (1991) succinctly describes the Fitzpatrick Mausoleum as "a square building with an ogee dome, like a conduit".

Recently, I spoke to the park manager and asked whether it was possible to have a look inside the mausoleum; his answer was a simple yet good humoured "no"—the wooden entrance door, which appears to be modern, is just a fronting to a sealed place of rest.

The Fitzpatrick Mausoleum appears to be the only building of its kind in the whole of Westminster. A short, factually thin piece on the mausoleum in the *Daily Telegraph* and *Morning Post* for 31 March 1964, puts the mausoleum into the following context: "The family [Fitzpatrick] is fortunate. Most of these attractive memorials have long since vanished from inner London." This point is reinforced by Lynn F Pearson's *Mausoleums* (2002), where there is only one entry—the Fitzpatrick Mausoleum—for Westminster in the book's national gazetteer. Here Pearson describes it as an "unprepossessing little classical structure".

The only published illustration—an attractive line drawing—of the mausoleum that I have come across anywhere is in the *Daily Telegraph* and *Morning Post* piece. Let us hope that this Grade II listed memorial survives for many centuries to come.

The rise and fall of Marylebone station

By Glyn Brown

MJ7.6, Dec-Jan 2011-12)

I'm very fond of several London railway termini. Waterloo—gateway to Hampshire and Dorset, Richmond and Barnes, and once upon a time to Paris; King's Cross, from where I would regularly set out to see my sister in Glasgow; Paddington, a bustle of escape to the translucent seas of Cornwall. But beside these giants, there's another favourite— Marylebone. It's a charmer. Last of all the central London rail termini to be built, it was the smallest too, until recently, and still has just six platforms. Though it's increasingly popular, there's a neat, genteel air— as John Betjeman observed, it looks like a public library.

Wander through the archway onto the concourse and you're already in a dappled suburban town—past the red 1960s post box, the branch of WH Smith's (here since 1899), the cream clapboard information box, like a Bexhill beach hut, and a florist whose rainbow wares take up almost a whole wall. There's refreshment too, at patisserie Paul (bien sûr), the International Cheese Centre and the Victoria & Albert pub, supplier of cask ales and fine wines. And of course, step under the porte cochère and you're in the Landmark, one of London's most astonishing hotels. Little Marylebone station itself doesn't seem astonishing—until you look at how much it now achieves, at its history, and at the fact that in the 1980s it was nearly closed down altogether.

Ceremonially opened on 9 March 1899, Marylebone was built as the London extension of the Manchester, Sheffield and Lincolnshire Railway (MSLR), which was tired of handing lucrative traffic to rivals for the journey south. The line was the vision of Sir Edward Watkin, chairman of the Metropolitan and South Eastern Railways. Watkin was a firebrand with big ideas; he envisaged a rail link between the north of England all the way to Europe via a channel tunnel (to be built by a company of which he was also chairman). Once the plan was passed by parliament, the MSLR changed its name to reflect its national status: it was now the Great Central Railway (you can still see the insignia on station railings).

But the channel tunnel idea bit the dust. Horrifically, the cost of building the new railway nearly bankrupted the GCR. The line linked London to Aylesbury, Rugby, Leicester, Nottingham, Sheffield and Manchester: 92 new connecting miles of superbly engineered double-track lines, with a gentle gradient of one in 176, achieved by long sections of viaduct or tunnels through Nottingham and Leicester. By the time it came to the locomotives and coaches, the company had to buy them on hire purchase. The station, last to be built, had to face cuts before it even existed. Instead of the 10 planned platforms, four were put in, with space left for the remaining six.

Finding a location for Marylebone was another headache. Over 37 acres of prime inner London in the only spot available, immediately to the west of Regent's Park, had to be cleared, an area that 19th century expansion had filled with homes and businesses. To replace 507 houses "of the labouring classes", occupied by 3,073 people, the GCR built Wharncliffe Gardens, six five-storey blocks off St John's Wood Road.

Far more controversial was the upset over Lord's cricket ground, where works had to tunnel under a corner. To placate hostile St John's Wood inhabitants, it was agreed the work would be started and finished between one cricket season and the next. Two cut-and-cover tunnels were built in that time, and the field returned to perfect order. Elsewhere Blandford Square, once home of Wilkie Collins, and Harewood Square, where George Eliot wrote Silas Marner, were razed. Much of this was space for platforms that never materialised.

The station took shape, neat and dapper, in the 'Wrennaissance' style of English baroque, but adapted to suit the residential surroundings, with Dutch gables, warm brick and cream-coloured stone. The concourse was ridiculously long (lots of extra platforms soon!) and, confident of enlargement, there were assorted extra buildings. Biggest of these, a vast goods warehouse on five storeys. It held stables to accommodate 650 horses on three floors (the equine equivalent of a multi-storey car par), an electric and hydraulic power station(in miniature, presumably) and two cast-iron water tanks on the roof holding 22,500 gallons between them, in case of a very big fire.

Who was invited to the station's unveiling? We don't know—but northern guests for a ceremonial dinner, held on the concourse, travelled in three special trains from Manchester, Sheffield and Nottingham. The six-course lunch was served to 734 people, sitting at tables stretching as far as the eye could see, to the accompaniment of a military band playing a programme of Brahms, Wagner and Strauss. And while the lunch (including such delights as Damier de Foie-Gras Lucullus and Balotine de Dinde) was in progress, the inaugural train, an immaculate locomotive adorned with the GCR arms on the smokebox, sat waiting for its starting signal in the misty morning light.

But business was slow. Trains were seldom full, and the GCR struggled to compete with the Metropolitan line, whose tracks it partly used, for second and third class local journeys. Marylebone became known as the quietest London terminal—despite the beauty and comfort of travel it provided, at least in first class. Coaches had electric lights, and there were restaurant cars on most expresses.

C Hamilton Ellis, Victorian writer on railways, describes it: "Jason fought for the Golden Fleece in mezzotint panels on the dining-car ceilings, and as you lounged on a splendiferous pew of carved oak and figured plush, the sun, shining through coloured glass deck lights, gave a deliciously bizarre quality to the complexion of the lady opposite." But it was cargo that paid the bills, and in 1903 there were still only 14 daily passenger arrivals.

And so to that hotel, initially intended as part of the station. When the money ran out, the site where the Landmark stands was sold to Sir John Blundell Maple, of furnishing company Maples, for ninepence a square foot. As the building rose from the ground it became increasingly opulent, with a clock tower, palm-fringed courtyard for the arrival and departure of carriages, a cycle track on the roof—and some rooms even had the innovative formation of a "bathroom and lavatory attached, screened off by an artistic arrangement".

From 1923 to the mid-1940s things picked up, and locomotives like the Flying Scotsman and the Mallard occasionally even ran from Marylebone. Nationalisation changed all that. The Landmark (at that time called the Great Central) had been used during the wars for convalescing officers; now it was requisitioned by the British Railways Board, dubbed "the Kremlin" by staff and not used again as a hotel until 1993. As for the station, express services were downgraded to semi-fasts. Freight services were curtailed. In the mid-1960s, the board's chairman Dr Richard Beeching took his famous 'Beeching Axe' to Marylebone with vigour, closing the Great Central main line between Aylesbury and Rugby and leaving Marylebone the terminus for Aylesbury, High Wycombe and Banbury only—one of the largest single railway closures of the era.

With no investment, the station became dog-eared, the best place in London to see out-of-date, heritage trains. Finally, in the 1980s, it was proposed to close it altogether and turn it into a bus station, rerouting services to Paddington. And that nearly happened—closure notices went up—but there was an outcry. The plan was dropped, and Marylebone at last was given a spruce-up, financed by selling the western part of the station, where so many extra lines might have been, and where the bank Paribas now stands.

And Marylebone has more than proved itself. With privatisation in 1996, the newly-formed Chiltern Railways took over, and has been remarkably successful. With its Evergreen projects, financed by £600m of its own money (well, borrowed from Network Rail, but steadily paid back), Chiltern has reinstated track torn up by British Rail, put in a modest two new platforms and purchased snazzy Clubman trains. A direct line to Oxford is set to open in spring 2016, the first new rail link from London to a major British city since 1910.

Lastly, despite—or maybe because of—the fact that it's cute and civilised, Marylebone Station, like the High Street, is hip. It was beloved of Betjeman as the gateway, with Baker Street, to Metroland ("Gaily into Ruislip Gardens/Runs the red electric train"). Film scenes have been shot there: Ringo, John and George were pursued down the platform by fans in A Hard Day's Night while Paul, in disguise, lurked by the ticket office; Michael Caine sauntered across the concourse in The Ipcress File; I'm afraid Marylebone even featured in Carry On Girls. Its dinky size and helpful staff mean it's still a favourite for movies, as well as TV series (Magnum, Spooks, Doctor Who) and high-end ads.

And strangely, all those time frames still fit. At Marylebone station you still sense the swinging sixties, the suburban 1940s, 20s palm court flappers, even the Victorians.

John Castles and Grotto Passage

By Oliver Bradbury

MJ2.5, Oct-Nov 2006

Grotto Passage is an intriguing narrow alleyway off Paddington Street which broadens out into a courtyard of a street. Its distinctive name and unusual layout were enough to invite curiosity. Investigating their source uncovered an intriguing story.

The passage owes its origin to John Castles, grotto-builder, shell-work artist and entrepreneur. Castles' skilled work enjoyed royal acknowledgement: "In his early days he presented to His Majesty King George III his Arms beautifully executed in shell work, and he also erected a grotto for Sir Robert Walpole at Chelsea."

In this period, coats of arms executed in shells were not unusual—there is one at Skipton Castle, Yorkshire in the room on the top floor above the gate-house—but contemporaneous newspapers published glowing reports of Castles' achievements, elevating him swiftly to the status of celebrity.

Castles then leased a one and a half acre site of pasture land on the west side of Marylebone High Street, where he erected wooden sheds and tents for the exhibition of the numerous elaborate displays of shellwork. And it was here in 1737 that Castles "finish'd a new Grotto". Fortunately for Castles, the exhibition happened to be situated opposite the entrance to Marylebone Gardens, a major place of entertainment of the time, similar to the pleasure gardens at Ranelagh and Vauxhall, which flourished on the other side of Marylebone High Street until 1772.

At a one shilling entrance fee, Castles' Great Grotto took off with immediate success. The exhibition received a boost in popularity after a visit by members of the Royal Family, which also provided an opportunistic excuse to raise the entrance fee to half a crown. A typical mention—one of many—that I have come across of Castles' Great Grotto dates from a 1756 newspaper cutting, a year before he died:

"To be lett and entered on immediately, at Marybone, Castles's Great Grotto, together with the house, long room, cold bath, and garden-ground, with a very good trade, and capable of improvement. The only reason Mr Castles is desirous of letting the same, is occasioned by his bad state of health. Note, breakfasting with coffee, tea, hot rolls, &c as usual." However, a description more evocative of an actual grotto is to be found in Thomas Smith's *A Topographical and Historical Account of the Parish of St Mary-le-Bone* (1833): "Grotto Passage, in Paradise Street; the lock-up cells, with some adjacent cottages, having been erected on the site of an exhibition of shell-work, called the Great Grotto, the property of one John Castles, who died in 1757; the ingenuity of this artist appears to have been duly appreciated by the public, his exhibition having been a celebrated place of fashionable resort."

The mention of 'shell-work' is instructive, as this was a popular and socially approved hobby (especially for ladies of leisure) throughout the 18th century—an especially fertile period for grotto-building—particularly in country houses all over Great Britain. Moreover, by the 1730s Castles' shell-work might have indicated a move towards a naturalism not found in earlier, Baroque grotto-building.

However, "an exhibition of shell-work" would imply that this was not a conventional grotto, which might have been subterranean and vaulted. Therefore, Castles' grotto is likely to have been built only as a semi-permanent structure. The cold bath mentioned in the newspaper article is a typically 18th century feature. This would have been used for medicinal purposes. Frustratingly, no pictorial view of the grotto has ever come to light.

John Castles enjoyed some 20 years of fame before passing away in 1757. Thomas Smith's *Account* also lists Castles in the list of the interred in the former Paddington Street Gardens cemetery: "John Castles (late of the Great Grotto, whose great ingenuity in shell-work gained him universal applause.) 1757". After Smith's passing, the Great Grotto continued to attract a diminishing crowd but without the leadership of its creative master the sparkle behind the attraction had gone.

It soon became unviable and was closed in 1772, having been in existence for only 35 years. However, it had clearly enjoyed its fair share of publicity during its short lifetime: Westminster City Archives keeps a collection of around 20 contemporary newspaper clippings relating to the

Grotto, dating from 1737 to 1769. In 1811 Lysons noted in *Environs of London* that it was: "Frequently advertised in the newspapers about the year 1744", suggesting a peak in popularity at this point.

Elsewhere, Castles was responsible for a grotto dating from the 1740s or 1750s at Wimborne St Giles, Dorset. Swiftly returning to Marylebone, though, Gwyn Headley and Wim Meulenkamp's *Follies, Grottoes & Garden Buildings* (1999) mentions: "a Mr Castle [sic] of Marylebone, no doubt a specialised workshop."' And in their earlier tome, *Follies* (1986), they wrote: "Grotto Passage [...] commemorates a long vanished grotto built as a commercial undertaking by John Castle [sic] in 1738. It appears to have been enormous, built on one and a half acres of land, offering wining, dining and entertainment for an admission charge of half-a-crown—a stupendous sum in those days. Castle died in 1757, and the Royal Grotto, as it had become known, was demolished shortly afterwards. Castle also built Sir Robert Walpole's vanished grotto in Chelsea."

The sparkle never returned to Grotto Passage and today it forms a curious backwater. In the middle of today's Grotto Passage is The Grotto Ragged and Industrial Schools Estabd 1846, a seven bay wide and two storey high brick Victorian educational building. Although the school was established in 1846, the current building was erected in 1860. At either end are entrances, with the overhead inscriptions: 'Girls and Infants' and 'Boys'. By 1895 it was known as the Grotto Passage Home for Lads. This building—as well as the unusual street name—helps to keep the grotto's name alive.

However, it seems that prior to 1923 the 18th century grotto had been pretty much forgotten. On 20 January 1923, a long article, The Royal Grotto in High Street, Marylebone: An Historical Sketch, was published in *The Marylebone Mercury*, in which the author, Arthur Ashbridge, district surveyor for the St Marylebone district from 1884 to 1918, reflected that "the Royal Grotto has been entirely overlooked by authors of books and plans and also by engravers." Sadly, it seems that Castles' Great Grotto has remained pretty much overlooked ever since.

The Marylebone street fight

By Tom Hughes

MJ9.1, Feb-Mar 2013

In 1971, an American writer had a caution for his countrymen who might wish to explore the precincts of Marylebone. "You are walking along James Street. All of a sudden it's Mandeville Place, which becomes Thayer Street, which becomes Marylebone High Street, and you've never turned a corner." Nearly half a century later, that same perplexing succession of names for what appears to be the same street has not changed. And frankly, the residents and merchants are quite chuffed to keep it that way. After all, their ancestors stared down the once almighty London County Council over that very issue.

Once upon a quaint old time, Marylebone was terra incognita—a small village in the fields somewhere north of "the Oxford Street". The village high street was connected to the West End only by Marylebone Lane, a twisting path that followed the River Tyburn. The lane, such as it was, hard by the fetid stream, was a squalid shambles of a place. It was thought best that a more direct route south to Oxford Street be found. It began with Thayer Street, a "modern elongation", named after a since-forgotten local heiress. Thayer Street was never too grand, merely a respectable terrace of Georgian storefronts, with rooms over the shop. By comparison, the next bit, Mandeville Place, was a grand Victorian development.

The name Mandeville is associated with the Duke of Manchester—his eldest son was styled the Viscount Mandeville. The postal address was quite haughty: "Mandeville Place, Manchester Square". It retains its appeal today. Modern architectural historians will tell us that if the walker wishes to stop staring at his mobile for a second and look up, he will enjoy the "highly decorative roofscape". Mandeville Place was "constructed of red brick with stone dressings with a French style mansard". Now, mansards are all well and good but you won't find any on James Street—the final stretch of macadam linking the old Marylebone Village to Oxford Street.

Have you ever stopped to count how many James Streets, Roads,

Terraces, Closes, Places, and Lanes there are in greater London? Don't even think of adding in those named for the blessed St James. You may not have counted them but the LCC did (or at least tried to) and hence, in 1936, the Socialist-controlled council resolved to do something about this vexing, confusing aspect of London's street names. A grand list of proposed name changes was submitted to the population living under its benign charge and, as almost always will happen, what was the bureaucrat's reward? A raspberry.

In few places was the chorus of disapproval as loud as it was in Marylebone over the LCC's plans to pull down the street signs from Thayer Street, Mandeville Place and James Street and, from now on, by council decree, everything from Marylebone Road to Oxford Street would be re-numbered and re-named Marylebone High Street.

The planning boffins thought it made eminent sense as the four streets formed a direct north-south route and the streetscapes were "more or less uniform". The *Times* reported that the LCC's plan was in for, well, a difficult road: "While geographically simple, it is strongly objected to by residents."

A good deal of the opposition came from the denizens of Mandeville Place who, from behind their rococo battlements, could hardly agree that any uniformity existed between their grand address and the ironmongers and chemists to their north and south. Mandeville Place had become home to many members of the medical profession, who strongly felt that the tone of their address was essential to place them on the same plane as their exalted colleagues on nearby Harley and Wimpole Streets. To suddenly have to change out their meticulously polished bronze doorplates and expensive embossed stationery and replace it with something as tatty as "Marylebone High Street" was unthinkable. What mandarin of medicine could hope to attract the right patients to a surgery beset with such "a clumsy and unattractive name suited only to a shopping street".

The opposition forces mobilised quickly—Mr C Rodmell, secretary of The Trinity College of Music (on Mandeville Place at Hinde Street) offered the school's performance hall for a protest meeting. It was well-attended. Dr Taylor Milton said he spoke for all his Mandevillian colleagues and declared their adamant opposition to the re-naming proposal.

It was also clear that the new name found little support either from the shopkeepers along Thayer and James Streets. Mr CE Paul, of James Street, estimated that 98 per cent of his neighbouring merchants opposed the change to Marylebone High Street. As he said, James Street enjoyed a reputation of being convenient to "the Ladies Mile" on Oxford Street and just a few steps from the fashionable Bond Street tube station. To be now burdened with the "Marylebone" name would confuse their toff clientele who would likely now associate them with the much grittier Marylebone Road and the hectic Baker Street Underground. Horrors. Beyond the class conscious Mr Paul, other merchants expressed their displeasure for the rather more mundane reasons of cost, having to change their billing addresses, rubber-stamps, shopping bags and "other paraphernalia of the retail trade".

Let history record the voice of Mr B Denton, who from the distant high street toddled down to the protest meeting to express his support for the LCC's plan. Denton said that a thriving extended high street would be a boon to the entire Marylebone community. Property values would rise. The existing higgledy-piggledy nomenclature was intolerable and an untold amount of trade was lost simply from people not knowing how to get there from Oxford Street.

To try to give anyone directions was a recipe for confusion. Why, Denton bravely asked, could people not see that Marylebone High Street "is a far more dignified name than four driblets of names". The *Times* reported that Mr Denton's doughty appeal was "interrupted with dissent". In the end, the vote was not in doubt. The meeting ended with the overwhelming passage of a resolution opposing the LCC's scheme.

As stated, the opposition in Marylebone was matched elsewhere throughout the vast domain of the London County Council. Accused of acting from "a wave of misplaced energy", the council had taken its remit to go about London expunging centuries old street names of local significance. Henry Berry, the council's embattled director of town planning, defended the action, which he insisted was not being done out of "sheer wantonness". Instead, he said the Fire Brigade and the Post Office had pleaded that something be done at last about London's baffling maze of changing street names and the muddle of duplicate, nay, sextuplicate, names.

In the end, the council won most of their battles. From Westminster to West Ham, hundreds of streets were re-named. But the council lost a few battles, including that in Marylebone. The names of James Street, Mandeville Place and Thayer Street can still be found in the index pages of a well-thumbed A-to-Z.

Marylebone did suffer the loss of one or two historic names. For instance, George Street, from Gloucester Place to the Edgware Road, used to be called "Upper George Street". The council, in its wisdom, declared that the length of the street be uniformly known as George Street. Critics said that the old socialist gang that ruled the council went about London taking special egalitarian glee in removing as many "Uppers" as they could. King Street also became part of an extended Blandford Street, though there's no evidence that this was an act of republicanism.

The workhouse of St Marylebone

By Viel Richardson

MJ2.1, Feb-Mar 2006

A glance at the recipe is a sobering experience. "Take a pint of water and a large spoonful of oatmeal. Stir it together and let it boil up three or four times, do not let it boil over; then strain it through a sieve, salt it to your palate." This recipe for 'water gruel' appears in *The Art of Cookery Made Plain and Easy*, published in 1796, and inmates of Marylebone's workhouse could look forward this breakfast five days a week. Other culinary delights on the workhouse menu included boiled mutton or meatless pease soup for the main meal, and bread and butter for supper. With meal times often being the highlight of a day, it is no wonder that many saw the workhouse as little better than prison. This was not the way it was supposed to be. Like many others, Marylebone's workhouse was the result of an Act of Parliament passed in 1723. Known as The Knatchbull's Act, after its author Sir Edward Knatchbull, this bill was by no means the first attempt by parliament to deal with the poor.

Poorhouses, where those in desperate poverty could find accommodation, had been administered by England's parishes for over 100 years. But two specific 'permissions' in Knatchbull changed everything, resulting in the transformation of the 'poorhouse' into the 'workhouse'. After Knatchbull, parishes could withhold relief from those refusing to enter a poorhouse, meaning that for the first time since the introduction of Poor Relief, parishes had a legally enshrined right to refuse help to those genuinely in need. Even more tellingly, parishes were granted the right to sell the labour of the poorhouse residents and retain the proceeds, an arrangement known as 'farming the poor'. It was seen as a win-win situation: a system of poor relief that not only cared for those in need, but one that would pay for itself in the process. The workhouse had been born. When on 4 September 1732 the St Marylebone Vestry Committee under the chairmanship of Thomas Gilbert Esquire met at the Queen's Head Inn on Holland Street, it was with a keen sense of philanthropy that they ordered "that the east side of the burying ground be set out for alms houses. To the piece of ground set out for a workhouse... be enclosed with a brick wall."It was the official first step in the construction of a workhouse that would one day boast the largest inmate population of any in the country.

Things did not begin well. The project was beset with such political and financial wrangling that Marylebone's first permanent workhouse did not open until 1752, 20 years after that meeting in Holland Street. The new building could house forty paupers; a number that shows the limited scale of parish pauperism when the Earl of Oxford had bequeathed the land back in 1731. The workhouse stood on an area of land bequeathed by the Earl of Oxford on the south side of Paddington Street. The new building replaced The Golden Lion, an abandoned alehouse in Marylebone Passage, which had served as the parish's first poorhouse.

With the new premises opened with a real sense of professionalism. The committee established to run the workhouse appointed a workhouse master to handle the daily affairs. This first master was Francis Parent, and his responsibilities reveal some of the altruistic motives behind the initial workhouse. His main duties were the provision of board, lodging and nourishment for the residents. He was also to teach any foundlings raised by the workhouse reading, writing and arithmetic, so that when they entered the world at 14-16 years of age, they had the skills to progress in society.

Under the practice of 'farming' laid out in Knatchbull's Act the master was required to organise both the adults' and children's work. This consisted mainly of spinning, winding silk, and some labouring. For this Parent received 1s 6d a head per week, plus any income gained from the work the residents had done. Unfortunately Mr Parent lived up to neither his name, nor his employers' hopes.

Within a year he was dismissed for constant drunkenness, frequent absences, misappropriation of supplies, and perhaps worst of all—the residents of a workhouse being technically in the care of the church—the discovery of one of his sons in bed with a 'female inmate'. Parent's behaviour had shown the inherent temptations that result from having an unsupervised workhouse master in charge of what was essentially his own private workforce. Succeeding masters were thereafter employed on an annual salary of 20 pounds. However the practice of farming continued, with the proceeds deposited in a workhouse account.

As the century progressed and London's expansion continued, pressure on the workhouse mounted and by the 1770s conditions had deteriorated markedly. In less than 20 years, circumstances had rendered the original building wholly inadequate for the task. Rats from the nearby burial ground and sewers had moved in. A building designed for 40, now housed over 200. Something had to be done about Marylebone's increasing vagrant population, and this time there was a genuine sense of crisis.

The new building was designed by Alexander Allen, a local Guardian of the Poor, and showed how much things had changed in just 20 years. Designed to accommodate up to 1000 inmates, it included a new main building running along Northumberland Street, with separate blocks at each end. Work began in 1775 and the inmates were transferred to their new accommodation in the spring of 1776. The old workhouse was converted to an infirmary. However its proximity to the sewers led to regular disease outbreaks.

Action was finally taken after an outbreak of fever in 1791 in which both the matron and apothecary died. In 1792, a new infirmary block accommodating 300 was built at the northwest of the main workhouse site. The original workhouse building was finally demolished. Begun with high hopes and good intentions, it had become a by-word for misery and injustice, before finally being killed off by disease. It is doubtful that many mourned its passing.

Both the poor and those who administered them had other issues to concern them. Alexander Allen's building was itself coming under strain. Within five years of the demolition of a workhouse designed to hold 40 paupers, one designed to hold 1,000 was full. Years of continental conflicts had taken their toll on the economy and population alike, and pauperism across Britain was on the rise. In 1797 Marylebone's workhouse population hit 1,168.

During this rapid population increase it was deemed that the original solution to the problems raised by Francis Parent's behaviour was not working. Removing the master's monetary incentive had resulted in a drop in the earnings brought in by the workhouse inmates, and this revenue was being missed. An official known as the 'taskmaster' was introduced and was placed in charge of the farming process. By now workhouses offered a full variety of services including spinners, nurses, domestic servants, tailors, carpenters, shoemakers and teachers.

The taskmaster had no fixed wage, but a look at his earnings is very revealing. In 1798, receiving 2s for every pound earned by his workers, the taskmaster received £151 19s 6d. The highest paid salaried member of staff was the chaplain, who commanded £80 a year teaching and conducting his spiritual duties. The workhouse master himself only received £60 annually. The taskmaster was clearly onto a winner.

With these levels of income available the inmates were pushed hard. Working days lasted from 6am to 6pm in the summer, with a half hour break for breakfast and one hour for dinner. In the winter, work carried on for as long as the workers could see. Hard work undertaken in poor conditions for no pay inevitably led to resentment, but any ill-discipline was treated harshly. When Anne Rollinson and Sarah Saunders were recaptured after running away, their punishment summed up Marylebone's workhouse regime.

They were stripped naked from the waist up and whipped, 'until their backs were bloody'. They were then placed on hard labour, and fed bread and water for a week. By the 1790s a pattern had been established. In 1856, the Poor Law Commission was informed that women were being flogged at the St Marylebone Workhouse—something strictly forbidden under an act of parliament. During one disturbance, girls as young as 17 had been severely beaten in the attempt to restore order. After an investigation proved the allegations to be true, the commission publicly called on the workhouse directors to dismiss the workhouse master, Richard Ryan, at once; overturning their earlier decision to merely reprimand him. The directors refused. The resulting standoff was only resolved after intense public pressure forced the directors to accept Ryan's 'resignation'.

What had started out as an attempt to help the poor, had descended into a system of ruthless exploitation. In less than 50 years Marylebone's workhouse had become a place where cold economics ruled, and inmates were seen as fodder to be farmed out for profit. It was a situation, repeated across the nation, which would last for generations. It would take another social revolution, nearly two centuries after birth of the workhouse movement—the creation of the Welfare State—to finally consign the workhouse to the dark and murky world of Dickensian London.

Profile: Alfred Waterhouse (1830-1905)

Architect, lived at 61 New Cavendish Street

Alfred Waterhouse was one of the most successful and respected architects of the 19th century. Although completely at home with a variety of architectural styles, Waterhouse has become most closely associated with the Victorian gothic revival.

Born into a wealthy Quaker family in Aigburgth, Liverpool, young Alfred was sent to London to be educated in the Quaker run Grove school near Tottenham before leaving to study architecture in Manchester under the architect and sculptor Richard Lane. Alfred made good use of the freedom afforded him by his parent's wealth and spent much of his youth travelling around Europe.

Waterhouse set up an architectural practice in 1853 working on general domestic commissions. His move into commercial buildings came through winning a competition to design the Manchester Assize courts held in 1859. It was a prestigious award for a young architect, but Alfred rose to the challenge. The finished building not only showed his ability to plan and execute a large and complex structure, it was a clear statement of his commitment to the increasingly fashionable gothic style. From this point onwards his high profile as a designer of public buildings was assured.

In 1860 Alfred married Elizabeth Hodgkin, sister of the historian Thomas Hodgkin, and five years later the couple moved to London where Alfred now chose to base his growing practice. He was one of the architects invited to compete for the design of the Royal Courts of Justice and though he lost out to George Edmund Street, the invitation showed the professional respect that he now commanded.

In 1867 he was asked to design the modifications at Balliol College Oxford and the following year was involved in rebuilding part of Caius College Cambridge, thus adding his mark to two of the world's oldest universities.

Waterhouse's position as Britain's leading gothic architect was confirmed in 1873 when he was invited to design the new Natural History Museum.

There had been a competition for the design in 1864 which had been won by the military architect and engineer Captain Francis Fowke, but he had died the following year and the project had stalled. When the project re-started Waterhouse was given Fowke's original designs which were much more renaissance in style, but he re-designed the plans along the romantic gothic lines for which he was known. The resulting building made extensive use of architectural terracotta and the Natural History Museum is widely regarded as the high watermark of this style. Waterhouse's original design contained a wing on each end, turning the main building into a central edifice overlooking a grand courtyard. But this idea was abandoned for financial reasons.

Waterhouse's success led to great recognition during his career. He became a fellow of the Royal Institute of British Architects (RIBA) in 1861, and was its president from 1888 to 1891. He obtained a grand prix for architecture at the Paris Exposition of 1867 and RIBA's Royal Gold Medal in 1878. In 1885 he was made a full member of the Royal Academy and was also a member of the academies of Vienna, Brussels, Antwerp, Milan, and Berlin, and a corresponding member of the Institut de France. In 1887 he was part of the international jury appointed to adjudicate on the designs for the west front of Milan Cathedral and in 1890 he served on a Royal Commission examining the proposed enlargement of Westminster Abbey as a place of burial.

Alfred Waterhouse's buildings can be found throughout Britain—from Strangeways prison in Manchester, through the National Liberal Club in London, to the Town Clock and covered market in Darlington. However it is perhaps fitting that a man whose life displayed such an international approach to his art, should best be remembered for the Natural History Museum—a building dedicated to a truly international science.

INDEX